THE MOTOROLA MC68000
An introduction to processor, memory and interfacing

Jean Bacon

Computer Laboratory, Cambridge University
Formerly at Hatfield Polytechnic

Prentice/Hall International

Englewood Cliffs, NJ   London   Mexico   New Delhi   Rio de Janeiro
Singapore   Sydney   Tokyo   Toronto   Wellington

Library of Congress Cataloging in Publication Data

Bacon, Jean, 1942 –
  The Motorola MC68000

  Bibliography: p.
  Includes index
  1. Motorola 68000 (Microprocessor) I. Title.
QA768.M6895B33   1986   004.165   85–25659
ISBN 0–13–604109–4 (pbk)

British Library Cataloguing in Publication Data

Bacon, Jean
  The Motorola MC68000: an introduction to
  processor, memory and interfacing.
  1. Motorola 68000 (Microprocessor)
  I. Title.
  004.165   QA76.8.M6895

  ISBN 0–13–604109–4

© 1986 Prentice-Hall International (UK) Ltd

Prentice-Hall Inc., Englewood Cliffs, New Jersey
Prentice-Hall International (UK) Ltd, London
Prentice-Hall of Australia Pty Ltd, Sydney
Prentice-Hall Canada Inc., Toronto
Prentice-Hall Hispanoamericana S.A., Mexico
Prentice-Hall of India Private Ltd, New Delhi
Prentice-Hall of Japan Inc., Tokyo
Prentice-Hall of Southeast Asia Pte Ltd, Singapore
Editora Prentice-Hall do Brasil Ltda, Rio de Janeiro
Whitehall Books Ltd, Wellington, New Zealand

Printed and bound in Great Britain for Prentice-Hall
International (UK) Ltd, 66 Wood Lane End, Hemel
Hempstead, Hertfordshire HP2 4RG, at the
University Press, Cambridge

2 3 4 5 90 89 88 87

ISBN 0-13-604109-4

Contents

6   Addressing modes   70

7   Stacks and subroutines   94

8   Instruction set summary   110

PART TWO
The Conventional Machine Level – Devices

9   Connection of input and output devices   131

10   Serial input and output (ACIA)   153

11   Example programs   166

Preface

This text introduces software aspects of the Motorola MC68000. It is based on a foundation course in Computer Systems Organisation at Hatfield Polytechnic which supports later specialist courses in both hardware and systems software. The material presented here is designed specifically to support later software courses. A complementary study of basic hardware principles supports further hardware courses.

Contemporary computer systems may be viewed as a series of levels as follows:

Problem oriented language level
Assembly Language level
Operating System Machine level
Conventional Machine level
Microprogramming level
Digital Logic level

This approach is used by A. Tanenbaum in *Structured Computer Organization*, Prentice-Hall 1976, 2nd edn, 1984.

This text is largely concerned with the conventional machine level with particular emphasis on how the hardware is controlled by program. A foundation is also provided for showing how a software system may be layered above the basic machine hardware and emphasis is given to areas in which the hardware has been designed specifically to support higher levels of software.

In Part One, Chapters 1–8, the processor and memory are introduced. In Part Two, Chapters 9–15, device interfacing and device programming are brought in and some aspects of the microprogramming and digital logic levels are included. Complementary hardware-oriented study would provide a comprehensive coverage of these levels together with some aspects of the conventional machine levels.

No previous knowledge of computer architecture, machine code or assembly language programming is assumed. However, the context described above shows that the material was designed for the serious student of computer science. The material presented is used for foundation study in Computer Systems Organisation at Diploma and Bachelor's level, and forms part of foundation study in this area at (conversion) Master's level.

The text is appropriate for students who have studied a simpler machine at foundation level, for example, an 8-bit microprocessor and who wish to progress to a 16-bit machine for subsequent courses or for project work. It is also appropriate for those in a professional computing environment who are familiar with other computer systems, for example, 8-bit microcomputer systems, minis and main-frames and who need to use the 68000.

Since the MC68000 has an advanced architecture, a fully general discussion would prove over-complex as an introduction. In those areas where it is helpful to have a physical system in mind as a basis for examples, a simple configuration has been used—a single board computer system, Motorola's educational board. This provides the TUTOR monitor program. The commands available in TUTOR are typical of microprocessor single-board systems and facilitate the loading, running under TUTOR control, and debugging of programs. A host-target environment is assumed rather than a self contained, complete microprocessor development system. Device programming is illustrated initially through use of a serial interface with simple input and output devices and a more complex parallel interface is subsequently introduced and programmed. The sections in which this configuration is referenced are self-contained and the bulk of the material can be read without reference to a specific configuration. An additional point is that it is desirable that the programmer should have an empty machine available in order to learn about hardware functions and system software construction. The TUTOR program is a minimal software system and, for this reason, preferable to a large operating system through which the hardware must be used.

The emphasis in this text is the development of software systems. A simpler processor, such as a typical 8-bit microprocessor, although providing a good basis for introducing hardware principles, would lack many desirable features which support the construction of operating systems, compilers and other utilities which are present in the 68000 series of microprocessors. The material presented here introduces the 68000 gradually so that at any stage the complexity is not over-whelming.

It is now generally recognized that assembly language programming should not be used for general problem solving. A high level language should be used wherever possible for ease of developing, reading, testing, debugging and maintaining programs. The use of assembly code in this text is, at the conventional machine level, as a shorthand for machine code and its purpose is to illustrate the functions of the hardware; to show how the hardware is controlled by program. To understand the control of devices in particular, it is necessary to have some experience at low level. Such a study also provides a basis for the understanding of system software functions such as operating system kernels, device drivers and the run-time support required for programs originally written in a high level language, for example, run-time storage management for block structured languages and support for input and output.

Part One (Chapters 1–8) is concerned with the conventional machine level covering the processor and memory.

- Chapter 1 introduces the 68000 series of microprocessors and provides a framework for the rest of the text.
- Chapter 2 develops a simple machine code program selecting a small number of instructions for study at this level.
- Chapter 3 shows how such a program is loaded, tested and run using the TUTOR development system.
- Chapter 4 introduces the concepts of assembling and loading. Assembly language is used subsequently since knowledge of the detailed bit patterns of object code is not needed. A host-target environment is assumed and the concepts of cross-assembling and down-line loading are introduced.
- Chapter 5 covers program control instructions associated with use of the user byte of the status register, the condition flags. Jump and branch instructions are incorporated into simple programs.
- Chapter 6 covers addressing modes. All are summarized and programs are developed to show applications of the more complex modes.
- Chapter 7 describes the 68000 stack, subroutine call and return mechanisms and the use of subroutines as a program structuring tool. It is emphasized that correct use of subroutines must be enforced as a discipline in circumstances when assembly language must be used.
- Chapter 8 summarizes the 68000 instruction set.

Part Two (Chapters 9–15) introduces device interfacing and input and output programming. Although the main emphasis is programming at the conventional machine level some aspects of the microprogramming and digital logic levels are included for completeness.

- Chapter 9 introduces device interfacing.
- Chapter 10 illustrates the programming of two simple devices via a single interface (ACIA) using busy status programming.
- Chapter 11 presents some example programs.
- Chapter 12 gives algorithms for conversion between the external and internal representations of data and presents further example programs.
- Chapter 13 presents device interrupt programming as an alternative to busy status programming. The ACIA is used as an example.
- Chapter 14 describes the full range of exceptions available in the 68000, their implementation and application.
- Chapter 15 discusses and develops programs for the PIA.

Appendices are as follows:

A: 'Number Systems for Computers' gives background information on binary, hexadecimal etc., gives conversion algorithms and explains two's complement representation.
B: Gives the manufacturer's specification of the serial interface chip (ACIA) used in the text.
C: Gives the manufacturer's specification of the parallel interface chip (PIA) used in the text.
D: Lists some available MC68000 peripherals.

The requirements of some categories of reader may best be met by selecting from the material presented here:

A complete beginner is advised to proceed to the example programs in Chapter 11 as quickly as possible, indeed, to make forward references to at least the simpler examples while progressing through the text. Such a reader would require:

Chapter 1 — a thorough grasp is essential.
Chapter 2 — machine code could be omitted, but is desirable for a thorough understanding.
Chapter 3 — use of a practical system could be omitted but see *.
Chapter 4 — most of this is required for the understanding of subsequent programs written in assembly language.
Chapter 5 — is necessary for program construction.
Chapter 6 — the basic ideas are necessary but the more complex modes will seem incomprehensible to a beginner on a first read-through. Sections 6.1 through 6.9 are recommended.
Chapter 7 — the basic concepts are very important but an initial attempt could stop after 7.5.2
Chapter 8 — could be omitted and referenced as required.
Chapter 9 — could be omitted if knowledge of hardware is not sought.
Chapter 10 — is important for understanding input and output.

For a reader with experience of other machines at this level:

Chapter 1 summarizes the 68000 architecture and gives useful reference material.
Chapters 5, 6, 7, and 8 expand on aspects of the conventional machine level.
Chapters 9, 10, 13 and 15 outline device interfacing and programming.
Chapter 14 gives a full coverage of exception handling.

Those readers who have no practical system in mind may wish to omit Chapter 3 on developing, running and debugging programs and those sections of Chapter 4 concerned with cross-assembling and down-line loading.

Chapter 9 is the most hardware-oriented in the text and could be omitted by anyone determined to avoid even an outline of hardware functions yet requiring to program devices in a microprocessor system.

Chapter 14 on exception handling is of interest to those concerned with the construction of the operating system level. Supervisor and user state are introduced and an initial indication of how supervisory software may be developed is given.

Chapters 5–8 are the main areas of interest for the support of the problem oriented language level. Aspects of this are highlighted in Sections 5.7, 6.11 through 6.14, and 7.6.

---

* It is the experience of the author that, having reached this point, it is essential for a beginner to reinforce the knowledge gained by writing some programs. The more practical experience that can be obtained throughout, the stonger the reinforcement.

I should like to acknowledge the help of my more hardware-oriented colleagues, Gordon Steven and Mike Bacon; Gordon as our resident microprocessor expert and source of all knowledge in this area and Mike for the material presented in Chapters 9 and 15.

BIBLIOGRAPHY

1. Lippiatt, A.G. and Wright, G.G.L., *The Architecture of Small Computer Systems*, 2nd edn, London: Prentice-Hall, 1985.
2. Tanenbaum, A.S., *Structured Computer Organization*, 2nd edn, Englewood Cliffs, NJ: Prentice-Hall, 1984.
3. Tanenbaum, A.S., *Computer Networks*, Englewood Cliffs, NJ: Prentice-Hall, 1981.
4. Motorola Inc., *Motorola M68000 16/32-bit Microprocessor Programmer's Reference Manual*, 4th edn, Englewood Cliffs, NJ: Prentice-Hall, 1984.
5. Knuth, D., *The Art of Computer Programming: Seminumerical Algorithms*, 2nd edn, Reading, Ma.: Addison-Wesley, 1981.
6. Halsall, F., *Introduction to Data Communications and Computer Networks*, Addison-Wesley, 1985.

The Conventional Machine Level — Processor and Memory

Part One, Chapters 1–8, introduces the MC68000 processor. At the end of Part One the reader will understand how a 6800 program is represented, stored and executed.

1

Introduction

Motorola is one of a number of companies who manufacture a large range of integrated circuits (IC's). The IC's include processors (called microprocessors), memories, device handlers for interfacing to peripherals for input and output, and communications interfaces. The MC68000 is one of a series, or family, of 16-bit microprocessors first introduced during the early 1980's. All members of this family have a 32-bit internal architecture, the MC68000 has a 16-bit external data bus.

This text introduces the MC68000. The emphasis is on control of the hardware by program. It is not intended to be a text on applications programming at assembly language level since applications software should be developed in a high level language wherever possible. Neither is it intended to be a full description of all aspects of the hardware. The aims are:

- To show the fundamentals of how software is developed building on the basic hardware.
- To show how the design of the hardware has been influenced by the requirements of the software.

The material presented is therefore located at the hardware–software boundary and shows the close interrelation of hardware and software.

In this chapter, choice of the 68000 is discussed and a context for its study is given showing how the material to be presented is structured. Although the material is quite general, it is helpful in places to have a basic system configuration in mind on which to base examples. Such a configuration is discussed in Section 1.3. The remainder of the chapter introduces basic concepts and concludes with some material which will be used for reference throughout the text.

1.1   THE MOTOROLA MC68000

In this text the MC68000 is introduced to the reader on the assumption that it may be the first machine to be studied in any detail. The justification for studying a machine which may be regarded as advanced and complex is as follows:

- It is widely used.
- It forms the basis for a large number of commercial systems with a range of operating systems and languages.
- It has a clean design.
- It has a comprehensive instruction set.
- It does not impose tiresome limits on system configuration, for example, 16 Mbytes (16 megabytes or 16 million bytes) of memory are addressable by the basic processor.
- Although earlier, simpler microprocessors provide a good basis for introducing hardware principles, they lack many important features which support software systems. Examples are, protection for operating systems and support for a wide range of data structures required by compiler writers and high-level language programmers.
- Further advances in technology will cause microprocessor design to continue to increase in complexity. A higher starting point will become increasingly desirable.

The author's experience over three years of teaching the 68000 to large numbers of students, at widely varying educational levels and experience, is that it is possible to present the machine gradually so that at any stage the complexity is manageable.

1.2   A COMPUTER SYSTEM AS A SERIES OF LAYERS

Contemporary computer systems may be viewed as a series of levels or layers, commonly called a layered or hierarchical model, as follows:

The problem-oriented language level

The assembly language level

The operating system level

The conventional machine level

The microprogramming level

The digital logic level

Fig. 1.1

This approach is used by A. Tanenbaum in *Structured Computer Organization*, Prentice-Hall 1976, second edition 1984. A hardware-oriented approach would concentrate on and expand the three lowest layers.

In this text, emphasis is given to the conventional machine level and above. Support for the higher layers provided by the 68000 is of particular interest and will be highlighted where appropriate. A detailed description of each level will not be presented here, rather, when a topic is introduced it will be related to this basic model. The aim of the remainder of this chapter is to explain basic concepts:

- The stored program.
- Instructions and data.
- Addressing memory.
- How the processor executes a program.

First, a basic 68000 configuration is outlined so that the concepts may be related to a physical system.

1.3   A SIMPLE 68000 SYSTEM CONFIGURATION

A simple representation of a computer consists of a processor connected to some memory and some input and output devices by a bus or data highway.

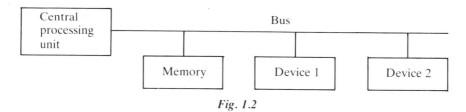

Fig. 1.2

If this representation is related to a single-board system such as Motorola's educational board which will be used to illustrate this text, the following, slightly more detailed, diagram is obtained:

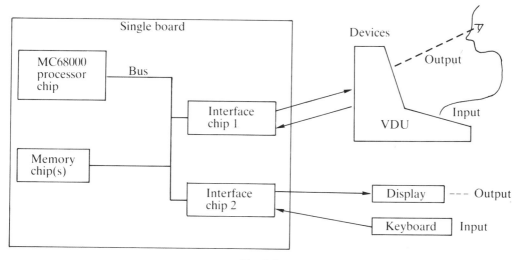

Fig. 1.3

Fig. 1.3 shows the MC68000 processor, some memory and some input and output devices. Programming input and output is difficult to understand at machine level and will be covered in later chapters. The first program to be developed in Chapter 2 will illustrate how the MC68000 processor executes a program stored in the memory. In this chapter, knowledge of the processor and the memory will be developed. A more abstract picture will be used and extended.

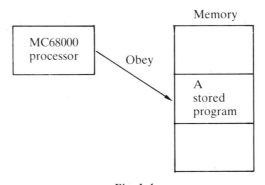

Fig. 1.4

1.4   THE MEMORY

The memory is used for storing programs which are executed (or run or obeyed) by the processor. A program consists of some data and some instructions to tell the processor how to process the data. Data may take the form of numbers, on which some arithmetic must be done, or characters, constituting text to be processed by means of the instructions.

In Fig. 1.5 a program is shown located at some arbitrary place in the memory.

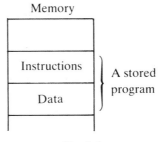

Fig. 1.5

The following questions are addressed in the rest of this chapter:

- What do instructions look like?
- What does data look like?
- How is the processor informed *where* the program is stored in the memory, so that it can execute the instructions?

1.4.1 Representation of data

It is assumed that the reader is familiar with some of the basic methods of coding information. Binary and hexadecimal representation of numbers and the ASCII character code will be used in this text. Appendix A gives introductory material on number systems for computers. Binary, octal and hexadecimal are introduced and conversion algorithms are given. The representation of positive and negative integers is explained and a brief introduction to real numbers is given. Finally, some character codes are summarized.

This chapter concludes with a summary of useful information presented as figures. Fig. 1.15 gives the decimal, binary and hexadecimal representation for numbers appropriate to this study of the 68000 and Fig. 1.16 is a table of the ASCII character codes.

The primitive data types of the 68000, i.e., the data types known by the processor, are as follows:

$$
\begin{aligned}
\text{byte} &: 8 \text{ bits (8 binary digits)} \\
\text{word} &: 16 \text{ bits} \\
\text{long word} &: 32 \text{ bits}
\end{aligned}
$$

1.4.2 Addressing memory

The smallest unit which can be addressed is the byte (8 bits). In this text memory will be drawn as an array of words (i.e. 16 bits wide) as follows:

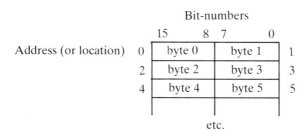

Fig. 1.6 ·

When memory is used to store words (16 bits) they are addressed as follows:

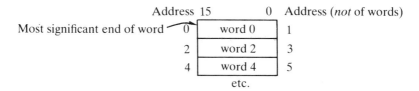

Fig. 1.7

When longwords (32 bits) are stored they are addressed as follows:

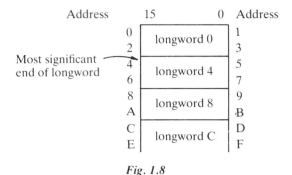

Fig. 1.8

It should be noted that a word and longword can only start at even addresses (at even byte numbers) i.e. there is *no* word 1, word 3, or longword 1, longword 3 etc. We shall see later that instructions also can only start at an even address.

Throughout this text, $ before a number indicates that the number is hexadecimal.

Important note
The importance of appreciating the difference between an address (or location) and what is stored at that address (its contents) cannot be over-emphasized; e.g. address $1000 may contain any bit pattern.

Hex contents $A2F0

1.4.3   Locating a program in memory

The program can now be shown located at some specific place in the memory. For example, the instructions may start at address $1000 and the data $1200. (See Fig. 1.9.)

The single board computer used as an example in this text has a memory size of 32 kbytes (32 × 1024 = 32768 bytes). Reference to Fig. 1.15 shows that the address range is therefore 0 to $7FFF. It should be noted that this range of addresses can be stored in 16 bits (in fact 16 bits can address 64 kbytes).

Single board computers of this type are intended as small evaluation systems. The design of the 68000 allows for an eventual address size of 32 bits although currently 24 bits are employed as the maximum address size. Fig. 1.15 again shows that 16 million bytes (16 megabytes or 16 Mbytes), can be addressed by 24 bits.

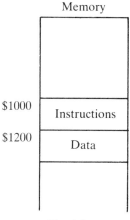

Memory

Fig. 1.9

1.5 INSTRUCTIONS

The 68000 is a powerful processor with a large, rich instruction set. The complete instruction set is given as Fig. 1.17. An instruction consists of at least one 16-bit word. The first word of an instruction, which is a control word or operation word, indicates to the hardware:

- What kind of instruction, for example add or subtract.
- Whether it is to operate on data words, bytes or long words.
- How many words of memory the complete instruction occupies.
- Where the data on which the instruction is to operate is to be found.

An instruction may consist of more than one word. If so, the extension words contain such things as constants and memory addresses to be used in executing the instruction.

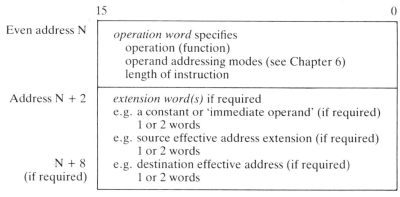

Fig. 1.10

1.5.1   Instruction format

The terms used in the above diagram are the formal ones from the manufacturer's handbooks and will be explained later. Examples illustrating the need for and use of extension words are given throughout this text. Some instructions will consist of a single word:

control word

Examples of the format of instructions with extension words are as follows:

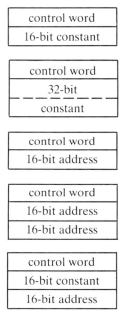

Fig. 1.11

The maximum instruction size is five words. Some examples of the detailed bit-coding of instructions are given in Chapter 2 where a complete program is developed.

1.6   THE PROCESSOR

Sections 1.4 and 1.5 have introduced the idea of a program located in memory. The function of the processor is now developed, in particular, how a program in the memory is executed. Since memory is merely a passive store, all the instructions of the program, i.e. operations on the data, must be carried out within the processor. Chapter 9 gives more details of processor architecture.

1.6.1   Processor registers

Fig. 1.13 shows the 68000 processor registers of which the programmer is aware. Since memory is passive, data must be fetched into data registers (D0 to D7) before operations can be performed on it. The registers labeled A0 to A7 are used for holding memory addresses but these will not be discussed until more complex programs are developed. Stack and status registers will also be discussed later. Data and address registers are 32 bits wide. Data and address register operations are given in 1.8 below. Chapter 9 gives more details of processor architecture.

1.6.2   The program counter

The program counter is a 32-bit register which is used to hold the address (or location) in memory of the next instruction to be executed. Since a program is a list of machine instructions, the program counter must be set up initially to contain the address of the first instruction of the program.

Since instructions always start on a word boundary, the least significant bit of the program counter is always zero.

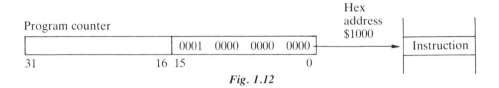

Fig. 1.12

1.7   THE INSTRUCTION CYCLE

When the processor is started off executing a program, it performs the following cycle, called the instruction cycle or fetch–execute cycle, indefinitely:
First, in outline:

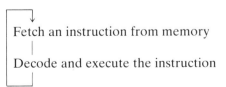

The program counter (sometimes called the sequence controller) must be managed during the instruction cycle so that at the start of each cycle the next instruction of the program is pointed to by the PC. If each instruction was exactly one word long this would be easy:

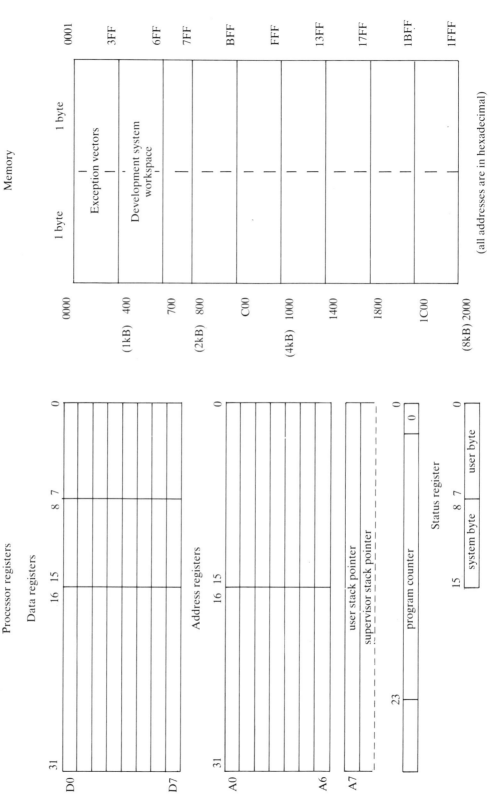

Fig. 1.13 68000 programmable registers and 8k bytes of memory

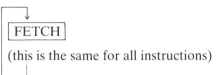

Fetch an instruction from memory

Increment the PC (by 2 bytes) to point to the next instruction

Decode and execute the instruction

As shown in 1.5 instructions may vary in length from one to five words. Once the control word has been fetched, however, the total length of the instruction is known, the rest of the instruction can be fetched and finally, the program counter can be set up ready for the next instruction.

The 68000 is called a 16-bit microprocessor because it fetches 16 bits at a time from memory.

FETCH

(this is the same for all instructions)

Copy the instruction pointed to by the program counter (PC) from memory into an internal processor register (the instruction register) ready for decoding. The instruction register is not shown in Fig. 1.13 since it is not programmable, i.e. is not accessible to the programmer. Increment the program counter to *the next instruction*.

EXECUTE

(this is different for each instruction)

Decode the instruction and obey it, e.g. carry out the required data transfers which may be between processor registers or between registers and memory.

The remaining sections of this chapter are included mainly for reference throughout later chapters and may be omitted at first reading.

1.8 DATA AND ADDRESS REGISTER OPERATION SUMMARY

Data registers
- 8, 16 or 32 bits are used as specified in the instructions.
- Only the bits used are changed, there is no extension or propagation.

Address registers
- Only word (16-bit) or long-word (32-bit) operations are valid.
- Word results loaded into an address register are extended to 32 bits, i.e. there is extension and propagation.

- Flags (condition codes – see Chapter 5) are not set by address register operations.
- Limited operations are available: LEA, MOVEA, ADD, SUB, NEG, CMP, NOT, CLR.
- Address registers can be used to access bytes, words and long words addressed as shown in section 1.4.3.

1.9   SIGNED AND UNSIGNED INTEGERS

In 'Number Systems for Computers', see Appendix A, the range of integers that can be represented by a given number of bits is discussed. The 68000 provides instructions that allow a number of bits to be used to store positive integers only (*unsigned* integers) or, alternatively, to be used for both positive and negative integers (*signed*).

```
        8 bits unsigned                              8 bits signed

2^8-1  │ 1 1 1 1 1 1 1 1 │ +255      2^7-1  │ 0 1 1 1 1 1 1 1 │ +127
       │ 1 1 1 1 1 1 1 0 │                  │ ⋮
       │ ⋮
2^7    │ 1 0 0 0 0 0 0 0 │ +128        0    │ 0 0 0 0 0 0 0 0 │  0
2^7-1  │ 0 1 1 1 1 1 1 1 │ +127             │ 1 1 1 1 1 1 1 1 │ -1
       │ ⋮                                 │ ⋮
 0     │ 0 0 0 0 0 0 0 0 │  0       -2^7+1  │ 1 0 0 0 0 0 0 1 │ -127
                                    -2^7    │ 1 0 0 0 0 0 0 0 │ -128
```

Fig. 1.14

8 bits

unsigned	0 to 2^8-1
signed	-2^7 to 2^7-1

16 bits

unsigned	0 to $2^{16}-1$
signed	-2^{15} to $2^{15}-1$

32 bits

unsigned	0 to $2^{32}-1$
signed	-2^{31} to $2^{31}-1$

1.10   THE ASCII CHARACTER CODE

Fig. 1.16 gives the complete ASCII character set in binary and hexadecimal. In the simple examples in Chapters 1 and 2, integer data has been used. In practice, data might equally well take the form of ASCII characters and the table is given here for convenient reference.

When input and output are discussed in Part Two it will be seen that data is usually transferred in the form of characters.

1.10.1 Parity

Fig. 1.16 gives the 7-bit representation of the ASCII characters which is the form used when character data is stored internally in memory. When characters are being transmitted, for example on input or output, an extra check digit can be inserted before transmission and checked (and removed) after transmission by hardware. This allows a transmission error in a single bit (or an odd number of bits) to be detected but not corrected. An 8-bit representation of the character is constructed. The additional eighth bit, the (even) parity bit, is inserted to make the total number of one's in the code even.

EXAMPLES

Character	Hex code	7-bit code	8-bit code (even parity) (most significant bit is even parity digit)
A	$41	1000001	01000001
C	$43	1000011	11000011
8	$38	0111000	10111000
9	$39	0111001	00111001

If an 8-bit character arrives with an odd number of one's an error has occurred.

Decimal	Binary	Hexadecimal
0	0	0
1	1	1
2	10	2
3	11	3
4	100	4
5	101	5
6	110	6
7	111	7
8	1000	8
9	1001	9
10	1010	A
11	1011	B
12	1100	C
13	1101	D
14	1110	E
15	1111	F
16	10000	10
17	10001	11
	etc.	
1023 = 1k–1	11 1111 1111	3FF
1024 = 1k	100 0000 0000	400
2k	1000 0000 0000	800
4k	1 0000 0000 0000	1000
8k–1	1 1111 1111 1111	1FFF
8k	10 0000 0000 0000	2000
16k–1	11 1111 1111 1111	3FFF
16k	100 0000 0000 0000	4000
32k–1	111 1111 1111 1111	7FFF
32k	1000 0000 0000 0000	8000
64k–1	1111 1111 1111 1111	FFFF
64k	1 0000 0000 0000 0000	10000
128k	10 0000 0000 0000 0000	20000
256k	100 0000 0000 0000 0000	40000
512k	1000 0000 0000 0000 0000	80000
1024k = 1M	1 0000 0000 0000 0000 0000	100000
2M	10 0000 0000 0000 0000 0000	200000
4M	100 0000 0000 0000 0000 0000	400000
8M	1000 0000 0000 0000 0000 0000	800000
16M–1	1111 1111 1111 1111 1111 1111	FFFFFF
16M	1 0000 0000 0000 0000 0000 0000	1000000

Note: 24-bit address for 0 → 16M–1
        32k machine – address range 0 → 7FFF.

Fig. 1.15

The form of the code is

3 bits	4 bits
most sig.	least sig.

		least sig.															
most sig.		**0**	**1**	**2**	**3**	**4**	**5**	**6**	**7**	**8**	**9**	**A**	**B**	**C**	**D**	**E**	**F**	hexadecimal
hex	**binary**	0000	0001	0010	0011	0100	0101	0110	0111	1000	1001	1010	1011	1100	1101	1110	1111	binary
0	000	NUL	SOH	STX	ETX	EOT	ENQ	ACK	BEL	BS	HT	LF	VT	FF	CR	SO	SI	
1	001	DLE	DC1	DC2	DC3	DC4	NAK	SYN	ETB	CAN	EM	SUB	ESC	FS	GS	RS	US	
2	010	SP	!	"	#	$	%	&	'	(	)	*	+	,	-	.	/	
3	011	0	1	2	3	4	5	6	7	8	9	:	;	<	=	>	?	
4	100	@	A	B	C	D	E	F	G	H	I	J	K	L	M	N	O	
5	101	P	Q	R	S	T	U	V	W	X	Y	Z	[	\	]	^	_	
6	110	`	a	b	c	d	e	f	g	h	i	j	k	l	m	n	o	
7	111	p	q	r	s	t	u	v	w	x	y	z	{	|	}	~	DEL	

Fig. 1.16 American Standard Code for Information Interchange (ASCII)

Mnemonic	Operation	Assembler syntax	X	N	Z	V	C
ABCD	Add Decimal with Extend	ABCD Dy,Dx ABCD (Ay),(Ax)	*	U	*	U	*
ADD	Add Binary	ADD ⟨ea⟩,Dn ADD Dn,⟨ea⟩	*	*	*	*	*
ADDA	Add to Address Register	ADDA ⟨ea⟩,An	—	—	—	—	—
ADDI	Add Immediate	ADDI #⟨data⟩,⟨ea⟩	*	*	*	*	*
ADDQ	Add Quick	ADDQ #⟨data⟩,⟨ea⟩	*	*	*	*	*
ADDX	Add Extended	ADDX Dy,Dx ADDX (Ay),(Ax)	*	*	*	*	*
AND	AND Logical	AND ⟨ea⟩,Dn AND Dn,⟨ea⟩	—	*	*	0	0
ANDI	AND Immediate	ANDI #⟨data⟩,⟨ea⟩	—	*	*	0	0
ASL,ASR	Arithmetic Shift Left, Right	ASd Dx,Dy ASd #⟨data⟩,Dy ASd ⟨ea⟩	*	*	*	*	*
Bcc	Branch Conditionally	Bcc ⟨label⟩	—	—	—	—	—
BCHG	Test a Bit and Change	BCHG Dn,⟨ea⟩	—	—	*	—	—
BCLR	Test a Bit and Clear	BCLR Dn,⟨ea⟩ BCLR #⟨data⟩,⟨ea⟩	—	—	*	—	—
BRA	Branch Always	BRA ⟨label⟩	—	—	—	—	—
BSET	Test a Bit and Set	BSET Dn,⟨ea⟩ BSET #⟨data⟩,⟨ea⟩	—	—	*	—	—
BSR	Branch to Subroutine	BSR ⟨label⟩	—	—	—	—	—
BTST	Test a Bit	BTST Dn,⟨ea⟩ BTST #⟨data⟩,⟨ea⟩	—	—	*	—	—
CHK	Check Register Against Bounds	CHK ⟨ea⟩,Dn	—	*	U	U	U
CLR	Clear an Operand	CLR ⟨ea⟩	—	0	1	0	0
CMP	Arithmetic Compare	CMP ⟨ea⟩,Dn	—	*	*	*	*
CMPA	Arithmetic Compare Address	CMPA ⟨ea⟩,An	—	*	*	*	*
CMPI	Compare Immediate	CMPI #⟨data⟩,⟨ea⟩	—	*	*	*	*
CMPM	Compare Memory	CMPM (Ay)+,(Ax)+	—	*	*	*	*

Mnemonic	Description	Syntax					
DBcc	Test Condition Decrement and Branch	DBcc Dn,⟨label⟩	—	—	—	—	—
DIVS	Signed Divide	DIVS ⟨ea⟩,Dn	—	·	·	·	0
DIVU	Unsigned Divide	DIVU ⟨ea⟩,Dn	—	·	·	·	0
EOR	Exclusive OR Logical	EOR Dn,⟨ea⟩	—	·	·	0	0
EORI	Exclusive OR Immediate	EORI #⟨data⟩,⟨ea⟩	—	·	·	0	0
EXG	Exchange Registers	EXG Rx,Ry	—	—	—	—	—
EXT	Sign Extend	EXT Dn	—	·	·	0	0
JMP	Jump	JMP ⟨ea⟩	—	—	—	—	—
JSR	Jump to Subroutine	JSR ⟨ea⟩	—	—	—	—	—
LEA	Load Effective Address	LEA ⟨ea⟩,An	—	—	—	—	—
LINK	Link and Allocate	LNK An,#⟨displacement⟩	—	—	—	—	—
LSR,LSL	Logical Shift Right, Left	LSd Dy,Dy LSd #⟨data⟩,Dy LSd ⟨ea⟩	·	·	·	·	0
MOVE	Move Data from Source to Destination	MOVE ⟨ea⟩,⟨ea⟩	—	·	·	0	0
MOVE from SR	Move from the Status Register	MOVE SR, ⟨ea⟩	·	·	·	·	·
MOVE to CC	Move to Condition Codes	MOVE ⟨ea⟩,CCR	·	·	·	·	·
MOVE to SR	Move to the Status Register	MOVE ⟨ea⟩,SR	·	·	·	·	·
MOVE USP	Move User Stack Pointer	MOVE USP,An MOVE An,USP	—	—	—	—	—
MOVEA	Move to Address Register	MOVEA ⟨ea⟩,An	—	—	—	—	—
MOVEM	Move Multiple Registers	MOVEM ⟨register list⟩,⟨ea⟩ MOVEM ⟨ea⟩,⟨register list⟩	—	—	—	—	—
MOVEP	Move Peripheral Data	MOVEP Dx,D(Ay) MOVEP d(Ay),Dx	—	—	—	—	—
MOVEQ	Move Quick	MOVEQ #⟨data⟩,Dn	—	·	·	0	0
MULS	Signed Multiply	MULS ⟨ea⟩,Dn	—	·	·	0	0
MULU	Unsigned Multiply	MULU ⟨ea⟩,Dn	—	·	·	0	0

Mnemonic	Operation	Assembler syntax	Cond codes				
			X	N	Z	V	C
NBCD	Negate Decimal with Extend	NBCD ⟨ea⟩	*	U	*	U	*
NEG	Two's-Complement Negation	NEG ⟨ea⟩	*	*	*	*	*
NEGX	Negate with Extend	NEGX ⟨ea⟩	*	*	*	*	*
NOP	No Operation	NOP	—	—	—	—	—
NOT	Logical Complement	NOT ⟨ea⟩	—	*	*	0	0
OR	Inclusive OR Logical	OR ⟨ea⟩,Dn	—	*	*	0	0
ORI	Inclusive OR Immediate	ORI #⟨data⟩,⟨ea⟩	—	*	*	0	0
PEA	Push Effective Address	PEA ⟨ea⟩	—	—	—	—	—
RESET	Reset External Devices	RESET	—	—	—	—	—
ROL,ROR	Rotate without Extend Left, Right	ROd Dx,Dy ROd #⟨data⟩,Dy ROd ⟨ea⟩	—	*	*	0	*
ROXL,ROXR	Rotate without Extend	ROXd Dx,Dy ROXd #⟨ea⟩,Dy ROXd ⟨ea⟩	*	*	*	0	*
RTE	Return from Exception	RTE	*	*	*	*	*
RTR	Return and Restore Condition Codes	RTR	*	*	*	*	*
RTS	Return from Subroutine	RTS	—	—	—	—	—

Mnemonic	Description	Operands	X	N	Z	V	C
SBCD	Subtract Decimal with Extend	SBCD Dy,Dx SBCD (Ay),(Ax)	·	U	·	U	·
Scc	Set according to Condition	Scc ⟨ea⟩	–	–	–	–	–
STOP	Stop Program Execution	STOP #xxx	–	–	–	–	–
SUB	Subtract Binary	SUB ⟨ea⟩,Dn SUB Dn,⟨ea⟩	·	·	·	·	·
SUBA	Subtract from Address Register	SUBA ⟨ea⟩,An	–	–	–	–	–
SUBI	Subtract Immediate	SUBI #⟨data⟩,⟨ea⟩	·	·	·	·	·
SUBQ	Subtract Quick	SUBQ #⟨data⟩,⟨ea⟩	·	·	·	·	·
SUBX	Subtract with Extend	SUBX Dy,Dx SUBX (Ay),(Ax)	·	·	·	·	·
SWAP	Swap Register Halves	SWAP Dn	–	·	·	0	0
TAS	Test and Set an Operand	TAS ⟨ea⟩	–	·	·	0	0
TRAP	Trap	TRAP #⟨vector⟩	–	–	–	–	–
TRAPV	Trap on Overflow	TRAPV	–	–	–	–	–
TST	Test an Operand	TST ⟨ea⟩	–	·	·	0	0
UNLK	Unlink	UNLK An	–	–	–	–	–

Fig. 1.17 68000 instruction set summary

The condition code values are coded as follows:
· Set according to the result of the operation
– Not affected by the operation
0 Cleared
1 Set
U Undefined after the operation.

2

Machine code introduced by means of a program

2.1 INTRODUCTION

In this chapter, the machine level language of the 68000 is introduced. A brief look at a small number of instructions is sufficient to illustrate this conventional machine level in the machine's hierarchy (see Fig. 1.1). Full details of the machine code for all instructions is given in Motorola's M68000 16/32-bit Microprocessor Programmer's Reference Manual. In later chapters a higher level notation which is convenient for humans (as opposed to computers) will be employed.

One aim of this text, however, is to illustrate how the hardware is controlled by program. To understand this, it is essential to take one look at least at the detail of machine code. A simple but complete machine code program will be developed in this chapter.

2.2 A SIMPLE PROGRAM

The example to be used to illustrate machine code is a program which adds together two words of data, taken from the program's data area and stores the result in the program's data area. In a high level language this program would implement one statement with a syntax such as:

$$z : = x + y;$$

As indicated in Section 1.4, the program may be located at some arbitrarily chosen place in the memory of the 68000 system, say at address $1000 (the '4k'th byte). Fig. 2.1 shows the instruction area of the program starting at address $1000 and the data area, again chosen arbitrarily, starting at address $1200. This data will consist of 16-bit integers stored in standard two's-complement form (see Appendix A, Number Systems for Computers).

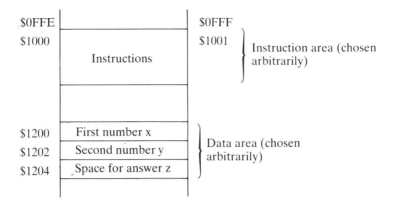

For example, the data might be:

address				contents
$1200	0001	0010	0011 0100	$1234 = decimal 4660
$1202	0100	0011	0010 0001	$4321 = decimal 17185
$1204	0000	0000	0000 0000	

Fig. 2.1

(8-bit or 32-bit numbers may also be used as data when required as explained in Chapter 1.)

2.3   THE PROCESSOR AND THE MEMORY

The memory of a computer is a passive store and processing of data almost always takes place within the processor. The fetch–execute cycle was explained in Chapter 1 and it was shown that instructions are copied from memory into a processor register, the instruction register, for decoding and execution. The data which are processed as a result of execution of the instructions also have to be fetched into processor registers, typically the data registers.

The program to implement $z := x + y$ therefore takes the following form:

- Copy the first word of data (x) from memory into a processor register, e.g. D5.
- Add the second word of data (y) onto the same processor register D5.
- Copy the sum formed in D5 into the memory.
- Stop fetching and executing instructions from this program.

Fig. 2.2 shows these instructions located in the memory together with the associated data.

Details will now be given of the coding at machine level of the three instructions.

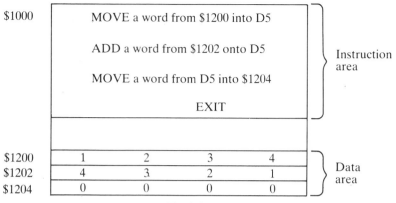

Fig. 2.2

2.4   A DATA TRANSFER INSTRUCTION (MOVE)

The MOVE instruction is used for transferring data from some source to some destination. The transfer might be between memory and processor registers, but a simple example is the instruction to MOVE (transfer or copy) the contents of some data register into some other data register. Fig. 1.17 gives the full 68000 instruction set including a number of MOVE instructions.

2.4.1   An example of the effect of a MOVE

E.g. MOVE.W D0,D3
   Copy a word (16 bits) from D0 to D3
   The effect of the instruction is as follows:

	31	16	15			0
D0	Not used		1	2	3	4
D1						
D2						
D3	Not affected		Copied			

Fig. 2.3

Instructions also exist to MOVE (i.e. copy) bytes or longwords.

E.g. MOVE.B D0, D3   (Copy a byte)

	31	16	15	8	7	0
D0	Not used				3	4
D3	Not affected				Copied	

Fig. 2.4

E.g. MOVE.L D0, D3   (Copy a longword)

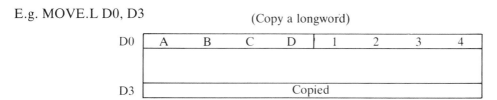

Fig. 2.5

The method of writing down the instructions used above, i.e.:

MOVE.W D0, D3
MOVE.B D0, D3
MOVE.L   D0, D3

employs assembly code mnemonics which will be introduced in Chapter 4. The *effect* of the instruction to move data between data registers has been shown. The instruction itself is now examined.

2.4.2   The MOVE instruction

The general definition of a MOVE instruction is as follows (see Fig. 1.17):

MOVE ⟨ea⟩, ⟨ea⟩

where ⟨ea⟩ means 'effective address' and may be a processor register or memory. The definition indicates that data of size byte (MOVE.B), word (MOVE or MOVE.W) or longword (MOVE.L) is to be transferred from any source to any destination using the syntax:

MOVE source, destination

The instruction is coded as follows:

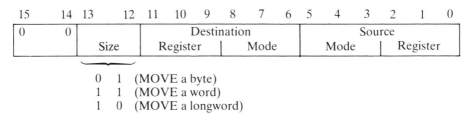

Fig. 2.6

To MOVE a word from D0 to D3 we can fill in:

15	14	13	12	11	10	9	8	7	6	5	4	3	2	1	0
0	0	1	1	0	1	1		?			?		0	0	0

MOVE a word   to D3   from D0

Fig. 2.7

The fields not yet filled in are named:

- Destination mode.
- Source mode.

These are the means by which the instruction word indicates to the hardware whether it has to move a word between data or address registers or between registers and memory and if so, to look at the extension words to find the required memory address.

In the above example, the source and destination are both data registers, for which the code happens to be 0. A full discussion of addressing modes is given in Chapter 6. The complete instruction is:

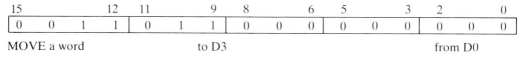

MOVE a word   to D3   from D0

Fig. 2.8

Writing the contents of the word in hexidecimal gives $3600 which is not very helpful if the individual fields are required but it provides a shorthand notation instead of using binary.

2.5 THE ADD INSTRUCTION

The definition of the ADD instruction contains only one general effective address. There are several ADD instructions of which one is required which ADDs to a data register. See Fig. 1.17.

ADD ⟨ea⟩ , Dn

i.e. ADD from any source effective address onto a data register, Dn←Dn + ⟨ea⟩. The same basic instruction may be used to add from a data register into memory,

i.e. ADD Dn, ⟨ea⟩   where the effect is ⟨ea⟩←⟨ea⟩ + Dn.

The basic instruction is coded as follows:

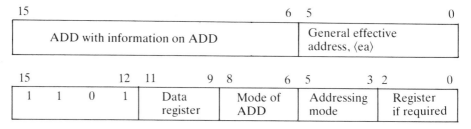

Fig. 2.9

Bits 6 to 8, the mode of ADD, are used to encode whether the instruction is ADD ⟨ea⟩, Dn or ADD Dn, ⟨ea⟩, and the size of the data to be added, as follows:

Byte	Word	Long	operations
000	001	010	ADD ⟨ea⟩, Dn
100	101	110	ADD Dn, ⟨ea⟩

Bits 0–5 are the general effective address ⟨ea⟩ as used in the MOVE instruction and will be discussed fully in Chapter 6.

2.6   A PROGRAM TO ADD TWO NUMBERS

We are now in a position to return to the short program described in Sections 2.2 and 2.3. The instructions (in outline) will look like:

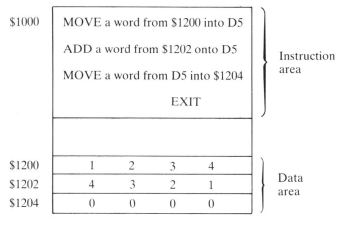

Fig. 2.10

The three instructions must now be filled in in detail.

The first instruction
MOVE from memory address $1200 to D5

is another example of the MOVE instruction introduced in 2.4. This time the 'source address mode' must indicate that the data is to be found in memory. An extension word is used to hold the memory address.
The operation word is:

Function				Destination						Source		Source	
0	0	1	1	1	0	1	0	0	0	?		?	

MOVE a word	into D5	from memory

Fig. 2.11

It will be shown in Chapter 6 that the source fields and extension word are set up as follows:

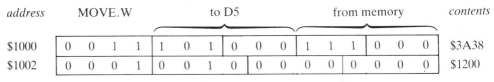

address	MOVE.W				to D5			from memory						contents
$1000	0	0	1	1	1	0	1	0	0	0	1	1	1	0 0 0	$3A38
$1002	0	0	0	1	0	0	1	0	0	0	0	0	0	0 0 0	$1200

i.e. address $1200 contains the source data

Fig. 2.12

The second instruction

ADD the contents of address $1202 onto D5 was introduced in Section 2.5 and is coded as follows:

address	ADD a word				to D5			from memory						contents
$1004	1	1	0	1	1	0	1	0	0	1	1	1	1	0 0 0	$DA78
$1006	0	0	0	1	0	0	1	0	0	0	0	0	0	0 1 0	$1202

i.e. address $1202 contains the source data

Fig. 2.13

The third instruction

MOVE from D5, into memory location $1204 is coded as:

address	MOVE.W				to memory			from D5						contents
$1008	0	0	1	1	0	0	0	1	1	1	0	0	0	1 0 1	$31C5
$100A	0	0	0	1	0	0	1	0	0	0	0	0	0	1 0 0	$1204

i.e. address $1204 is the destination of the data transfer

Fig. 2.14

2.6.1   The complete machine code program

Figure 2.15 shows the whole program in memory. EXIT at the end of the list of instructions indicates to the processor that it should no longer FETCH and EXECUTE from here as it has come to the end of the instructions.

The code that will be used for EXIT is $4E40. This is not a STOP or HALT instruction, i.e. it does not halt the processor. Its effect will be described in Chapter 3.

hex address	hex contents				
1000	3	A	3	8	MOVE.W $1200, D5
1002	1	2	0	0	
1004	D	A	7	8	ADD.W $1202, D5
1006	1	2	0	2	
1008	3	1	C	5	MOVE.W D5, $1204
100A	1	2	0	4	
100C	EXIT				EXIT has code $4E40
.	.				
.	.				
.	.				
1200	1	2	3	4	x
1202	4	3	2	1	y
1204	0	0	0	0	z for z:=x+y

Fig. 2.15

2.7   THE FETCH–EXECUTE CYCLE FOR THIS PROGRAM

In Chapter 1, the fetch–execute cycle was explained in general terms. Detailed execution of the first instruction of the program just developed will now be shown. Only the processor registers used during the course of the execution are shown.

(i)   Initially:

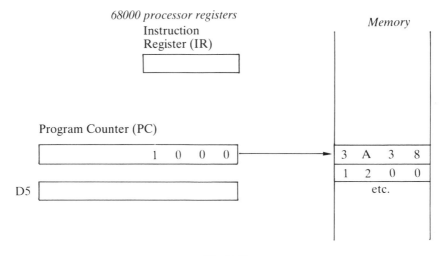

Fig. 2.16

(ii)   After the first instruction is fetched (control word only):

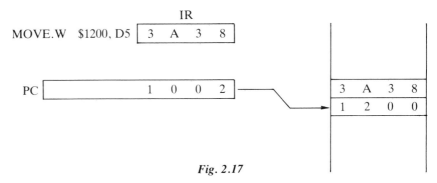

Fig. 2.17

(iii)   After decode of the control word:

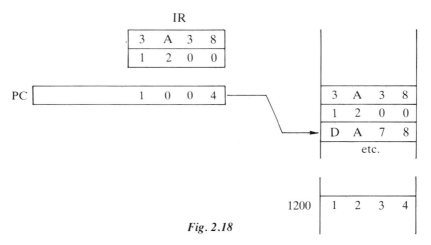

Fig. 2.18

(iv)   After execution of the first instruction:

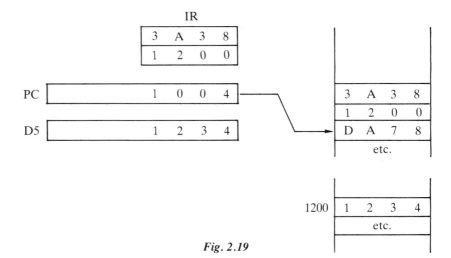

Fig. 2.19

The steps shown in Figs. 2.16 to 2.19 are as follows:

- Fetch the instruction pointed to by the PC into the instruction register (IR) (an internal register of the processor which is not programmable).
- Increment the PC by 2 (bytes).
- Decode the control word of the instruction. In this case, the addressing mode indicates that there is an extension word so fetch this from memory.
- Increment the PC by 2 (bytes).
  (The PC now points to the next instruction.)
- Execute the instruction.
  Use the address contained in the extension word of the instruction to fetch the word of data from memory into D5.
- The processor is now ready to fetch and execute the next instruction.

2.8 THE MOVE INSTRUCTION TO MOVE A CONSTANT

In order to provide material for further exercises, a variation of the MOVE instruction with an 'immediate' addressing mode is introduced. In the program developed in Section 2.6, an extension word was used to hold the address of a data value as follows:

	MOVE.W						to D5						from memory			
$1000	0	0	1	1	1	0	1	0	0	0	1	1	1	0	0	0
$1002	0	0	0	1	0	0	1	0	0	0	0	0	0	0	0	0
							address $1200									
$1200	0	0	0	1	0	0	1	0	0	0	1	1	0	1	0	0

(This bit pattern indicates that the extension word is a single word address.)

contents data $1234

Fig. 2.20

If, in a more extensive program, such a data value is computed by the instructions of the program, i.e. it is a variable, this addressing method is suitable. If, however, the data value is constant, then the extension word of the instruction can be used to hold the constant rather than its address. The technical term for this usage is 'immediate mode' addressing, for example:

MOVE.W						to D5						from memory			
0	0	1	1	1	0	1	0	0	0	1	1	1	1	0	0
0	0	0	1	0	0	1	0	0	0	1	1	0	1	0	0
						constant $1234									

(This bit pattern indicates that the extension word is an 'immediate mode' constant.)

Fig. 2.21

When the instruction is executed, the constant \$1234 is copied into the least significant 16 bits of D5. This illustrates that constants can be embedded within the instructions of the 68000. It should be noted, however, that 16 bits are used to hold the constant and 6 bits to tell the hardware it is the first extension word of the instruction.

2.9   THE MOVEQ INSTRUCTION FOR SMALL CONSTANTS

A common requirement is for the manipulation of small integer constants. The MOVEQ instruction is a single word instruction where the immediate data is an 8-bit integer constant incorporated into the control word as follows:

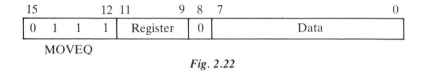

Fig. 2.22

Movement is always into a data register. The range of the data is −128 to +127, see Section 1.9, which is sign-extended to fill the 32 bits of the data register when it is transferred at run-time, i.e. the sign-bit (most significant bit) of the 8-bit data field is propagated to fill the most significant 24 bits of the destination data register, thus preserving the sign of the data.

2.10   SUMMARY

The detailed binary coding of a small number of instructions has been explained as fully as possible at this stage. The concept of addressing modes has been briefly touched upon and this topic is treated systematically in Chapter 6. In practice, only hardware designers need to be constantly aware of this level of detail and in the rest of this text, machine code will be brought in only when necessary for illustration. Assembly code will be used as a shorthand notation for machine code and this is introduced in Chapter 4.

For those using the 68000 for serious programming, however, there will be occasions when it is necessary to examine the machine code of an instruction. The Motorola M68000 16/32-bit Microprocessor Programmer's Reference Manual, 4th edition, specifies the detailed bit coding of every instruction.

Chapter 3 takes the program developed in Section 2.6 and shows how to load it into a 68000 system and execute it.

3

The TUTOR single board computer development system

3.1 INTRODUCTION

The emphasis in this chapter is on how to use a 68000 system. Although a particular single board development system, Motorola's TUTOR, is used the requirements for setting up and executing a program are quite general. It has been found, for example, that the facilities available in TUTOR, 'Macsbug' and 'Versabug' (also single board development systems) are virtually identical with slight variations in syntax.

A complete specification of the full set of TUTOR commands is not given in this text. It is assumed that readers will obtain details of their particular development systems from elsewhere. Sufficient is included to indicate the likely range of facilities provided. TUTOR is a program which is always in the 68000 memory, see Fig. 3.1, and which is entered when the RESET button is pressed. In the words of the manufacturer: 'TUTOR is a resident firmware package (stored in two 8k × 8 ROM or EPROM devices) which provides a self-contained programming and operating environment'.

The user interacts with TUTOR via the console VDU using a simple set of commands. By giving appropriate commands, a program may be set up in the memory, executed under the control of TUTOR and the results stored in the memory may be examined. The program developed in Section 2.6 is used as an example.

This chapter may be omitted by readers without a practical requirement.

The general format of a TUTOR command, typed in response to the TUTOR prompt is:

TUTOR 1.X > ⟨command⟩ [⟨parameters⟩] [;⟨option⟩]

i.e.   TUTOR 1.X > ⟨command mnemonic⟩ ⟨parameter list with spaces as separators and any option on a parameter preceded by;⟩

In the following sections, sufficient TUTOR commands will be introduced to allow the program developed in Chapter 2 to be entered into the memory and executed. User input is underlined for clarity. In each case the general format is given, followed by some simple examples.

In Chapter 4, further commands, associated with loading larger programs, are explained. (See Fig. 3.2.)

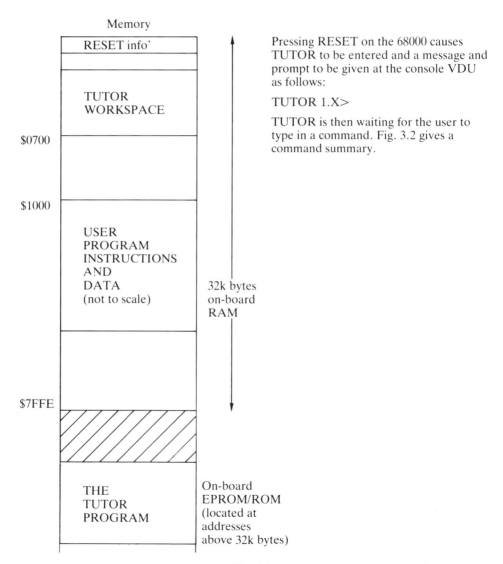

Pressing RESET on the 68000 causes TUTOR to be entered and a message and prompt to be given at the console VDU as follows:

TUTOR 1.X>

TUTOR is then waiting for the user to type in a command. Fig. 3.2 gives a command summary.

Fig. 3.1

Command mnemonic	Description
MD	Memory Display
MM, M	Memory Modify
MS	Memory Set
.A0–.A7	Display/Set Address Register
.D0–.D7	Display/Set Data Register
.PC	Display/Set Program Counter
.SR	Display/Set Status Register
.SS	Display/Set Supervisor Stack Pointer
.US	Display/Set User Stack Pointer
DF	Display Formatted Registers
OF	Display Offsets
.R0–.R6	Display/Set Relative Offset Register
BF	Block of Memory Fill
BM	Block of Memory Move
BT	Block of Memory Test
BS	Block of Memory Search
DC	Data Conversion
BR	Breakpoint Set
NOBR	Breakpoint Remove
GO, G	Go
GT	Go Until Breakpoint
GD	Go Direct
TR, T	Trace
TT	Temporary Breakpoint Trace
PA	Printer Attach
NOPA	Reset Printer Attach
PF	Port Format
TM	Transparent Mode
*	Send Message to Port 2
HE	HELP
DU	Dump Memory
LO	Load
VE	Verify

Fig. 3.2 The TUTOR Commands

3.2 MEMORY DISPLAY MD

MD ⟨address⟩ [⟨count⟩] [;⟨options⟩]

The MD command is used to display a section of memory beginning at ⟨address⟩ and displaying the number of bytes given as ⟨count⟩. The default option is hexadecimal together with equivalent ASCII but :DI gives a disassembled form.

E.g. TUTOR 1.X > MD 1000

asks TUTOR to display the contents of address $1000 at the console VDU. The output gives a minimum of sixteen bytes as follows:

TUTOR 1.X > MD 1000

```
0010000    00    00    . . . . . . . . . . . . . . . .    00    00    . . . . . . . . . . . . . . . .
            ↑     ↑                                        ↑     ↑
Address    byte  byte                                    byte  byte    ASCII equivalent
           1000  1001                                    100E  100F
```

Several options are available with this command but perhaps the most useful is that pressing carriage return (CR) after this display is output will cause another sixteen lines to be output.

3.3   MEMORY SET MS

MS ⟨address⟩ ⟨data . . . . .⟩

The MS command alters memory by setting data into the specified address. The data can take the form of an ASCII string or hexadecimal data.

E.g. TUTOR 1.X > MS 1000 3A38
                        ↑   ↑
                     address contents

3.4   MEMORY MODIFY MM

MM ⟨address⟩ [;options]

The MM command is used to display memory and, if required, to change the contents of the displayed addresses. The default unit of display is one byte but W and L options may be used to display words or long words.

E.g. TUTOR   1.X >   MM 1000;W
```
      001000    3A38?                  to leave unchanged press CR
      001002    0000?    1000          enter new contents and press CR to continue
      001004    0000?    DA78          enter new contents and press CR to continue
        .
        .
      00100C    0000?    4E40.         enter new contents then . to terminate and return
                                       to a TUTOR prompt.
```

3.5   TO RUN A PROGRAM, GO

GO ⟨address⟩

E.g. TUTOR 1.X > <u>GO 1000</u>

Causes the program counter to be set to $1000 and execution to proceed from that address. The fetch–execute cycle continues through the instructions of the program until the EXIT instruction is fetched. This instruction causes a return to TUTOR and a TUTOR prompt to be given.

3.6   SETTING THE PROGRAM COUNTER, .PC

If the address is omitted from the GO command execution proceeds from the current value of the program counter. An alternative procedure is as follows:

TUTOR 1.X > <u>. PC 1000</u>   sets the program counter to 1000
.PC = 000010000
TUTOR 1.X > <u>GO</u>   starts execution

3.7   TO LOAD AND RUN A PROGRAM

The program developed in Chapter 2 can now be set up in memory and executed.

TUTOR	1.X >	MM 1000;W	
001000	0000?	<u>3A38</u>	<u>return</u>
001002	0000?	<u>1200</u>	<u>return</u>
001004	0000?	<u>DA78</u>	<u>return</u>
001006	0000?	<u>1202</u>	<u>return</u>
001008	0000?	<u>31C5</u>	<u>return</u>
00100A	0000?	<u>1204</u>	<u>return</u>
00100C	0000?	<u>4E40</u>.	
TUTOR	1.X >	MM 1200;W	
001200	0000?	<u>1234</u>	<u>return</u>
001202	0000?	<u>4321</u>	<u>return</u>
001204	0000?	<u>.</u>	

TUTOR 1.X > <u>MD 1000</u>
001000 3A 38 12 00 DA 78 12 02 31 12 04 4E 40 00 00 etc.

TUTOR 1.X > <u>MD 1200</u>
001200 12 34 43 21 00 00 00 00 etc.

TUTOR 1.X > GO 1000

at the end of the program on exit to TUTOR is followed by some output, see Section 3.8, and a prompt

TUTOR 1.X > MD 1200

001200 12 34 43 21 55 55 00 00 etc.

Note that after executing the program the result of the addition is stored in word $1204.

3.8   DISPLAY REGISTERS DF AND TUTOR OUTPUT ON PROGRAM EXIT

Individual registers may be displayed and set if required as described in 3.6 for the PC.

.An is used for address register n, n = 0 – 7
.Dn is used for data register n, n = 0 – 7
.PC for the program counter
.SR for the status register, see Chapter 5
.SS for the supervisor stack pointer, see Chapter 12
.US for the user stack pointer, see Chapter 12.

E.g. TUTOR 1.X > .A0
      .A0 = 00000000
      TUTOR 1.X > .A0 1000
      .A0 = 00001000

All the registers may be displayed using DF (display formatted registers).

TUTOR 1.X > DF

```
PC=00001010    SR=2704=.S7..Z..   US=00002000   SS=00001300
D0=00000000    D1=00000000  D2=00000000   D3=00000000
D4=00000000    D5=00000000  D6=00000000   D7=00000000
A0=00000000    A1=00000000  A2=00000000   A3=00000000
A4=00000000    A5=00000000  A6=00000000   A7=00001300
---------------------------------------------
001010       0C000030      CMP.B        #48,D0
```

This output is also given automatically on program exit into TUTOR and when ABORT is pressed. SR, US and SS will be discussed in later chapters.

The instruction at the address to which the PC points is disassembled and shown as the last line.

3.9   TRACING THROUGH A PROGRAM, TR

TR ⟨count⟩

The TR command causes instructions to be executed, one at a time, beginning at the location pointed to by the program counter. After execution of each instruction, the registers are displayed as shown in Section 3.8. If ⟨count⟩ is included, ⟨count⟩ instructions are traced before a TUTOR prompt is given. After trace mode is entered, the TUTOR prompt includes a colon (:). Pressing return in response to such a prompt causes one further instruction to be traced. To exit from trace mode, any command may be given. Tracing the program in Section 3.7 gives:

e.g.   TUTOR 1.X > .D5 = 0
.D5 = 00000000

     TUTOR 1.X > .PC 1000
.PC = 00001000

     TUTOR 1.X > TR

PC = 1002	SR = ...	US = ...	SS = ...
D0 = ...	D1 = ...	D2 = ...	D3 = ...
D4 = ...	D5 = 00001234	D6 = ...	D7 = ...

A0
A4 etc.

               PC 1002   ADD.W 1202, D5   (next instruction)

     TUTOR 1.X : > CR   (carriage return pressed)
PC = 1004
registers as above except
          D5 = 00005555

            PC 1004   MOVE.W D5. 1204

     TUTOR 1.X : > CR
PC = 1008
registers as above

     TUTOR 1.X : > MD 1200 etc.

3.10   BREAKPOINTS, BR

     BR [⟨address⟩[;⟨count⟩]]

Tracing through a program is a useful method of checking the correctness of its logic at run time. For a long program however, tracing is tedious and it is more convenient to execute a program at full speed without trace output until a point is reached where tracing is required. A breakpoint may be set at such a point. Execution ceases before the instruction at the breakpoint is executed, the registers are displayed and a TUTOR prompt is output, e.g.:

     TUTOR 1.X > BR 1008
BREAKPOINTS 1008

TUTOR 1.X > <u>GO 1000</u>
AT BREAKPOINT
PC = 1008   SR =   etc.
D0 = ...
D4 = ...   D5 = 00005555
A0 = etc.

TUTOR 1.X > <u>GO</u>   continue from current PC
i.e. proceed from breakpoint.

Breakpoints may be removed by:

TUTOR 1.X > <u>NOBR 1008</u>
or
TUTOR 1.X > <u>NOBR</u> to remove all.

Up to eight simultaneous breakpoints may be set.

4

Assembling and loading

4.1 INTRODUCTION

In Chapters 2 and 3, programs were written in machine code and were concerned with detailed bit-patterns. Although this approach is good as an introduction to the machine it is not a viable method of writing, loading and running realistic programs.

Instead of hexadecimal patterns of machine code, as in Chapter 2, loaded manually into the machine as shown in Chapter 3, programs are written in a mnemonic form called an Assembly Language. This requires:

- A translating program – an *assembler*
  so that programs may be written in a convenient mnemonic form and be automatically translated into the bit patterns required by the machine. The assembler creates the assembly language level of Fig. 1.1.
- A *loader*
  so that large programs can be set up quickly in the memory (instead of repeated use of the MM or MS commands).

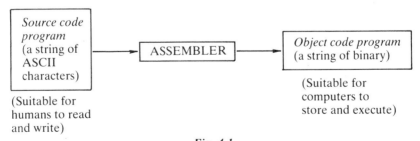

Fig. 4.1

In this text, the method of *cross-assembling* and *down-line loading* will be assumed. This method avoids purchasing 68000 systems with large amounts of software for editing, file handling, etc. and discs for file storage. Instead, the powerful editing and file storage facilities of a mainframe or *host* computer are used to create and store source code files in 68000 assembly code. A cross-assembler program runs on such a host machine. Its input is source-code files in 68000 assembly code and its output is object-code files which are the binary patterns to be loaded into the 68000 as machine code programs together with some control and formatting information. An object code file can then be down-line loaded from the host's file store into the memory of a selected 68000 system.

This method is useful in an educational environment since the 68000 systems are not occupied while source code is being entered at the host. It is also used in industrial microprocessor applications where the host machine is used for program development. Here, the microprocessors are target machines into which software is loaded and which runs for long periods controlling industrial processes.

The assembler presented here is Motorola's standard MC68000 assembler. It is included in most development systems as a resident assembler and cross-assembler versions are available for most hosts.

4.2   MNEMONIC INSTRUCTIONS

Fig. 1.17 gives the full list of 68000 operation codes. Translation of this fixed length list of instruction mnemonics into the corresponding bit-patterns is a process ideally suited to automation by a computer. In detail, the assembler reads a sequence of ASCII characters such as MOVE terminated by a non-alphabetic character such as a space, matches MOVE with a table entry and looks up the corresponding binary pattern to build up the object code.

As an example, consider the source code and object code for:

   MOVE.W D0, D3

The source code form of this instruction is a string of ASCII characters (excluding tab before the instruction and carriage return, line feed after it) as follows:

$4D	$4F	$56	$45	$2E	$57	$20	$44	$30	$2C	$44	$33
M	O	V	E	.	W	space	D	0	,	D	3

It should be noted that eight bits are required to represent each character, 96 bits for the instruction without formatting or comment.

The object code, developed in Section 2.6 is the one-word instruction

0011	011 000	000 000
MOVE.W	to D3	from D0

4.3   SYMBOLS DEFINED BY THE PROGRAMMER

It would be very tedious if assembly language programs only allowed operation codes to be written in symbolic form, leaving the programmer to work out all addresses in hexadecimal. The editing of programs, inserting and deleting instructions, would be virtually impossible. Assemblers therefore allow symbolic names to be given to addresses. For example:

MOVE.W D5, DATA   instead of   MOVE.W D5, $1200
             ↑   ↑
      (symbolic address)   (hex address)

The assembler will accept two methods of giving a symbolic name or label to some address or location. First, implied by format:

LABEL   MOVE.W D5, DATA
DATA   DC $1234

Second, by terminating the label with a colon(:):

LABEL: MOVE.W D5, DATA

The latter method is used in the body of the text where formatting may not be clear. The former method is used in general in the program listings. A user-defined symbol must start with an alphabetic character and may consist of alphanumeric characters. A specific assembler implementation will probably place a limit on the total number of characters allowed.

There are therefore two kinds of symbol:

- Defined as part of the mnemonic assembly language, for example mnemonics for operation codes (but other kinds will be introduced below).
- Defined by the user.

A precise specification of all aspects of the assembler will not be given in this chapter, but instead, assembler features will be introduced as required.

4.4   EXAMPLE OF AN ASSEMBLY CODE PROGRAM

```
            TTL      FIRST          * optional title
            ORG      $1000          * base address for subsequent instructions
START:      MOVE.W   DATA,D5        * move contents of location DATA into D5
            ADD.W    NEXT,D5        * add contents of location NEXT onto D5
            MOVE.W   D5, ANSWER|    * move contents of D5
                                    * into location ANSWER

            MOVE.W   #$1234,D2      * move constant into D2 (immediate mode)

            MOVEQ    #1,D3          * move short constant into D3
            MOVE.W   #1,D4          * two word instruction used for same

EXIT:       TRAP     #0            * end of instructions (EXIT)
                                    * (transfer into TUTOR)
            ORG      $1200          * base address for subsequent words
DATA:       DC.W     $1234          * declare a word constant
NEXT:       DC.W     $4321
ANSWER:     DC.W     0

            END
```

Fig. 4.2

4.4.1   General points on the program syntax

* precedes a comment which is ignored by the assembler.

$ indicates that a number is in hexadecimal.

\# precedes an immediate operand (constant) and distinguishes it from an address (see Chapter 6).

D0 to D7 are data registers.

ORG (origin) gives a base address from where what follows is to be loaded.

START, EXIT, DATA, NEXT and ANSWER are defined by the programmer.

DC (see Section 4.6 below) asks the assembler to set up data.

TRAP #0 is the EXIT instruction. It will be described fully in Chapter 12.

4.4.2   Symbols

The symbols used in this program which are defined as part of the language are:

Operation codes:	MOVE.W
	ADD.W
	MOVEQ
	TRAP
Register names:	D2, D3, D4, D5
Assembler directives:	TTL (see Section 4.5 below)
	ORG
	DC
	END

The symbols used in this program which are defined by the programmer are given in the following symbol table:

symbol	hex value
START	1000
EXIT	1016
DATA	1200
NEXT	1202
ANSWER	1204

Fig. 4.3

E.g. START is the name for location $1000 or the symbol START has value $1000, etc. One task the assembler must carry out is to work out the values of the user-defined symbols. This symbol table is made available to the user, see Section 4.7, Fig. 4.4, etc.

The source code file

```
          TTL FIRST
          ORG $1000

          MOVE      DATA,D5
          ADD       NEXT,D5
          MOVE      D5,ANSWER

          MOVE      #$1234,D2

          MOVEQ     #1,D3
          MOVE      #1,D4

          TRAP      #0

          ORG       $1200
DATA:     DC        $1234
NEXT:     DC        $4321
ANSWER:   DC        0

          END
```

The list file

	object code		source code	
	00001000		ORG	$1000
location	contents			
001000	3A381200		MOVE	DATA,D5
001004	DA781202		ADD	NEXT,D5
001008	31C51204		MOVE	D5,ANSWER
00100C	343C1234		MOVE	#$1234,D2
001010	7601		MOVEQ	#1,D3
001012	383C0001		MOVE	#1,D4
001016	4E40		TRAP	#0
	00001200		ORG	$1200
001200	1234	DATA:	DC	$1234
001202	4321	NEXT:	DC	$4321
001204	0000	ANSWER:	DC	0
			END	

****** TOTAL ERRORS   0 —   0 — TOTAL LINES 19

APPROX   2116 UNUSED SYMBOL TABLE ENTRIES

ANSWER   001204 DATA   001200 NEXT   001202

The object code file (not readable)

```
S00600004844521B
S11310003A381200DA78120231C51204343C123430
S10B10107601283C00014E405A
S109120012344321000003A
S9030000FC
```

Fig. 4.4

4.4.3   Data types and default values

The instructions MOVE.W and ADD.W were used in the program. In general:

OPCODE.B indicates that the operation is on data of type byte (8 bits).
OPCODE.L indicates that the operation is on data of type longword (32 bits).
OPCODE.W indicates that the operation is on data of type word (16 bits).

If the data type is not specified it is assumed to be of type word.

MOVE   DATA, D5
MOVE.W DATA, D5 have the same effect.

4.5   ASSEMBLER DIRECTIVES

The program in Fig. 4.2 contains statements such as:

MOVE.W DATA, D5

which are a mnemonic form of a single 68000 instruction.
The program statements:

TTL   FIRST
ORG $1000
DC.W $1234
END

do not correspond to 68000 instructions but are directives from the programmer to
the assembler.
Some assembler directives cause no object code to be generated, for example:

TTL FIRST asks the assembler to note the program title on output listings.
END   tells the assembler there are no more statements to translate.
ORG $1000 tells the assembler where the next section of program is to be
                loaded in the memory so that the assembler can work out the
                values of symbolic addresses.

Some assembler directives cause object code to be generated, for example:

DC.W $1234 asks the assembler to set up a 16-bit word of data as described in
                Section 4.6.

4.6   SETTING UP DATA AREAS (DC AND DS)

DC is a directive to the assembler to set up one or more data values, for example:

DC.B	$12	*set up the 8-bit byte 00010010
DC.W	$1234	*set up a 16-bit word
DC	$1234	*set up a 16-bit word (word by default)
DC.L	$12345678	*set up a 32-bit longword

DC may be used to request the assembler to set up a list of data values in contiguous locations, for example:

```
DC.B        $12,  $34,  $56,  $78,  $9A,  $BC
DC          $1234,  $5678,  $9ABC,  $DEF3
```

DC.B may also be used to set up the ASCII value of characters, for example:

```
DC.B 'A'              *set up the ASCII value of the character A
```

This is equivalent to DC.B $41
Also for a string   DC.B 'HATFIELD'* set up ASCII values for the 8 bytes
is equivalent to   DC.B $48, $41, $54, $46, etc.
and also to   DC.B 'H', 'A', 'T', 'F', etc.

DC may also be used to ask the assembler to insert the values of symbols defined by the programmer as constants, for example:

```
POINTER:  DC   DATA
```

would cause the assembler to set up a word constant with value $1200 in the program in Section 4.4. The location with symbolic name POINTER contains the value $1200. The difference between 'DATA', a string of ASCII characters and DATA, the value of a user defined symbol should be noted.

As before, a list may be set up:

```
POINTER_TABLE:  DC  ROUTINE1,  ROUTINE2, etc.
```

DS is a directive to the assembler to reserve locations which will be used to hold data when the program runs, for example, input data or computed values. The initial contents are unspecified.

```
DS.B   4     *reserve four bytes
DS.W  10     *reserve ten (decimal) words
DS    10     *reserve ten words
```

Care must be taken in using DC and DS for an odd number of bytes. If word or longword data or an instruction is to follow, it must always start on a word boundary, an even address. A good assembler implementation should check this for the programmer. Assembler directives which do not appear in the program are discussed in Section 4.8 and Fig. 4.7 shows the complete range and their effect in the object code.

4.7   SOURCE CODE, OBJECT CODE AND LIST FILES

An example of a source code program is given in Fig. 4.2 and Section 4.4. This is typed into a mainframe or host computer using an editor. The cross-assembler is then run and the source code file to be translated is specified.

The cross-assembler attempts to translate the source code into object code and if there are no errors an object code file is produced. As this is a string of binary, a

readable representation of the object code is also produced by the assembler (called
the list file). If the assembler has found errors in the source code, these are given in
the list file. It is therefore essential to examine the list file in order to detect and
correct errors in the source code. The list file is also essential when the program is
loaded into the target 68000 and run since it contains the object code and the values of
all user-defined symbols. Fig. 4.4 shows a source code file, and the corresponding
list file and object code file. The list file should be examined in detail as an exercise,
in particular, the object code and the symbol table (see also Section 4.7.1). Fig. 4.5

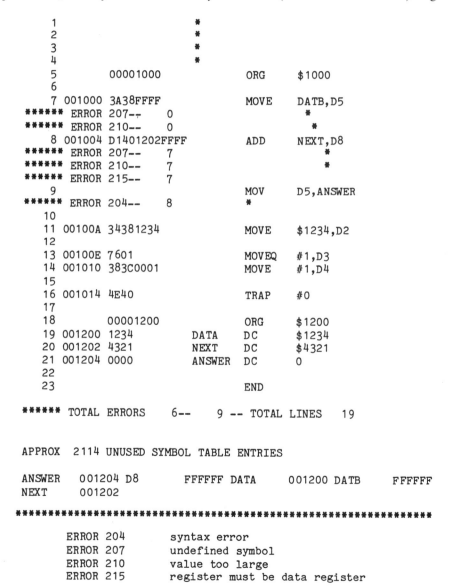

```
      1                             *
      2                             *
      3                             *
      4                             *
      5           00001000              ORG     $1000
      6
      7 001000 3A38FFFF               MOVE    DATB,D5
****** ERROR 207--     0              *
****** ERROR 210--     0                        *
      8 001004 D1401202FFFF           ADD     NEXT,D8
****** ERROR 207--     7              *
****** ERROR 210--     7                        *
****** ERROR 215--     7
      9                             MOV     D5,ANSWER
****** ERROR 204--     8              *
     10
     11 00100A 34381234              MOVE    $1234,D2
     12
     13 00100E 7601                  MOVEQ   #1,D3
     14 001010 383C0001              MOVE    #1,D4
     15
     16 001014 4E40                  TRAP    #0
     17
     18           00001200              ORG     $1200
     19 001200 1234      DATA       DC      $1234
     20 001202 4321      NEXT       DC      $4321
     21 001204 0000      ANSWER     DC      0
     22
     23                             END

****** TOTAL ERRORS    6--    9 -- TOTAL LINES    19


APPROX  2114 UNUSED SYMBOL TABLE ENTRIES

ANSWER     001204 D8      FFFFF DATA       001200 DATB       FFFFF
NEXT       001202

**********************************************************************
           ERROR 204        syntax error
           ERROR 207        undefined symbol
           ERROR 210        value too large
           ERROR 215        register must be data register
```

Fig. 4.5   Assembly listing showing errors

shows a similar source code file with some deliberate mistakes introduced together with the corresponding list file (see Section 4.7.2).

Using the DECSYSTEM 10 as an example, the sequence of activities is:

Create TEST.M68 using an editor
./M68XAS   TEST.M68
run the cross-assembler; tell it what to assemble

the assembler will output a message, e.g.:

0 ERRORS
ASSEMBLY COMPLETE

The user's file directory will then contain:

TEST.M68   the source code file
TEST.OBJ   the object code file
TEST.LST   the list file

Using VAX Berkeley 4.1 UNIX as an example, the sequence is:

Create test.m68 using an editor

%m68k m 1 x test.m68
run the cross-assembler and tell it what to assemble

After which the user's file directory will contain:

test.m68   the source code file
test.s   the object code file
test.1   the list file

4.7.1   Some details from a list file

Taking Fig. 4.4 as an example, consider the first instruction as shown in the list file:

location   contents   source code
1000   3A381200   MOVE   DATA,D5

Through the list file, the assembler informs us that the instruction will be loaded from location 1000 and will occupy four bytes, value 3A381200. In detail (see also Section 2.4.2):

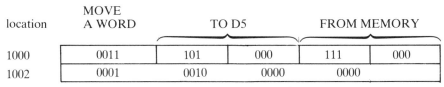

location	MOVE A WORD	TO D5		FROM MEMORY	
1000	0011	101	000	111	000
1002	0001	0010	0000	0000	

address in memory $1200

Fig. 4.6

The symbol DATA has been translated by the assembler into the value $1200. This can be seen from the list file statement where the symbol is defined:

location	contents	source code
1200	1234	DATA:DC $1234

or from the symbol table at the end of the list file which gives the values of all the user defined symbols. In Fig. 4.4, the symbol table is:

symbol	value
ANSWER	001204
DATA	001200
NEXT	001202

4.7.2   Errors detected by the assembler

The assembler translates correct 68000 source code into object code. If there are mistakes in the source code, the assembler will be unable to complete this task. Fig. 4.5 shows the list file for a source file containing source code errors. There will be no object code file in this case. By means of the list file the assembler indicates to the programmer which source code statements it was unable to translate and attempts to specify what the error is. Fig. 4.5 shows that the assembler is not very good at doing this, for example, ERROR 207, is not a very helpful message. The complete list of error messages is not given here since it is implementation specific.

The errors in Fig. 4.5 are as follows:

1.   MOVE   DATB,   D5
     DATB was typed instead of DATA. There is no symbol DATB defined by the programmer so the 'undefined symbol' message is appropriate. The second error message was in case the programmer was trying to specify a data register with allowed range D0 to D7.
2.   ADD   NEXT,   D8
     In this case a slip was probably made, the programmer intended to use the highest data register and forgot the range was D0 to D7; 'value too large' is appropriate. The other error messages tell the programmer that the symbol D8 has not been defined for an address in memory and if it had the instruction would still be incorrect since only a data register is allowed in the field in ADD ⟨ea⟩, Dn
3.   MOV   D5,   ANSWER
     Probably a slip in typing the program. The assembler cannot make sense of the format of the statements since it has not found an operation code to indicate the statement is an instruction, neither has it found a directive. It gives the general message 'syntax error'.

Finally, the assembler appears to indicate that there are six errors when there are only three. This is just a count of the error messages, but it can be quite disconcerting for a beginner. It is possible for a large number of 'errors' to be removed by a single edit of the source file. All the symbols found by the assembler are entered in the symbol table with value FFFFFF even though the symbols are undefined.

The message after the END statement of the program:

TOTAL ERRORS 6 – 9 – TOTAL LINES 19

indicates that six errors were found in this program. There are 19 lines of source excluding comments, and the highest line number in which an error is found is 9. The error message in line 9 contains the next highest line number containing an error. The error locations are therefore *chained* through the list file and this is helpful in locating the errors in very long programs.

4.8   THE EQU DIRECTIVE (EQUATE)

This directive allows a value to be assigned to a symbol directly by the programmer. An entry is made directly into the symbol table of symbol and value. No object code is generated and the symbol is *not* a name for a location. The general form is:

```
symbol                  EQU   expression
(string of alphanumeric       (combination of symbols, constants
characters)                   and operators, see Section 4.9)
```

The assembler works out the value of the expression which must be an integer.

A program will usually start with an EQU list of often-used constants, for example:

```
LENGTH   EQU   $8
MASK     EQU   $000F
DEVICE   EQU   $3FF01
```

When the assembler encounters the symbol in the program text, it replaces it with the value from the symbol table, thus:

```
MOVEQ   #LENGTH,   D1
```

can be used instead of:

```
MOVEQ   #8,   D1   (the object code is identical).
```

The aim is to use names in the program text to make it easier to read and to locate in one place those items which might need to be changed if a variation of the program is required.

A further example is:

```
LABEL   | EQU   *
```

which may be used to label a location where the contents are typed on the next line in the assembly language program. The * symbol can in this case be read as 'where you are now'. An example is:

```
* the function of ROUTINE is . . .
ROUTINE   EQU   *
          MOVE   A,B
          etc.
```

The purpose of this usage is to make the name of the routine stand out and to make the body easy to edit (without having to retype the name).

```
SYMBOL   EQU   *
```

may also be used to give two symbolic names to the same location. An example showing this is given in Chapter 7 and is as follows:

```
          ORG   $1000
STACK     EQU   *
START     LEA   STACK,  SP
```

The symbols STACK and START are entered into the symbol table each with the value $1000. The programmer is reminded by the names that START is where the instructions of the program start but also that a data area called STACK is being defined growing from where the program starts towards the low end of memory. This will be explained fully in Chapter 7. The point here is that it may be convenient to give two names to a location.

4.9   THE SET DIRECTIVE

The directive SET is used in a similar way to EQU. The difference is that when SET is used the symbol may be redefined in a later SET statement to a different value. This is illustrated in Fig. 4.7.

4.10   EXPRESSIONS

It has been explained that the assembler notes the user-defined symbols in a symbol table together with their values. Expressions may be used in assembly language programs which consist of symbols, constants and operators, for example:

```
DATA + 2
LENGTH – 1
```

The assembler computes a value for the expression. In the program introduced in Section 4.4, for example, DATA had value $1200. The expression DATA + 2

```
 1                               * The following list of statements is not a program
 2                               * It illustrates assembler directives
 3
 4                                       NOPAGE
 5                               * directive to suppress page headings
 6                                       G
 7                               * G requests all characters in lists and strings to
 8                               * be shown in the list file
 9                               * the default is that only the first element is shown
10
11         00001000                      ORG     $1000
12                               * locates the addresses in the program in memory
13
14                               * labels may be indicated by format
15                               * or be terminated by :
16 001000 1234                   DATA:   DC      $1234
17 001002 1234                           DC.W    $1234     * same since .W is default
18 001004 12                     LAB1    DC.B    $12
19 001006 12345678                       DC.L    $12345678
20 00100A 0A                     LAB2    DC.B    10,5,7    * decimal radix is default
20 00100B 05
20 00100C 07
21
22         0000000A             TEN     EQU     10        * note the symbol table entry
23 00100D 0A                             DC.B    TEN,5,7
23 00100E 05
23 00100F 07
24 001010 000A                           DC      TEN,5,7
24 001012 0005
24 001014 0007
25
26         00000005             SYM     SET     5         * like EQU but temporary
27 001016 0005                           DC      SYM
28         00000020             SYM     SET     $20       * new value for symbol SYM
29 001018 0020                           DC      SYM
30
31         0000101A             ADDRESS EQU     *
32                               * ADDRESS is entered in the symbol table
33                               * with the current location as its value
34 00101A 30381000                       MOVE    DATA,D0 * this has label ADDRESS
35
36         00001100                      ORG     $1100
37 001100 1000                   LAB3    DC      DATA
38 001102 1001                           DC      DATA+1 * expression
39 001104 1001                           DC      DATA+3-2
40
41 001106 41                             DC.B    'A'     * ASCII character
42 001107 4D                             DC.B    'MESSAGE'
   001108 45
   001109 53
   00110A 53
   00110B 41
   00110C 47
   00110D 45
```

```
43 00110E 41          LAB4    DC.W    'A'
   00110F 00
44 001110 41                  DC      'A'
   001111 00
45 001112 31                  DC.L    '1234'
   001113 32
   001114 33
   001115 34
46 001116 111E                DC      LAB5    * forward reference OK
47 001118 0000                DC      LAB8    * LAB8 requires >16 bits
****** ERROR 210--     0
48 00111A 00100000            DC.L    LAB8
49                     * DS does not initialize storage to 0
50 00111E 000A         LAB5    DS.B    10      * space for 10 bytes
51 001128 0014                DS      10      * space for 10 words
52 00113C 0014                DS.W    10      * same
53 001150 0028         LAB6    DS.L    10      * space for 10 longwords
54 001178 0001                DS.B    1
55 00117A 0002                DS.W    1        * word requested at odd
56                     * address, assembler uses next even address
57
58          00100000          ORG     $100000 * to force a long address
59 100000 0014         LAB8    DS      10       * LAB8 requires >16 bits
60
61                     * END indicates no more program statements
62                            END

****** TOTAL ERRORS   1--   47 -- TOTAL LINES   52
```

APPROX 2110 UNUSED SYMBOL TABLE ENTRIES

ADDRESS	00101A DATA	001000 LAB1	001004 LAB2	00100A LAB3	001100
LAB4	00110E LAB5	00111E LAB6	001150 LAB8	100000 SYM	000020
TEN	00000A				

Fig. 4.7 Assembly directives

therefore has value $1202. This could have been used in the program as follows:

> START: MOVE.W   DATA, D5
> ADD.W   NEXT, D5
> MOVE.W   D5, ANSWER

could have been written:

> START: MOVE.W   DATA, D5
> ADD.W   DATA + 2, D5
> MOVE.W   D5, DATA + 4

Although this would cause exactly the same code to be generated by the assembler, the program is less easy to read and it is very easy to make errors in calculating the size of the data. This usage is therefore *strongly discouraged*.

Expressions, therefore, should be used with care and only when their meaning is clear as for example LENGTH + 1. Some assemblers allow only the operators plus (+) and minus (−) in expressions, others allow multiply.

Fig. 4.7 shows the object code and the symbol table generated by the assembler as a result of program statements containing assembler directives. It is not intended to be a meaningful program.

4.11   LOADING A PROGRAM IN A HOST—TARGET ENVIRONMENT

In the introduction to this chapter it was established that to develop realistic programs, assistance from two pieces of system software, an ASSEMBLER and a LOADER, is required. The idea of developing programs on a host system and down-line loading into a target 68000 system was also introduced. The functions of the assembler have been explained throughout this chapter and in Section 4.7 the software development process on the host system was described. It now remains to show how an object code program may be transferred from a host system and be loaded into a target system.

As in Chapter 3, the specific commands available in the TUTOR single board development system are used as an illustrative example. Similar facilities are required for all host-target environments, but may be invoked by a slightly different command set. In outline, the procedure is as follows:

- Select a target 68000 system and establish a connection from it to the host system.
- Invoke the loader in the target system. The object code file is transferred from the host system and placed in the memory of the target system by the loader.

The development system, in this case TUTOR, must support both of these activities.

4.11.1   Establishing a connection to the host system

The TUTOR command for this purpose is TM (Transparent Mode). The effect of TM is that all subsequent input from the console VDU is passed to the host until an escape character, typically a control character, is typed. The host system may therefore be used with the target console VDU acting as a normal host terminal until the escape character is typed.

After transparent mode has been established, the user will log in to the host as usual making the user's files available to the target system, as to a normal terminal. The escape character is then typed, the connection having been established. Fig. 4.8 gives a schematic view.

The whole software development process at the host, using the editor and cross-assembler, may be carried out from the target system using transparent mode. Alternatively, the object code file may already have been created from some other terminal and all that is required is to make it available to the target system.

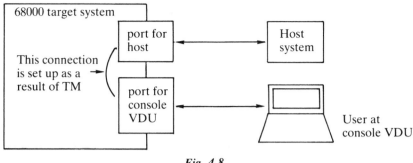

Fig. 4.8

4.11.2 Loading an object code file

It is assumed that a connection is established to the host, that the object code file is accessible to the target system, and that the user has returned from transparent mode to normal mode by typing the exit character. A command is then given to TUTOR to load a given object code file with the following general syntax:

LO [port number]   [; ⟨options⟩]   [= text]

The port number is that for the source of the object code file, the host port, and may be omitted for a standard configuration. A useful option, invoked by ;X, is that the object code is displayed on the console VDU screen as well as being loaded. This reassures the user that something is happening if the loading takes any length of time. The 'text' is passed to the host allowing a command appropriate to the particular host being invoked to be given, for example:

LO   ;X = TYPE   TEST.OBJ   (for the DEC 1091)
LO   ;X = 1s test.s   (for UNIX)

When the file has been loaded, TUTOR will output a prompt and the program may be executed as described in Chapter 3. Use of a simple absolute loader has been described here. Software support for assembling and loading a set of related program modules is described in reference 2.

5

Program control instructions

5.1 INTRODUCTION

The program developed in Chapter 2 consisted of a list of instructions. Execution of the program involved obeying the instructions, in sequence, once only. More realistic programs require that a given set of instructions should be executed repeatedly. Sometimes the number of times is known in advance (a constant number), sometimes it is computed when the program runs (a variable number, conditional on some run-time value). The instruction sets of all computers provide tools for controlling the order of execution of the instructions of a program, for determining the 'flow of control' through the program by building loops and testing conditions (see below) or calling subroutines (see Chapter 7). The 68000 provides a large and comprehensive set of such instructions.

In this chapter the 68000's instructions for effecting control flow and their interaction with the processor's status register are described. A high-level language's control structures are implemented, at run time, with these instructions as elements. To illustrate this, the chapter concludes with an implementation of Pascal's conditional and repetitive statements in terms of 68000 instructions.

5.2 UNCONDITIONAL TRANSFER OF CONTROL

5.2.1 The jump instruction (JMP)

The instruction is defined as:

    JMP ⟨ea⟩

⟨ea⟩ means 'effective address' and will be discussed in detail in Chapter 6.
    A simple example of the instruction is:

    JMP LOOP

which causes the address LOOP to be set up in the program counter so that the instruction in location LOOP is the next one to be obeyed. Because a fully general effective address is allowed, the instruction is at least two words long, of the form:

control word
address (16-bit)

5.2.2 The branch always instruction (BRA)

The instruction is defined as:

BRA ⟨label⟩

Note that the address is restricted to a simple label, for example:

BRA LOOP

In the JMP instruction described in Section 4.2.1 the address in the object code is an absolute address. In the BRA instruction, the address stored in the object code is calculated as a displacement from the value of the program counter, i.e. jump n locations forwards or backwards from this instruction.

In the case of short branches, PC–128 bytes to PC+127 bytes, a single word instruction can be used

8	8
BRA	displacement

If a greater displacement is necessary, the format is:

BRA	0
16-bit displacement	

PC ± 32k words.

The programmer, however, does not need to be concerned with the calculation of these displacements. The information is given here so that the object code in the list file can be understood.

5.3 THE 68000 STATUS REGISTER

In Section 1.6, some 68000 processor registers were introduced and Fig. 1.13 gave a diagram of processor registers including the STATUS REGISTER which will now be described in more detail. (See Fig. 5.1.)

The system byte will be discussed in Chapter 13.

The user byte, the 'condition code register' contains five flag bits that hold information about the result of the instruction that has just been executed. Fig. 1.17, which gives the full 68000 instruction set, contains information on how each of these flags is affected by execution of the instructions.

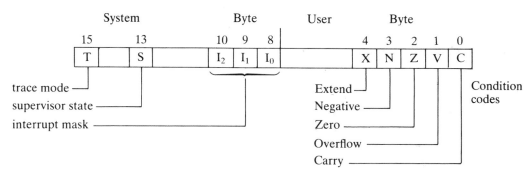

Fig. 5.1

Bit 0, Carry (C)

Set to 1 if an add operation produces a carry or a subtract operation produces a borrow, otherwise it is cleared to 0. Carry also holds the value of a bit that has been shifted out of a data register or memory location and reflects the result of a compare instruction.

Bit 1, Overlow (V)

This bit is useful only during operations on signed integers (see Section 1.9). It is set to 1 if the addition of two like-signed numbers (or the subtraction of two opposite-signed numbers) produces a result that exceeds the two's-complement range of the operand (see below), otherwise it is cleared to 0. Overflow is also set to 1 if the most significant bit of the operand is changed at any time during an arithmetic shift operation, otherwise it is cleared to 0.

Bit 2, Zero (Z)

This bit is set to 1 if the result of an operation is 0, otherwise it is cleared to 0.

Bit 3, Negative (N)

This bit is meaningful only during operations on signed numbers. It is set to 1 if an arithmetic, logical, shift or rotate operation produces a negative result, otherwise it is cleared to 0. The N flag follows the most significant bit of an 8-, 16- or 32-bit operand.

Bit 4, Extend (X)

This bit functions as a carry for multiple precision operations. It is affected by add, subtract, negate, shift and rotate operations during which it receives the state of the carry (C) bit.

5.3.1   Examples illustrating overflow and carry

Consider signed integers (two's-complement representation for negatives) of type byte. The range is:

decimal	binary
+127	01111111
.	
.	
.	
0	00000000
−1	11111111
.	
.	
.	
−127	10000001
−128	10000000

The following additions would take place as a result of, for example, ADD.B D0, D3.

- Addition of two positive signed integers with no overflow:

```
15    00001111
15    00001111
30    00011110
```

After the addition, V=0, C=0.

- Addition of two positive signed integers with overflow:

```
126               01111110
  3               00000011
129 (out of range)  10000001    (but this number is −127)
```

Note that the result of the addition is out of range so overflow has occurred. This can be detected by noticing that the sign of the result is different from the sign of the two positive numbers added together.
After the addition V=1, C=0

- Addition of two negative integers with no overflow:

```
−2          1111110
−3          1111101
−5    (1)   1111011
      carry
```

Note that the result of the addition has the same sign as the two numbers added therefore no overflow has occurred. The result requires 9 bits and not 8 therefore carry sets. After the addition V=0, C=1.

- Addition of two negative integers with overflow:

```
−127                 100000001
−   5                111111011
−132 (out of range)  (1)  011111100    (but this is +124)
                    carry
```

The result of the addition is out of range so overflow has occurred. Again the sign of the integers being added is the same and differs from the sign of the result. The result requires 9 bits. After the addition V=1, C=1.

It should be noted that overflow will not occur when integers of opposite sign are added.

Similar examples may be constructed for word and longword data types.

5.3.2   Example illustrating carry

Consider unsigned integers of type byte.
The range is:

decimal	binary
255	11111111
254	11111110
.	.
.	.
128	10000000
127	01111111
.	.
.	.
1	00000001
0	00000000

The following additions would take place as a result of, for example, ADD.B D0,D3

- Addition of two (positive) unsigned integers with no carry:

```
 .128   10000000
  15    00001111
 143    10001111
```

After the addition C=0.

- Addition of two (positive) unsigned integers with carry:

```
128           10000000
143           10001111
271     (1)   00001111
        carry
```

Note that the result requires 9 and not 8 bits therefore carry sets. The 9-bit representation is the correct result, however.

5.4   CONDITIONAL BRANCH INSTRUCTIONS

The general form of the instruction is:

Bcc ⟨label⟩

The object code contains a calculated displacement as described in Section 5.2.2.

In Bcc, the suffix cc represents the condition being tested, for example, BCS means branch if carry is set. If the condition is true the branch takes place; if the condition is false the program counter is unaffected and the next instruction in sequence is fetched and executed. Fig. 5.2 shows the range of conditional branch instructions. BEQ, for example, is true if the zero flag is set. Some of the conditions cannot be evaluated by examining only one of the flags and a logical expression is involved as shown in the right hand column. One of these, BLT, will be explained as an example.

Consider   ADD.B   D0, D3   *where D0 and D3 contain signed integers
                BLT   NEGATIVE

- $\begin{array}{r} -1 \\ \underline{-1} \\ \underline{-2} \end{array}$ (1) $\begin{array}{r} 11111111 \\ \underline{11111111} \\ \underline{11111110} \end{array}$ $C = 1, N = 1, V = 0, N \vee V = 1$

- $\begin{array}{r} +127 \\ \underline{+127} \\ \underline{+254} \end{array}$ $\begin{array}{r} 01111111 \\ \underline{01111111} \\ \underline{10000000} \end{array}$ $C = 0, N = 1, V = 1, N \vee V = 0$

Instruction	Signed or un-signed (two's-complement arithmetic?)	Condition	True if
BEQ	unsigned	Equal to zero	$Z = 1$
BNE	unsigned	Not equal to zero	$Z = 0$
BMI	unsigned	Minus	$N = 1$
BPL	unsigned	Plus	$N = 0$
BGT	signed	Greater than zero	$Z \wedge (N \veebar V) = 0$
BLT	signed	Less than zero	$N \veebar V = 1$
BGE	signed	Greater than or equal to zero	$N \veebar V = 0$
BLE	signed	Less than or equal to zero	$Z \vee (N \veebar V) = 1$
BHI	unsigned	Higher than zero	$C \wedge Z = 0$
BLS	unsigned	Lower than or same as	$C \vee Z = 1$
BCS	unsigned	Carry set	$C = 1$
BCC	unsigned	Carry clear	$C = 0$
BVS	signed	Overflow	$V = 1$
BVC	signed	No overflow	$V = 0$
BT		Always true	
BF		Always false	

$\wedge$ = AND
$\vee$ = inclusive OR
$\veebar$ = exclusive OR

Fig. 5.2

●	−128	10000000	
	−128	10000000	
	−256 (1)	00000000	$C = 1, N = 0, V = 1, N \vee V = 1$
●	+1	00000001	
	+1	00000001	
	+2	00000010	$C = 0, N = 0, V = 0, N \vee V = 0$

Only in the first and third cases has a negative result been obtained.

5.5 EXAMPLES OF THE USE OF BRANCH INSTRUCTIONS

```
SUB      D1,D0      * subtract D1 from D0 (16-bit word)
                    * leaving the result in D0 (low order word)
BEQ      SAME       * branch to SAME if the subtraction
                    * produces a zero result in D0 (low order word)
                    * otherwise continue execution in sequence

CMP      D1,D0      * subtract D1 from D0 setting the
                    * condition flags but do not change either (compare)
BEQ      SAME       * as above

CMPI.B  #$41,D0     * A CMP instruction on byte data with an immediate
                    * operand
BLT      BELOWA     * D0 contains a character with code <$41
BEQ      A          * D0 contains $41
BGT      ABOVEA     * D0 contains a character with code >$41

CMPI.B  #'A', D0    * The same as CMP.B #$41,D0

ADD      D0, D1     * Word addition of D0 onto D1
BCS      CARRYSET   * branch to CARRYSET if the ADD operation
                    *|produces a carry out of the low word of D1
```

5.5.1 To control a loop

Suppose a loop is to be executed five times

```
MOVEQ #5, D7   * set up a count in D7 to control the loop
LOOP:
    ↑
    instructions
    in loop
    ↓
SUBQ    #1, D7   * decrement the count each time round
BNE     LOOP     * go back to LOOP until count becomes 0
continue
```

```
 1                                    *
 2                                    *
 3                                    *
 4                                    * This program illustrates some control
 5                                    * instructions. The first section shows a
 6                                    * loop executed 5 times
 7                                    * NOP (no operation) is used in the loop body
 8                                    *
 9          00001000                          ORG      $1000
10 001000 7E05                 START   MOVEQ    #5,D7       * set up count
11                                    * for D7:=5 downto 1 do.....
12 001002 4E71                 LOOP    NOP                  * body of loop
13 001004 4E71                         NOP
14 001006 4E71                         NOP
15 001008 5347                         SUBQ     #1,D7       * decrement count
16 00100A 6EF6                         BGT      LOOP        * repeat until count 0
17 00100C 4E71                 OUTOFLOOP NOP               * exit from loop
18
19                                    * the next section tests a character
20 00100E 1C38102A                     MOVE.B   CHAR,D6     * character for test
21 001012 0C060030                     CMP.B    #$30,D6     * compare ASCII zero
22 001016 6D00000A                     BLT      NOTOCTAL
23 00101A 0C060037                     CMP.B    #$37,D6     * compare ASCII 7
24 00101E 6F000008                     BLE      OCTAL
25
26 001022 4E40                 NOTOCTAL TRAP    #0          * exit and look at PC
27 001024 4E71                         NOP
28 001026 4E71                         NOP
29 001028 4E40                 OCTAL    TRAP    #0          * exit and look at PC
30
31                                    * character to be tested set up in a data area
32 00102A 33                   CHAR     DC.B    $33
33
34                                             END

****** TOTAL ERRORS    0--    0 -- TOTAL LINES    26


APPROX  2113 UNUSED SYMBOL TABLE ENTRIES

CHAR       00102A LOOP       001002 NOTOCTAL 001022 OCTAL      001028
OUTOFLOO 00100C START       001000
```

Fig. 5.3   Some control instructions

Fig. 5.3 incorporates this basic structure. No operations NOP are substituted in the body of the loop to highlight the control instructions.

5.5.2   To test if a character is hexadecimal

A fragment of program is developed which tests a character assumed to be in D0 and passes control to instructions labelled HEX if the character is in the hexadecimal range 0–9, A–F, otherwise control is passed to NOTHEX.

Character as printed	ASCII code	(see Fig. 1.16)
0	$30	
·	·	
·	·	
9	$39	
A	$41	
·	·	
·	·	
F	$46	

The program must test for two ranges $30 to $39 and $41 to $46; the characters with codes below $30, above $46 and in the range $3A to $40 are not hexadecimal.

Alternatively

HEXTEST:	CMPI.B	#$30,D0	HEXTEST:	CMPI.B	#'0',D0
	BLT	NOTHEX		BLT	NOTHEX
	CMPI.B	#$39,D0		CMPI.B	#'9',D0
	BLE	HEX		BLE	HEX
	CMPI.B	#$41,D0		CMPI.B	#'A',D0
	BLT	NOTHEX		BLT	NOTHEX
	CMPI.B	#$46,D0		CMPI.B	#'F',D0
	BLE	HEX		BLE	HEX
	BGT	NOTHEX		BGT	NOTHEX

5.6 EXAMPLE PROGRAM

Fig. 5.3 shows the assembler listing of a complete program incorporating the loop structure discussed in Section 5.5.1 and a section to test whether a character is in the octal range 0 to 7, code $30 to $37. Since input and output have not yet been introduced, the program is somewhat artificial. The character to be tested is set up in a memory location CHAR instead of being input and after it has been tested control is passed to OCTAL or NOTOCTAL depending on the result. At these points a more realistic program would output an appropriate message.

However, the value of the program counter on exit from the program indicates the result of the test and this method may be used at present until output routines are developed in Chapters 10 and 12.

Only a basic framework for loop control is included in the first section. No operation NOPs are used in the body of the loop in place of useful processing instructions. The first section of the program, for example, could be rewritten to incorporate a loop which is executed 26 times and which generates successive letters of the alphabet. Again, the letters cannot be output or stored in an appropriate data structure, as developed in Chapter 6, but the instructions to generate them would be as follows:

```
START:  MOVEQ  #26,D7           *set up count in D7
        MOVEQ  #$41,D6          *set up code for A in D6

LOOP:   MOVE   D6, ALPHACHAR
        ADDQ   #1,D6            *form the next character
        SUBQ   #1,D7            *decrement the count
        BGT    LOOP             *go back until count=0
```

For readers who have a development system available, the following exercises are suggested, using TUTOR commands which were introduced in Chapter 3. For readers without a practical system a 'dry run' through the program would be valuable.

- Load and run the program shown in Fig. 5.3. Note the PC on exit and check whether the result was 'octal' or 'not octal'
- Change the character at CHAR using a TUTOR command and re-run the program.
- Test with a range of characters e.g. $2F, $30, $39, $3A in turn at CHAR.
- Trace the program through to completion. Take care not to trace past the exit into TUTOR.
- Set a breakpoint at 100C i.e. at OUTOFLOOP.
- Run the program from 1000 and examine the output at the breakpoint.
- Set breakpoints at 1022 i.e. NOTOCTAL and 1028 i.e. OCTAL and continue execution.
- Clear all breakpoints.
  Clear all data and address registers.
- Set a breakpoint with a count of 4 at 1008 and restart the program from 1000.

Further programs
In Chapter 11, graded example programs are given. Although these include some features which have not yet been introduced, some of the basic algorithms could be understood at this stage.

5.7   HIGH-LEVEL LANGUAGE CONTROL STRUCTURES

The control structures required in a high level language must be built from the conditional instructions in the machine's order code by the compiler. Pascal, for example, has the repetitive statements:

<u>while</u> ⟨expression⟩ <u>do</u> ⟨statement⟩
<u>repeat</u> ⟨statement⟩{; ⟨statement⟩}<u>until</u> ⟨expression⟩
<u>for</u> ⟨control variable⟩:=⟨initial value⟩ <u>to</u> ⟨final value⟩
                    <u>do</u> ⟨statement⟩

or,　for ⟨control variable⟩:=⟨initial value⟩ <u>down to</u> ⟨final value⟩
<u>do</u> ⟨statement⟩

and the conditional statements:

<u>if</u> ⟨expression⟩ <u>then</u> ⟨statement⟩
or,　<u>if</u> ⟨expression⟩ <u>then</u> ⟨statement⟩ <u>else</u> ⟨statement⟩
<u>case</u> ⟨expression⟩ <u>of</u> ⟨case label list⟩:⟨statement⟩;

.

.

.

⟨case label list⟩:⟨statement⟩

<u>end</u>

If programs must be written directly in assembly language, it is good policy to write them in high level 'pseudo code' as an aid to good structure and to translate the high level structures into machine level instructions.

Taking the <u>while</u> repetitive statement as an example, this can be built at assembly code level as follows:

WHILE_TEST:　　　　(instructions to calculate ⟨expression⟩ and set the condition code flags)
Bcc OUT_OF_WHILE * select Bcc to test for expression <u>false</u>
WHILE_BODY:　　　　(instructions to implement <u>while</u> statement(s))
BRA WHILE_TEST
OUT_OF_WHILE:　　.

.

.

The *if-then-else* conditional statement is constructed as follows:

IF_TEST:　　　　　　(instructions to calculate ⟨expression⟩ and set the condition code flags)
Bcc ELSE_CODE　　* select Bcc to test for expression <u>false</u>

THEN_CODE:　　　　(instructions to implement the <u>then</u> statements)
BRA OUT_OF_IF
ELSE_CODE:　　　　(instructions to implement the <u>else</u> statement)
OUT_OF_IF:　　　.

.

.

It is good practice to use high-level language statements to comment on the assembly language program as shown in the following examples:

EXAMPLE 1: FOR

* for D7 : = 26 downto 1 do ....

	MOVEQ	#26,D7
FORLOOP:		
	↑	
	instructions in loop	
	↓	
	SUBQ	#1,D7
	BGT	FORLOOP

EXAMPLE 2: WHILE

TERMINATOR	EQU $04	* control D character
INPUT:	assume a character	
	is input into D0	

* while D0 ⟨ ⟩ TERMINATOR do ....

	CMPI.B	#TERMINATOR, D0
	BEQ	OUTOFWHILE
WHILE:	↑	
	instructions for the case when D0 is not the terminator	
	↓	
	BRA	INPUT
OUTOFWHILE:	.	
	.	
	.	

EXAMPLE 3: REPEAT

	CLR	D3
	MOVEQ	#1, D4

* repeat D3 : = D3 + D4 until D4 > 100

REPEAT:	ADD	D4, D3	
	ADDQ	#1, D4	
	CMPI	#100, D4	
	BLE	REPEAT	* perform the '*until*' test

EXAMPLE 4: IF-THEN-ELSE

* <u>if</u> $'A' \leqslant D0 \leqslant 'Z'$ <u>then</u> output 'alphabetic' <u>else</u> output 'not alphabetic'

IFTEST:	CMPI.B	#'A', D0
	BLT	ELSE
	CMPI.B	#'Z', D0
	BGT	ELSE
THEN:	↑	
	instructions to output 'alphabetic'	
	↓	
	BRA OUTOFIF	
ELSE:	↑	
	instructions to output 'not alphabetic'	
	↓	
OUTOFIF:	.	
	.	
	.	

6
Addressing modes

6.1 INTRODUCTION

The instruction set of the MC68000 is given in Fig. 1.17. In the instruction definitions ⟨ea⟩ indicates a general 'effective address'. ⟨ea⟩ may appear as a source for a data transfer, for example:

    ADD   ⟨ea⟩,Dn   * add a word taken from ⟨ea⟩ onto a data register,

or as a destination, for example:

    ADD   Dn,⟨ea⟩   * add a word taken from a data register onto ⟨ea⟩

An effective address ⟨ea⟩ may be a data or address register or a word of memory. Examples of ADD ⟨ea⟩,Dn are:

    ADD   D2,D3   * ⟨ea⟩ is a data register

    ADD   A1,D3   * ⟨ea⟩ is an address register

    ADD   LABEL,D3   * ⟨ea⟩ is a word of memory.

The examples above illustrate three possible *addressing modes*. The MC68000 has twelve addressing modes which are summarized in Section 6.5 and which are described in the rest of this chapter.

6.2 EXAMPLES OF INSTRUCTION DEFINITIONS

Some instructions have no effective address, for example:

    BRA   ⟨label⟩

indicates that only a simple label may be used, for example:

    BRA   LOOP

Most instructions contain an effective address which may be a source or destination for a data transfer, for example:

ADD   ⟨ea⟩,Dn   * add a word to a data register from ⟨ea⟩

ADDA   ⟨ea⟩,An   * add a word to an address register from ⟨ea⟩

ADD   Dn,⟨ea⟩   * add a word from a data register to ⟨ea⟩

ADDI   #⟨data⟩,⟨ea⟩   * add a word constant to ⟨ea⟩

                                            ADDI (immediate) indicates that the constant to be added is to be found in an extension word of the instruction.

One instruction is defined to have two general effective addresses, this is:

MOVE   ⟨ea⟩,⟨ea⟩   * Move from source to destination.

In Chapter 2, machine code was introduced by selecting a few instructions to make a simple program. Some examples of the detailed bit-coding of ADD and MOVE instructions are given in Sections 2.5 and 2.4.

6.3 ORTHOGONAL INSTRUCTION SETS

An important principle of computer design is that considerations of how an address is calculated should be independent of which operation code the address calculation is associated with. This is called orthogonality. The MC68000 has an orthogonal instruction set with a very small number of exceptions.

6.4 AN INSTRUCTION WITH A SINGLE EFFECTIVE ADDRESS

The format of any instruction with a single effective address is:

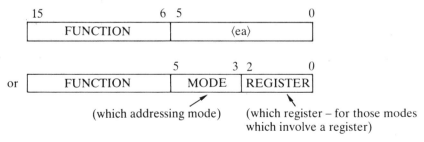

Fig. 6.1

In order to summarize and explain addressing modes, one form of one instruction ADD will be used as an example throughout this chapter.

The function field of the instruction contains the following information:

- The operation code is ADD
- The size of data to be added, byte, word or longword
- Whether the instruction is:

	ADD	⟨ea⟩, Dn,
or	ADD	Dn, ⟨ea⟩,
or	ADDA	⟨ea⟩, An.

The object code for the first two of these instructions is given in detail in Section 2.5, and is used in Figs. 6.21 and 6.22. Full details of all ADD instructions are given in Motorola's 68000 processor handbook and examples are given in Fig. 6.23.

The purpose of this chapter is to explain how the contents of the ⟨ea⟩ field, bits 0–5, determine the effective address calculation, independent of the particular function code.

	Addressing mode	Register		example ADD ⟨ea⟩,D3
Data Register Direct	000	Dn	1	ADD D0, D3
Address Register Direct	001	An	1	ADD A7, D3
Address Register Indirect	010	An	1	ADD (A0), D3
Address Register Indirect with Postincrement	011	An	1	ADD (A0)+, D3
Address Register Indirect with Predecrement	100	An	1	ADD –(A0), D3
Address Register Indirect plus (16-bit) displacement	101	An	2	ADD 4(A0), D3 ADD LABEL(A0), D3
Address Register Indirect plus index (data or address reg.) plus (8-bit) displacement	110	An	2	ADD 2(A0,D6.W), D3 ADD LABEL(A0,A6.W), D3
Absolute short (16 bits)	111	000	2	ADD LABEL, D3
Absolute long (24/32 bits)	111	001	3	ADD HIGHAD, D3
				PC relative after RORG
PC + 16-bit displacement	111	010	2	ADD LABEL, D3
PC + index (data or address reg.) + (8-bit) displacement	111	011	2	ADD 4(A0), D3 ADD LABEL(D0), D3
Immediate	111	100	2 or 3	ADD #9,D3 ADD.L #$123456, D3

length of instruction in words

Fig. 6.2

6.5   SUMMARY OF ADDRESSING MODES

The effective address field in the control word of an instruction consists of two three-bit fields. Both fields can hold an integer in the range 0–7. As shown in Fig. 6.2 modes 0–6 require an address or data register to be specified. The value 7 in the mode field is an escape or extension value. It indicates that the mode does not require use of a register and therefore that the register field can be used to indicate further modes, up to a maximum of eight; in fact five further modes are used.

6.6   ADDRESSING MODES USED IMPLICITLY IN CHAPTERS 1–5

In the rest of this chapter, the addressing modes introduced in Fig. 6.2 will be explained in detail. First, those modes which have already been encountered in the examples given in Chapters 1–5 will be explained and brought together in a program. After this, the remaining modes will be introduced and their use will be illustrated.

6.6.1   Data register direct

Using this mode,   ADD   〈ea〉, D3
becomes, for example,   ADD   D1, D3
i.e. add a word from any data register to D3 in this example.

The instruction format is:

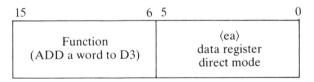

Fig. 6.3

6.6.2   Address register direct

Using this mode,   ADD   〈ea〉, D3
becomes, for example,   ADD   A0, D3
i.e. add a word from any address register to D3.

The instruction format is:

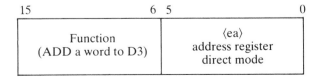

Fig. 6.4

6.6.3 Immediate mode

Using this mode,   ADD   ⟨ea⟩, D3
becomes, for example, ADD   #9, D3
i.e. add a word constant to D3.

The format of the instruction is:

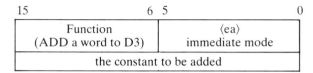

Fig. 6.5

If a longword constant is required the *function* ADD (ADD.W) may be replaced by ADD.L, for example. It should be noted that the function code and not the addressing mode indicates the size of data to be used.

ADD.L #$12345678,D3.

The format of the instruction is:

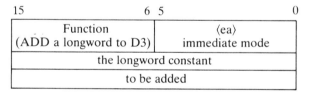

Fig. 6.6

6.6.4 Absolute short addressing mode

Using this mode,   ADD   ⟨ea⟩, D3
becomes   ADD   LABEL, D3
i.e. add the contents of the word at LABEL to D3.

The format of the instruction is:

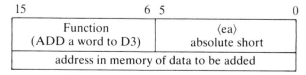

Fig. 6.7

6.6.5 Absolute long addressing mode

Using this mode,　　　　ADD　⟨ea⟩, D3
again becomes　　　　　ADD　LABEL, D3
but in this case the memory address LABEL is longer than 16 bits, i.e. is above
64 kbytes.

The format of the instruction is:

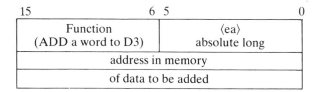

Fig. 6.8

To produce the correct object code for the hardware to execute, the assembler
must be able to detect whether an absolute address is short or long since the syntax is
the same in both cases. In the case of a reference to an address not already defined, a
forward reference, the assembler must 'decide' whether to allow space for a short
address or a long one. In this case the programmer informs the assembler by using
ORG as usual if only short addresses are to be allowed for and ORG.L if all forward
references should be assumed to be long addresses.

6.6.6 Example showing these modes

The reader is recommended, as an exercise, to type in a list of statements of the
addressing modes already covered and to examine the object code in the list file, for
example:

```
        TTL         ADDRESSING MODES
        ORG.L       $1000           * space for long address in forward references
        ADD         D0, D3          * data register direct
        ADD         A7, D3          * address register direct
        ADD         DATA, D3        * absolute short (16-bit address)
        ADD         HIGHADD, D3     * absolute long (24/32-bit address)
        ADD         #2, D3          * immediate (2 words)
        ADD.L       #$123456, D3    * immediate (3 words)

        ORG         $1200
DATA:   DC          $1234

        ORG         $1000000
HIGHADD: DC         $1234           * force a 2-word address

        END
```

Fig. 6.9

Fig. 6.21 gives such a program for the complete set of addressing modes for the function ADD ⟨ea⟩, D3. Fig. 6.22 gives a similar program for the function ADD D3, ⟨ea⟩. Fig. 6.23 illustrates the full range of ADD instructions. In the rest of this chapter, some of the addressing modes not already covered will be introduced. Since most of these involve the use of address registers we shall first see how to load addresses into address registers.

6.7   PUTTING ADDRESSES INTO ADDRESS REGISTERS

The addressing modes still to be described require the use of an address register containing a pointer to (address of) some location in memory. When an instruction invoking one of modes 2–6 is used, it is assumed that an address register has already been loaded with the relevant address.

The instruction LEA load effective address is designed for this purpose:

      LEA   ⟨ea⟩, An   * load the address ⟨ea⟩ into An

e.g. LEA   TABLEBASE, A1

Note that the address and not the contents of that address are loaded into the address register, unlike:

      MOVEA   ADDRESS, A1   * move to address register

where the contents of ADDRESS are moved into A1.

It may be appropriate to use a method involving MOVEA if pointers have been set up in memory, for example:

      POINTER: DC TABLE   * the address TABLE (a pointer to a
                                                table)
      TABLE: DS 100   * space for a 100-word table

              .
              .
              .

      MOVEA   POINTER, A1   * move the contents of POINTER
                               * i.e. the address TABLE into A1

Finally, for a simple label only and not a general effective address:

      MOVE   #TABLE, A2   * immediate mode

causes the value of the symbol TABLE i.e. the address TABLE to be set up by the Assembler as an immediate value and at run-time to be moved into A2.

6.8   ADDRESS REGISTER INDIRECT

Using this mode   ADD   ⟨ea⟩, D3

becomes, for example, ADD   (A0), D3

Before the instruction is executed at run time the appropriate address must have been loaded into A0 by one of the methods described in Section 6.7.

The format of the instruction is:

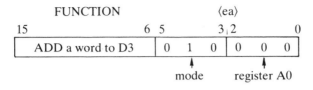

Fig. 6.10

The value 010 in the mode field indicates 'address register indirect'. The value 000 in the register field indicates that address register 0 is to be used.

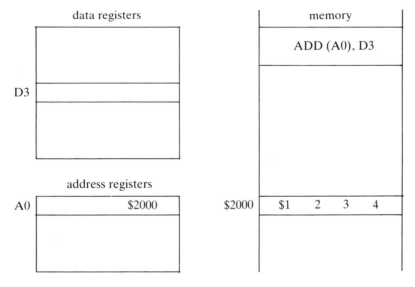

Fig. 6.11

The instruction adds the number $1234 onto the low 16-bit word of D3.

6.9 ADDRESS REGISTER INDIRECT WITH POSTINCREMENT

Using this mode   ADD   ⟨ea⟩,D3

becomes, for example,   ADD   (A0)+,D3

As in Section 6.8, it is assumed that an appropriate address has been loaded into A0. The address register is used as described in Section 6.8 but after use the address register is incremented. If, as in this example, a word operation has been carried out, A0 is incremented by 2 (bytes). If the operation was ADD.B the increment would be 1. If the operation was ADD.L the increment would be 4 (bytes). The postincrement facility is useful when a list of words, bytes or longwords are to be accessed in sequence. An example is given below in Section 6.9.1.

The format of the instruction is:

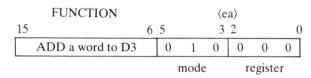

Fig. 6.12

6.9.1   Example using address register indirect with postincrement mode

Example: Write a program to add the elements of a word array containing 8 elements.
(or, add up a list of 8, 16-bit numbers).

The program has the following structure:

Initialize: Set a data register D0 as a count of the array length 8.
Clear a data register D1 to accumulate the sum.
Set the address of the base of the array (the first element) in an address register A0.

Process: Add, using A0 as a pointer, to D1 (the sum).
Increment address register A0.
Decrement the data register D0 holding the count and control the loop (execute 8 times).

Store result: Move the final value of the sum into memory.

The complete program is as follows. The list file is given as Fig. 6.24a. Figs. 6.24b and 6.24c show the same program modified to add the elements of a byte and longword array respectively. (See Fig. 6.13.)

As described in Section 4.8, the EQU directive could be used as follows:

```
              TTL etc.
LENGTH:       EQU 8
START:        MOVEQ   #LENGTH, D0
              etc.
```

This usage would be important for a longer program to increase readability and to make modification easier.

```
            TTL     ADD WORD ARRAY
            ORG     $1000
START:      MOVEQ   #8,D0           * set up the count in D0
            LEA     WARRAY,A0       * set up the pointer in A0
                                    * to the start of the word array
            CLR     D1              * clear D1 for the sum

LOOP:       ADD     (A0)+,D1        * add array element to D1
            SUBQ    #1,D0           * decrement the count and set cc's
            BNE     LOOP            * go back 7 times (while D0 > 0)

            MOVE    D1,TOTAL        * store result in memory

            TRAP    #0              * exit into TUTOR

* Data area
WARRAY:     DC.W    1, 2, 3, 4, 5, 6, 7, 8   * the word array
TOTAL:      DS.W    1               * space for the sum
            END
```

Fig. 6.13

6.10 ADDRESS REGISTER INDIRECT WITH PREDECREMENT

Using this mode   ADD   ⟨ea⟩,D3

becomes, for example,   ADD   −(A0),D3

As in Sections 6.8 and 6.9 it is assumed that A0 has been loaded with an appropriate address. When this addressing mode is invoked, the address register is decremented before it is used as a pointer. As in Section 6.9, the decrement is by 2, 1 or 4 (bytes) respectively for word, byte or longword operations. The predecrement facility, together with the postincrement facility is useful for manipulating a stack data structure. This is explained in Chapter 7.

The format of the instruction is:

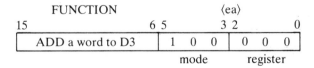

Fig. 6.14

6.11 ADDRESS REGISTER INDIRECT WITH 16-BIT DISPLACEMENT

Using this mode   ADD   ⟨ea⟩,D3

becomes, for example,   ADD   4(A0),D3
            or   ADD   LABEL(A0),D3.

The format of this instruction is:

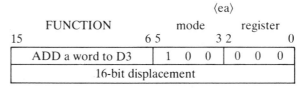

Fig. 6.15

In this case, the effective address is the contents of the address register specified plus the 16-bit displacement contained in the first extension word of the instruction. The displacement is interpreted as a signed integer giving a displacement of ± 32k bytes from the address contained in A0. The displacement, being part of the instruction word is constant, fixed at assembly time and not dynamically variable at run-time.

This mode could be used for accessing fields of a record, for example:

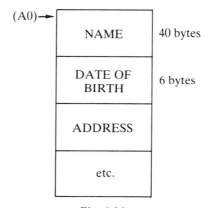

Fig. 6.16

The date of birth starts at a fixed displacement, in all similar records, of 40 bytes from the start of the record which is the address contained in A0.

Alternatively, using the form ADD LABEL(A0), D3, the value in A0 may be adjusted dynamically to provide required displacements from LABEL

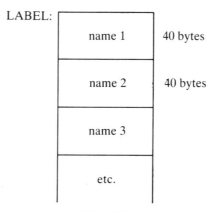

Fig. 6.17

In this case the data structure consists of a list of names each occupying 40 bytes. The names in the list could be accessed in turn by programming a loop, initializing A0 to zero and adding 40 to A0 each time round the loop. There is a restriction on this usage in that LABEL may only be a signed 16-bit quantity i.e. it must be located below 32k bytes in the memory.

6.12 ADDRESS REGISTER INDIRECT WITH INDEX AND 8-BIT DISPLACEMENT

Using this mode, ADD ⟨ea⟩,D3

becomes, for example, ADD 4 (A0, D6),D3
     or ADD LABEL(A0,D6),D3

in general, ADD d(An, Rn),D3

where d is an 8-bit displacement in two's-complement form.

An is a full 32-bit address register.
Rn is an address or a data register.
Rn or Rn.W indicates that the sign extended low order word of Rn must be used.
Rn.L indicates that all 32 bits of Rn must be used.

The effective address calculation is therefore:

⟨ea⟩ = An(32 bits) + Rn (16 or 32 bits as indicated) + d (8 bits)

The instruction format is:

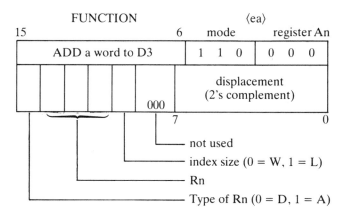

Fig. 6.18

This mode is useful for handling data in the form of records containing variable length fields as described above in Section 6.11. Since an extra register is available, the data structure could be manipulated as follows:

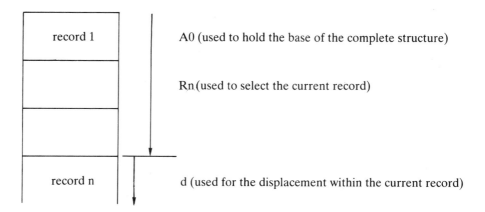

Fig. 6.19

The mode is not as useful as it might be for handling two-dimensional arrays. The 8-bit value for d prevents the following general usage:

ADD BASE(A0, A1), D3

It would be convenient to use d for a base address and to use A0 to select, for example, a row of a matrix then A1 to index within that row. The restriction on the size of d prevents this usage in most circumstances.

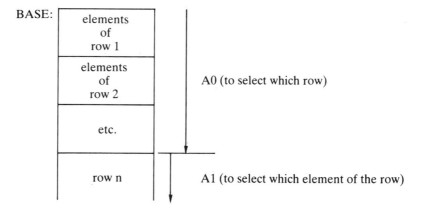

Fig. 6.20

The modes described in Sections 6.11 and 6.12 have been designed to be useful to compiler writers. The management of storage space at run-time for block structured high level language requires this type of addressing. Further relevant material is included in Chapter 7, Section 7.5.4.

6.13   PROGRAM COUNTER RELATIVE MODES

Two addressing modes have been provided, PC + 16-bit displacement and PC + index (in a data or address register) + 8-bit displacement, to allow position-independent code to be written. Such code will execute equally well wherever it is loaded in the memory. There is no special instruction syntax for this addressing mode and addresses in this format are generated by the assembler when RORG is used instead of ORG. Data may be set up provided it consists only of constants since code and data following RORG are restricted to be read only. A further restriction on data areas is that they must not include relative addresses since the assembler would produce absolute values for these as illustrated in Fig. 6.25.

Position-independent code may be developed in one area of memory and, when tested, may be replicated anywhere in memory and, in particular, may be moved into prom. Fig. 6.25 gives a list file showing comparable statements following ORG and RORG. The following example illustrates the use of the PC relative with index mode and also shows how a table of addresses may be avoided in movable code.

EXAMPLE:

* non-movable code

           ORG $1000

         .

         .

* a table of pointers (addresses of routines) is set up

ADDRESSTABLE: DC.W ROUTINE1, ROUTINE2, ROUTINE3, . . . etc.

         .

         .

         .

* assuming that which of N routines should be executed has been
* computed in D0 (multiplied by two for word entries in ADDRESSTABLE).

         .

         .

         .

           LEA   ADDRESSTABLE, A0

           MOVE 0(A0, D0), A1

           JMP   (A1)

Alternatively, the following instructions may be used

           MOVE D0, A0   * copy into an address register

           MOVE ADDRESSTABLE(A0), A1 * can only use an address register

           JMP   (A1)

● movable code

                    RORG $1000
                      .
                      .

* again, assume that which of N routines should be executed has been
* computed in D0 (multiplied by four for two-word instructions to be skipped)
                      .
                      .
                      .

                    JMP   JUMPTABLE (D0)   * PC relative
                                                     * allows index in Dn
                      .

JUMPTABLE: JMP   ROUTINE1
                    JMP   ROUTINE2
                    JMP   ROUTINE3
                      .

                    etc.


```
 1                         *         Figure 6.21
 2                         *
 3                         *
 4                         *
 5         00001000                  ORG     $1000
 6                         * Addressing Modes Example:
 7                         * ADD <ea>,D3  (add to data register)
 8                         * Function is:  <ea>+D3->D3
 9                         * Consider different modes for <ea>
10
11                         * Data Register Direct
12 001000 D640                       ADD     D0,D3
13
14                         * Address Register Direct
15 001002 D64F                       ADD     A7,D3
16 001004 D64F                       ADD     SP,D3
17
18                         * Absolute Short Address
19 001006 0001            DATA    DC 1
20 001008 D6781006                   ADD     DATA,D3
21
22                         * Absolute Long Address
23         00001100                  ORG.L   $1100
24 001100 D67900100000               ADD     HIGH,D3
25         00001200                  ORG     $1200
26
27                         * Immediate Data
28 001200 5C43                       ADD     #6,D3
29 001202 0643FFFA                   ADD     #-6,D3
30 001206 068300123456               ADD.L   #$123456,D3
```

```
31
32                          * Address Register Indirect
33 00120C D650                  ADD     (A0),D3
34
35                          * Address Register Indirect with Postincrement
36 00120E D658                  ADD     (A0)+,D3
37
38                          * Address Register Indirect with Predecrement
39 001210 D660                  ADD     -(A0),D3
40
41                          * Address Register Indirect with Displacement
42                          * (Indexed Addressing)
43 001212 D6680004              ADD     4(A0),D3
44 001216 D6681006              ADD     DATA(A0),D3
45
46                          * Address Register Indirect with Indexing
47 00121A D6706002              ADD     2(A0,D6.W),D3
48 00121E D6706802              ADD     2(A0,D6.L),D3
49 001222 D6706006              ADD     DATA(A0,D6),D3
****** ERROR 208--    0                 *
50                          * error since displacement needs > 8 bits
51
52 001226 D670E002              ADD     2(A0,A6.W),D3
53 00122A D670F000              ADD     0(A0,SP),D3
54                              ADD     (A0,SP),D3
****** ERROR 204--   49                 *
55                          * displacement does not default to zero
56
57                          * Program Counter with Displacement
58         00001500             RORG    $1500
59 001500 0004         LAB     DS      2
60 001504 D67AFFFA             ADD     LAB,D3
61 001508 D6781006             ADD     DATA,D3
62                          * Program Counter with Index
63 00150C D6680006             ADD     6(A0),D3
64 001510 D67BE0EE             ADD     LAB(A6),D3
65 001514 D66E1006             ADD     DATA(A6),D3
66
67         00100000             ORG     $100000
68 100000 0001         HIGH    DC      1
69
70                              END

****** TOTAL ERRORS   2--   54 -- TOTAL LINES   66


APPROX  2116 UNUSED SYMBOL TABLE ENTRIES

DATA    001006 HIGH    100000 LAB    001500
```

Fig. 6.21 Addressing modes 1

```
 1                          *          Figure 6.22
 2                          *
 3                          *
 4                          * Addressing Modes Example:
 5                          * ADD D3,<ea>    (add D3 to memory)
 6                          * Function is:   D3+<ea>-><ea>
 7                          * Consider different modes for <ea>
 8
 9          00001000              ORG     $1000
10
11                          * Data Register Direct
12 001000 D043                    ADD     D3,D0
13
14                          * Address Register Direct
15 001002 DEC3                    ADD     D3,A7
16 001004 DEC3                    ADD     D3,SP
17
18                          * Absolute Short Address
19 001006 0001            DATA    DC      1
20 001008 D7781006                ADD     D3,DATA
21
22                          * Absolute Long Address
23          00001100              ORG.L   $1100
24 001100 D77900100000            ADD     D3,HIGH
25          00001200              ORG     $1200
26
27                          * Immediate Data
28                          * NOT APPROPRIATE
29
30                          * Address Register Indirect
31 001200 D750                    ADD     D3,(A0)
32
33                          * Address Register Indirect with Postincrement
34 001202 D758                    ADD     D3,(A0)+
35
36                          * Address Register Indirect with Predecrement
37 001204 D760                    ADD     D3,-(A0)
38
39                          * Address Register Indirect with Displacement
40                          * (Indexed Addressing)
41 001206 D7680004                ADD     D3,4(A0)
42 00120A D7681006                ADD     D3,DATA(A0)
43
44                          * Address Register Indirect with Indexing
45 00120E D7706002                ADD     D3,2(A0,D6.W)
46 001212 D7706802                ADD     D3,2(A0,D6.L)
47 001216 D770E002                ADD     D3,2(A0,A6.W)
48 00121A D7706006                ADD     D3,DATA(A0,D6)
****** ERROR 208--   0                                  *
49                          * error since displacement needs > 8 bits
50
51 00121E D770F000                ADD     D3,0(A0,SP)
52                                 ADD     D3,(A0,SP)
****** ERROR 204--  48                                  *
53                          * displacement does not default to zero
```

```
54
55                          * Program Counter with Displacement
56         00001500               RORG     $1500
57 001500 0004          LAB      DS       2
58 001504 D77AFFFA               ADD      D3,LAB
****** ERROR 231--    52
59 001508 D7781006               ADD      D3,DATA
60
61                          * Program Counter with Index
62 00150C D77BE0F2               ADD      D3,LAB(A6)
****** ERROR 231--    58
63 001510 D76E1006               ADD      D3,DATA(A6)
64 001514 D76E0004               ADD      D3,4(A6)
65
66         00100000               ORG      $100000
67 100000 0001          HIGH     DC       1
68
69                               END
```

****** TOTAL ERRORS   4--   62 -- TOTAL LINES   61

APPROX   2116 UNUSED SYMBOL TABLE ENTRIES

DATA   001006 HIGH   100000 LAB   001500

Fig. 6.22   Addressing modes 2

```
 1                              *          Figure 6.23
 2                              *
 3                              *
 4                              *
 5                              *   ADD INSTRUCTION EXAMPLES:
 6                              ********************************
 7                              * the destination is always on the right
 8                              * any addressing mode can, in general,
 9                              * be substituted for DATA
10                              * all operations using data registers apply
11                              * equally to bytes, words and longwords
12                              * address register operations may only use
13                              * words and longwords
14           00001000                    ORG     $1000
15                              * ADD to data register
16 001000 D0781204             START     ADD     WDATA,D0   * default word op
17 001004 D0381206                       ADD.B   BDATA,D0   * byte operation
18 001008 D0B81200                       ADD.L   LDATA,D0   * longword op
19                              * ADD to memory
20 00100C D3781204                       ADD     D1,WDATA
21                              * ADD to address register
22 001010 D2F81204                       ADDA    WDATA,A1
23 001014 D4F81204                       ADDA.W  WDATA,A2
24 001018 D0021206                       ADDA.B  BDATA,A3   * byte op. illegal
****** ERROR 217--    0
25                              * ADD immediate to <ea>
26 00101C 067800241204                   ADDI    #36,WDATA
27 001022 06400024                       ADDI    #36,D0
28                              * ADD quick-generalized increment
29 001026 54781204                       ADDQ    #2,WDATA
30 00102A 067800021204                   ADDI    #2,WDATA   * force immediate
31                              * ADD with extend
32 001030 DB40                           ADDX    D0,D5
33                              * ADD with extend in memory
34                              * only a limited format is available:-
35 001032 D948                           ADDX    -(A0),-(A4)
36
37           00001200                    ORG     $1200
38 001200 0004               LDATA       DS.L    1
39 001204 0002               WDATA       DS.W    1
40 001206 0001               BDATA       DS.B    1
41                                       END
****** TOTAL ERRORS    1--   24 -- TOTAL LINES    28


APPROX  2114 UNUSED SYMBOL TABLE ENTRIES

BDATA     001206 LDATA    001200 START     001000 WDATA     001204
```

Fig. 6.23 Examples of ADD instructions

```
 1                                  *
 2                                  *
 3                                  *
 4                                  *
 5                                  * This program adds the elements of a word
 6                                  * array and it illustrates the use of the
 7                                  * addressing mode address register indirect
 8                                  * with postincrement
 9                                      G
10                                  * G asks for full array to be shown in listing
11
12                                  *
13            00001000                  ORG     $1000
14            00000008    LENGTH      EQU     $8        * max 256 with MOVEQ
15 001000 7008            START       MOVEQ   #LENGTH,D0
16 001002 41F81100                    LEA     ARRAY,A0   * address of base
17 001006 4281                        CLR.L   D1         * to accumulate sum
18                                  * for D0:=8 downto 1 do   sum:=sum+element
19 001008 D258            LOOP        ADD     (A0)+,D1
20 00100A 5340                        SUBQ    #1,D0      * decrement count
21 00100C 66FA                        BNE     LOOP
22 00100E 31C11110                    MOVE    D1,TOTAL   * save in memory
23 001012 4E40                        TRAP    #0         * exit from program
24
25            00001100                  ORG     $1100
26                                  * Data area
27 001100 0001            ARRAY       DC.W    1,2,3,4,5,6,7,8
27 001102 0002
27 001104 0003
27 001106 0004
27 001108 0005
27 00110A 0006
27 00110C 0007
27 00110E 0008
28 001110 0002            TOTAL       DS.W    1
29                                    END
```

****** TOTAL ERRORS   0--   0 -- TOTAL LINES   17

APPROX 2114 UNUSED SYMBOL TABLE ENTRIES

ARRAY   001100 LENGTH   000008 LOOP   001008 START   001000
TOTAL   001110

Fig. 6.24a   Program to add a word array

```
 1                                 *          Figure 6.24b
 2                                 *
 3                                 *
 4                                 *
 5                                 * This program adds the elements of a byte
 6                                 * array and illustrates the use of the
 7                                 * addressing mode address register
 8                                 * indirect with postincrement
 9                                 *
10                                             G
11                                 * G asks for full list to be shown in list file
12
13           00001000                        ORG      $1000
14           00000008              LENGTH    EQU      $8         * max 256 with MOVEQ
15 001000   7008                   START     MOVEQ    #LENGTH,D0
16 001002   41F81100                         LEA      ARRAY,A0   * address of base
17 001006   4281                             CLR.L    D1         * to accumulate sum
18                                 * for D0:=8 downto 1 do   sum:=sum+element
19 001008   D218                   LOOP      ADD.B    (A0)+,D1
20 00100A   5340                             SUBQ     #1,D0      * decrement count
21 00100C   66FA                             BNE      LOOP
22 00100E   31C11108                         MOVE     D1,TOTAL   * save in memory
23 001012   4E40                             TRAP     #0         * exit from program
24
25           00001100                        ORG      $1100
26                                 * Data area
27 001100   01                    ARRAY     DC.B     1,2,3,4,5,6,7,8
27 001101   02
27 001102   03
27 001103   04
27 001104   05
27 001105   06
27 001106   07
27 001107   08
28 001108   0002                  TOTAL     DS.W     1
29                                           END
```

****** TOTAL ERRORS   0--   0 -- TOTAL LINES   17

APPROX 2114 UNUSED SYMBOL TABLE ENTRIES

```
ARRAY     001100 LENGTH    000008 LOOP      001008 START     001000
TOTAL     001108
```

Fig. 6.24b Program to add a byte array

```
 1                                    *          Figure 6.24c
 2                                    *
 3                                    *
 4                                    *
 5                                    * This program adds the elements of a long word
 6                                    * array and   illustrates the use of the
 7                                    * addressing mode address register
 8                                    * indirect with postincrement
 9                                    *
10                                            G
11                                    * G asks for full list to be shown in list file
12
13           00001000                         ORG      $1000
14           00000008           LENGTH  EQU      $8        * max 256 with MOVEQ
15 001000 7008                  START   MOVEQ    #LENGTH,D0
16 001002 41F81100                      LEA      ARRAY,A0  * address of base
17 001006 4281                          CLR.L    D1          * to accumulate sum
18                             * for D0:=8 downto 1 do   sum:=sum+element
19 001008 D298                  LOOP    ADD.L    (A0)+,D1
20 00100A 5340                          SUBQ     #1,D0     * decrement count
21 00100C 66FA                          BNE      LOOP
22 00100E 21C11120                      MOVE.L   D1,TOTAL  * save in memory
23 001012 4E40                          TRAP     #0        * exit from program
24
25           00001100                         ORG      $1100
26                             * Data area
27 001100 00000001             ARRAY   DC.L     1,2,3,4,5,6,7,8
27 001104 00000002
27 001108 00000003
27 00110C 00000004
27 001110 00000005
27 001114 00000006
27 001118 00000007
27 00111C 00000008
28 001120 0004                 TOTAL   DS.L     1
29                                     END

****** TOTAL ERRORS    0--    0 -- TOTAL LINES    17


APPROX  2114 UNUSED SYMBOL TABLE ENTRIES

ARRAY    001100 LENGTH   000008 LOOP      001008 START     001000
TOTAL    001120
```

Fig. 6.24c Program to add a longword array.

```
 1                              *           Figure 6.25
 2                              *
 3                              *
 4                              * The program illustrates position-independent cod
 5                              * This section is not position-independent
 6                              * the object code should be compared with
 7                              * the position-independent section below
 8              00001000                  ORG      $1000
 9 001000 0002         LAB1     DS.W     1
10 001002 1000                  DC.W     LAB1
11 001004 D0781000     START1   ADD      LAB1,D0
12 001008 D1781000              ADD      D0,LAB1
13 00100C 307C1000              MOVE     #LAB1,A0
14 001010 41F81000              LEA      LAB1,A0
15 001014 60EE                  BRA      START1
16 001016 4EFA00EC              JMP      START2
17 00101A 600000E8              BRA      START2
18 00101E 4EBA00E4              JSR      START2
19 001022 4EF81004              JMP      START1
20
21                              * PC relative addressing modes are used
22                              * automatically after RORG. Errors have been
23                              * included to illustrate assembler assistance
24                              * for writing position-independent code
25              00001100                  RORG     $1100
26 001100 0002         LAB2     DS.W     1
27 001102 1100                  DC.W     LAB2          * absolute address
28                              * error but no help in detection
29 001104 D27AFFFA     START2   ADD      LAB2,D1
30 001108 D2781000              ADD      LAB1,D1
31 00110C D57AFFF2              ADD      D2,LAB2       * error - read-only
****** ERROR 231--    0
32 001110 307C1000              MOVE     #LAB1,A0
33 001114 307C1100              MOVE     #LAB2,A0      * absolute address
****** ERROR 231--   31
34 001118 41F81000              LEA      LAB1,A0
35 00111C 41FAFFE2              LEA      LAB2,A0
36 001120 D27B10DE              ADD      LAB2(D1),D1
37 001124 D2691000              ADD      LAB1(A1),D1
38 001128 D27B80D6              ADD      LAB2(A0),D1
39 00112C 60D6                  BRA      START2
40 00112E 4EFAFFD4              JMP      START2
41                              END

****** TOTAL ERRORS    2--  33 -- TOTAL LINES   34


APPROX  2115 UNUSED SYMBOL TABLE ENTRIES

LAB1      001000 LAB2     001100 START1    001004 START2    001104
```

Fig. 6.25 Position independent code

6.14 SUMMARY

In this chapter, the range of addressing modes available in the 68000 has been described. Compared with earlier machines, there are a large number of modes and, together with the operation codes, they provide a very powerful machine.

The choice of addressing modes made by the designer of a processor is influenced by the requirement of systems and applications software. In this chapter, the range of data structures which are conveniently supported by the 68000 addressing modes has been shown. In later chapters, further indication will be given of how the 68000 addressing modes support the requirements of the writers of compilers and operating systems.

The general point is that provision of *addressing modes* at the conventional machine level support *data structures* at high level language level (see Fig. 1.1).

7

Stacks and subroutines

7.1 THE 68000 STACK

In Chapter 6, several data structures were introduced including arrays, records and structures consisting of arrays of records. A stack is a data structure in which the first element put in is the last one to be taken out (FILO) or conversely, the last item to be stacked is the first to be unstacked (LIFO). A simple use of a data stack is to reverse the order of a list of numbers or characters. The power and extent of use of this structure are developed throughout this chapter.

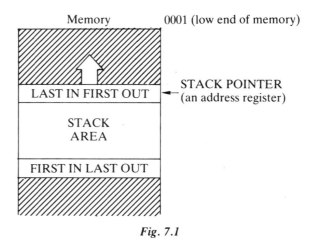

Fig. 7.1

Fig. 7.1 shows the 68000 stack; note that:

- The 68000 stacks grow towards the low end of memory (address 0).
- All eight address registers can maintain a stack i.e. be used as stack pointers.
- Address register 7 is only special in that it is used automatically by the hardware for subroutine linkage (see below). The mnemonic SP may be used for A7.

- The stack pointer contains the address of the last item on the stack (*not* the next free).

7.2   PROGRAMMING A STACK

In Section 6.9 the effect of automatic increment of an address register after use was illustrated. The complementary addressing mode of automatic decrement of an address register before use is helpful, together with postincrement, for maintaining a stack.

7.2.1.   Instructions to manipulate data stacks

> MOVE.W   D0, –(SP)   * stack or push D0, i.e. copy the contents of the low order word of D0 onto the stack (where SP is pointing after being decremented by two (bytes))
>
> MOVE.W   (A7)+, D0   * unstack or pop into D0, i.e. copy the contents of the top of the stack (where A7 is pointing) into D0 then increment A7 by two (bytes)
>
> ADD.L   (SP)+, D0   * unstack and add a longword to D0, increment SP by a longword.

In more detail, consider the stack before MOVE   D0, –(SP) is executed as follows:

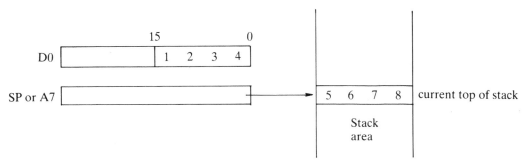

Then, after MOVE   D0, –(SP) is executed the stack will be

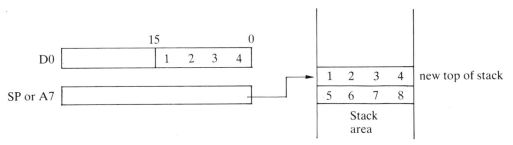

Fig. 7.2

7.2.2   Storage space for stacks

Since stacks are just data areas, space must be reserved for them in programs. For example:

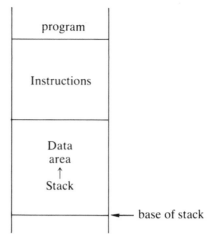

The data area might contain, for example:

```
                ORG    $2000
STACKEND:       DS.W   100        * reserve 100 words for the stack
   STACK:       EQU    *          * base of stack
```

The stack pointer is then initialized by the instruction:

```
        LEA        STACK, SP
```

Care must be taken that the stack does not grow to such an extent that it overwrites the instructions.

An alternative arrangement is to allow the stack to grow towards the low end of memory from the point at which the instructions start:

```
            TTL    PROGRAM
            ORG    $1000
STACK:      EQU    $1000
START:      LEA    STACK, SP    * initialize stack pointer.
```

7.3   SUBROUTINE CALL AND RETURN

In Chapter 5, some program control instructions, Jumps and branches, were introduced. Of far greater importance in program structure and design is the concept of the subroutine call and return.

A subroutine is a set of instructions which carries out a single task. Implementation details of how the task is done are expressed once only, within the subroutine. The subroutine can be called any number of times from any number of different places in a program. Subroutine call and return is supported by the 68000 processor through the provision of the two operation codes JSR, jump to subroutine, and RTS, return from subroutine, defined as:

    JSR ⟨ea⟩
    RTS

They are used as follows in a program:

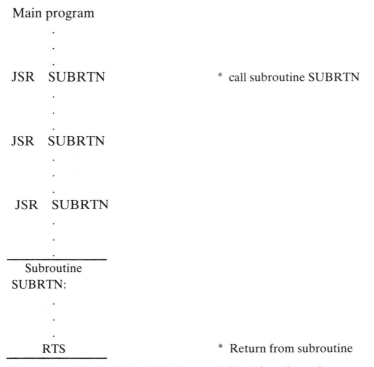

    Main program
        .
        .
        .
    JSR SUBRTN   * call subroutine SUBRTN
        .
        .
        .
    JSR SUBRTN
        .
        .
        .
    JSR SUBRTN
        .
        .
        .
    ─────────────
      Subroutine
    SUBRTN:
        .
        .
        .
    ─────────────
      RTS   * Return from subroutine

Examples of tasks that might be carried out in subroutines are:

- Numerical algorithms, e.g. root location.
- Input and output, e.g. read or print a character; read or print a string.
- Sort routines, e.g. sort an array into order.
- Validation, e.g. check that a character is alphabetic; check that a character is hexadecimal.

At the lowest level, the use of a subroutine saves the labour of typing in instructions, many times over, at each point of call. However, subroutines are valuable for imparting clarity even in cases where they are called only once. By their use, the high-level structure of the program can be segregated from the low-level coding detail.

When subroutines are used within a program it is important to enforce the discipline that a subroutine may only be left either through a return instruction RTS or by calling another subroutine. For clarity of structure and ease of testing, debugging and reading, jumps and branches should not be used to leave a subroutine. This is enforced by the compiler at high level and should be followed as a discipline at low level.

7.4   THE CALL AND RETURN MECHANISM

```
         *              Main program
                        .
                        .
                        .
                        JSR SUBRTN    * first call
         RET1:          .
                        .
                        .
                        JSR SUBRTN    * second call
         RET2:          .
                        .
                        .
         _____

         *              Subroutine
         SUBRTN:        .
                        .
                        .
                        RTS
```

After the first call of the subroutine the return, when RTS is executed, must be to the instruction labeled RET1. After the second call, the return must be to the instruction labeled RET2. A mechanism is needed to remember from where the call was made and to return to the following instruction.

7.4.1   Use of the stack for call and return

The mechanism used by the 68000 to 'remember' the return address is that the PC when the instruction JSR SUBRTN has been fetched (the return address) is stacked using A7 (also named SP) as stack pointer. The full 32-bit program counter is stacked and SP is first decremented appropriately by four bytes. The PC is then set up from the address field of the instruction JSR, i.e. the PC is set up to contain the address SUBRTN. The next instruction to be fetched is therefore that at SUBRTN.

On RTS, the PC is loaded with the longword at the top of the stack and SP is incremented by four bytes. The next instruction to be executed is therefore at the return address which was stacked (see Fig. 7.3).

7.5   EXAMPLES

Examples are now given showing complete programs incorporating subroutines. The first example illustrates setting up the stack pointer and calling a subroutine from two points in a main program section. It should be noted that the exit instruction TRAP #0 is at the end of this section.

After the instruction JSR SUBRTN has been fetched

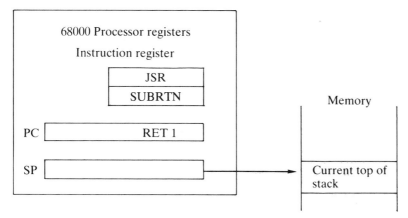

After the instruction JSR SUBRTN has been executed:

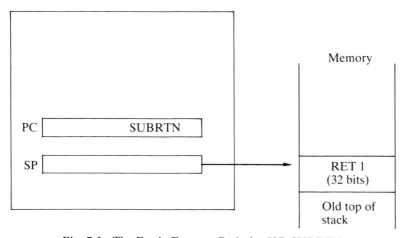

Fig. 7.3 The Fetch–Execute Cycle for JSR SUBRTN

Fig. 7.4 illustrates the mechanism provided by the 68000 to support subroutine call and return by showing two 'snapshots' of the stack, taken during execution of the program. The second example shows a program with two subroutines and illustrates a nested call from subroutine 1 to subroutine 2. Again, the stack is shown in Fig. 7.5 at a point during the execution after subroutine 2 has been entered. The third example is not a realistic program but illustrates that the stack mechanism can support recursive calls. The subroutine body contains a call to that subroutine. No attempt is made at this stage to explain the use of recursion; the point is to illustrate the mechanism.

In Fig. 7.6, the stack is shown after the subroutine has been called from the main program and has then called itself three times recursively.

7.5.1   Example showing the stack on subroutine call

The following program should be studied or, if possible, typed in and executed in trace mode. The stack and stack pointer, A7, should be examined at each subroutine call and return. The NOP (no operation) instruction is used in place of a specific example.

```
                                  TTL    SUBROUTINE CALL AND RETURN
      location

                          ORG     $1000
                  STACK:  EQU     $1000
      1000        START:  LEA     STACK, SP
      1004                NOP
      1006                JSR     SUBRTN

      100A        RET1:   NOP
      100C                NOP
      100E                JSR     SUBRTN

      1012        RET2:   NOP
      1014                TRAP    #0
                  *_____
                  * Subroutine
      1016        SUBRTN: NOP
      1018                NOP
      101A                NOP
      101C                RTS
                  *_____
                          END
```

The stack after the first call   **The stack after the second call**

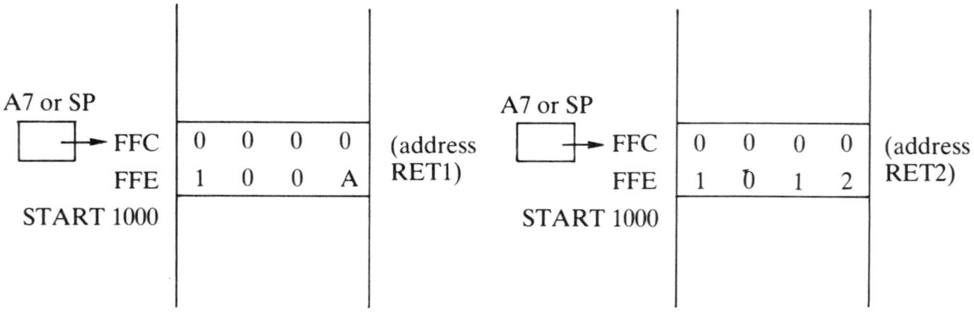

Fig. 7.4

7.5.2. Example with a nested subroutine call

The following program should be studied or, if possible, typed in and executed in trace mode. The stack and stack pointer should be examined at each subroutine call and return.

```
                     TTL NESTED SUBROUTINE
location              ORG    $1000
            STACK:    EQU    $1000
1000        START:    LEA    STACK, SP
1004                  NOP
1006                  JSR    SUB1
100A        RET1:     NOP
100C                  TRAP   #0
                     ------------------------
            *Subroutine 1

100E        SUB1:     NOP
1010                  JSR    SUB2
1014        RET2:     NOP
1016                  RTS
                     ------------------------
            *Subroutine 2

1018        SUB2:     NOP
101A                  NOP
101C                  RTS
                     ------------------------
                      END
```

The stack after JSR SUB2

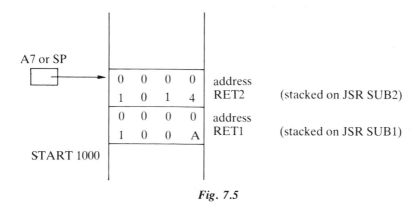

Fig. 7.5

7.5.3 Example with a recursive call

In the previous exercise SUB2 was called from within SUB1. For completeness, consider a call to a subroutine **from within that subroutine** – a *recursive* call. This example shows an uncontrolled recursive call. The program should be traced and the stack and SP examined for a few calls. If the program is executed at full speed the stack will grow indefinitely and write over all the low end of memory.

```
                        TTL     RECURSIVE CALL

                        ORG     $1000
             STACK:     EQU     $1000
location
1000         START:     LEA     STACK, SP
1004                    NOP
1006                    JSR     SUBRTN
100A         RET1:      NOP
100C                    TRAP  #0
             *_____

             *Subroutine SUBRTN

100E         SUBRTN:NOP
1010                    NOP
1012                    JSR     SUBRTN      * recursive call
1016         RET:       RTS
             _____

                        END
```

The stack after four calls of SUBRTN

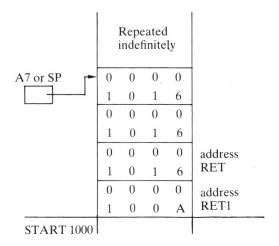

Fig. 7.6

7.6   PARAMETER PASSING

So far, the transfer of control between subroutines has been discussed. Since a subroutine performs a single operation, possibly on some data, we must now consider how such data may be passed as parameters to the subroutine. It is desirable that subroutine code should not access global data, data defined at the calling level, directly but only in a controlled way through the parameter passing mechanism so that the actions of a program can be understood and managed.

7.6.1   Parameter passing via the registers and MOVEM

Since the 68000 has a reasonably large number of registers, these may be used to pass call and return parameters for small assembly language programs. The problem with this method is keeping track of which registers are used by which subroutines in large programs. At the start of a subroutine, documentation should be given including what the input and output parameters are, what registers are used by the subroutine and which further subroutines may be called. For large programs it is a good idea to save the value of the registers not used to pass parameters on entry to a subroutine and restore them before returning. The 68000 has an instruction 'move multiple registers' MOVEM to support this requirement, of the form:

```
MOVEM   register list, ⟨ea⟩        * from registers to memory
MOVEM   ⟨ea⟩, register list        * from memory to registers
MOVEM   D3/D4/D5/A1, SAVEBLOCK
```

In this example, the subroutine uses registers D3, D4, D5 and A1. So that the calling program does not need to be aware of this, the subroutine itself saves the contents, on entry, of these registers by the above instruction and restores the contents, before return, by the instruction:

```
MOVEM   SAVEBLOCK, D3/D4/D5/A1
```

If the list includes a consecutive range of registers, the following may be used:

```
SUBRTN:   EQU   *
          MOVEM   D0 – D7/A0 – A6, SAVEBLOCK
          ——
          ——
          ——
          ——

          ——
          MOVEM   SAVEBLOCK, D0 – D7/A0 – A6
          RTS
```

Note that the stack pointer is not copied. It will be used for any subsequent subroutine calls.

Note also that SAVEBLOCK is local to this particular subroutine. A different 'saveblock' would be needed for every subroutine so that nested calls could be used. Even so, recursive calls would cause SAVEBLOCK to be overwritten. It is therefore more general, and safer, to save the registers on the stack.

```
SUBRTN:   EQU *
          MOVEM    D0 – D7/A0 – A6, –(SP)    ; stack the registers
            .
            .
            .
            .
          MOVEM    (SP)+, D0 – D7/A0 – A6   ; restore the registers
          RTS
```

7.6.2   Value and reference parameters

Parameters may be passed to procedures by value or by reference (*var* parameters in Pascal are reference parameters). Using the simplest 68000 method, of passing parameters in registers, the methods are illustrated by the example:

```
*                calling level
          .
          .
          .
          MOVE   DATA1, D0   * set up a value parameter in D0
          LEA    DATA2, A0   * set up a reference parameter in A0
          .
          .
          .
DATA1    :
DATA2    :
*_____
* subroutine name and function
* input parameters are:
* D0 value parameter
* A0 reference parameter
* etc
SUBRTN: EQU   *
```

Note that the location DATA1 at the calling level is not changed by the subroutine since its contents were passed as a value parameter. Note that the location DATA2 at the calling level may be changed by the subroutine since its address was passed as a reference parameter.

7.6.3   Data areas known to the called and calling routines

The body of a subroutine may have the following layout:

```
* Subroutine data area
INPUT-PARAMS:          ——

                       ——
                       ——
OUTPUT-PARAMS:         ——
                       ——
                       ——
LOCAL-VARIABLES:       ——
                       ——
                       ——
* Subroutine code
      SUBRTN:          EQU   *
                       ——
                       ——
                       RTS
```

The agreed convention may be that the calling routine fills in the input parameter area before calling the subroutine and picks up the output parameters after return.

Alternatively, the calling program may set up a call-parameter block corresponding to the input parameter area and pass its address in an agreed register. The subroutine, using the address register, will copy the parameters across. An address register may be used in a similar way for the return parameter. It should be noted that this arrangement could not be used for a recursive subroutine. There is only one place for the parameters and local variables and these would be overwritten on recursive calls.

7.6.4   Stacks for parameter passing

The most general method for parameter passing is to use a stack. The stack used by the hardware for subroutine linkage could also be used (with great care) for parameter passing. Alternatively, the subroutine linkage stack could be left as a 'control stack' and a separate stack, maintained by another address register, could be used for parameter passing.

The basic idea is that input parameters are stacked before the subroutine is called, the call causes the return address to be stacked. The code in the subroutine picks up the input parameters from the stack, uses the stack for local variables, and puts output parameters on the stack. Register values may also be stacked on entry and restored before exit. After return from the subroutine the output parameters are obtained from the stack.

It should be noted that the stack pointer must be pointing to the return address when RTS is executed.

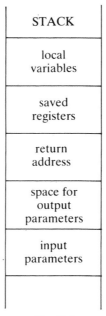

Fig. 7.7

Fig. 7.7 shows the layout of the stack for all the subroutine's data area.

Recursive subroutines may be supported using this method since a new area of the stack will be used for each recursive call. This chapter is not the place to explain in full how compilers allocate storage for variables and manage parameter-passing but it is worthwhile noting that the 'run-time stack' for block-structured high level languages is organized along the lines of the above description with parameters, local variables and link addresses residing on the stack within an 'activation record' for a subroutine. An example of two instructions specifically designed for this use is given in Section 7.6.5. This section may be omitted at first reading.

7.6.5 The LINK and UNLK instructions

    LNK An, #⟨displacement⟩

- The contents of An are pushed onto the stack.
- An is loaded from the updated stack pointer.
- The sign extended 16-bit displacement is added to SP

    UNLK An.

- The stack pointer is loaded from An.
- An is then loaded with the longword pulled from the top of the stack.

These two instructions are used together to manage a stack consisting of a series of frames and to allow easy access to individual data items within frames. They support the run-time storage management provided, through run-time support routines, by compilers for block structured languages. A stack frame (or activation record) for a procedure contains input parameters, output parameters, local variables and the link address.

Example – showing minimum overhead on procedure call:

Main program body

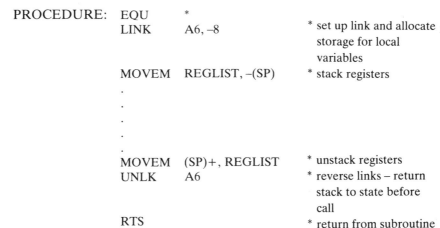

```
        MOVE    PARAM1, –(SP)      * push value parameter onto stack
        PEA     PARAM2             * push reference parameter onto stack
        JSR     PROCEDURE          * call subroutine (link address onto stack)
        ADDQ    #6, SP             * pop output parameters on return
                .
                .
                .
                .
                .
```

Procedure body

```
        PROCEDURE:  EQU     *
                    LINK    A6, –8          * set up link and allocate
                                              storage for local
                                              variables
                    MOVEM   REGLIST, –(SP)  * stack registers
                        .
                        .
                        .
                        .
                        .
                    MOVEM   (SP)+, REGLIST  * unstack registers
                    UNLK    A6              * reverse links – return
                                              stack to state before
                                              call
                    RTS                     * return from subroutine
```

See Fig. 7.8, p. 108, for the stack before and after the procedure call.

7.7 ASSEMBLY LANGUAGE PROGRAM STRUCTURE

Since the language itself provides little assistance in making programs readable it is important that the programmer should develop sensible conventions for program structuring. This text is not the place for a lengthy development of structure but that which has been established for high level language programming is, arguably,

the stack before the procedure calls is as follows:

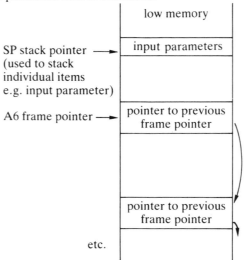

the stack after the procedure call is as follows:

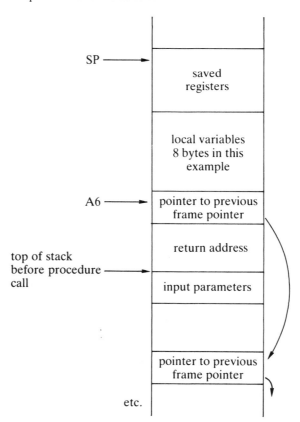

Fig. 7.8

even more important for low level. A few general rules are as follows:

- A subroutine should carry out one operation on some data.
- A subroutine should not access data directly at the calling level, i.e. there should be no global variables. Such accesses may be carried out in a controlled way through reference parameters.
- Each subroutine should be documented and clearly divided from the rest of the program. Input and output parameters should be described in a heading, including the registers used and further subroutines called.
- In some circumstances it is appropriate for a data structure not to be passed around from subroutine to subroutine but to be kept as local data in a module. The module may then provide all the operations appropriate to that data structure. Fig. 7.9 gives an outline layout, but a detailed discussion more appropriately belongs in a programming course.

* **initialization** section of main program

⋮

call subroutine in module to initialize data

⋮

* **main program body**

⋮

call subroutine performing operation 1 on data

⋮

etc.

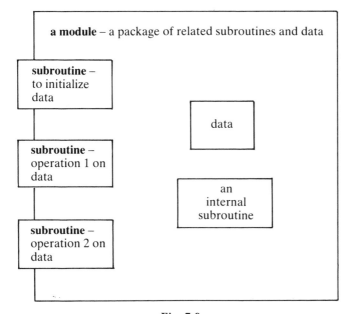

Fig. 7.9

8

Instruction set summary

8.1 INTRODUCTION

The approach taken so far has been to introduce instructions as needed to illustrate a particular point or write a specific program. A more general summary is now given so that information is easy to find. This chapter may be omitted at first reading since later chapters will refer back to this one when a particular instruction is used. The full instruction set is given in Fig. 1.17 and details of the object code for all instructions are available in Motorola's MC68000 16/32-bit Microprocessor Programmer's Reference Manual. The effect of the instructions on the condition flags is not in general reiterated here since this topic was discussed in Chapter 5.

8.2 INSTRUCTION TYPES

The 68000 instruction set types may be classified as follows:

Data Movement Instructions
– move data between memory locations, general purpose registers and input or output devices (see Part 2) in any combination.

Integer Arithmetic Instructions
– perform single precision and multiple precision arithmetic operations on binary numbers.

Logical Instructions
– perform logical AND, OR and Exclusive OR operations on memory locations and registers.

Shift and Rotate Instructions
– on memory locations and registers.

Bit Test and Manipulation Instructions
– test the state of individual bits, set the condition flags and perform some operation based on the result of the test.

Binary Coded Decimal (BCD) Instructions
- add and subtract BCD digits.

Program Control Instructions (see Chapters 5 and 7)
- perform branches, jumps and subroutine call to control the sequence of program execution.

System Control Instructions (see Chapter 12 in Part 2).

8.3 DATA MOVEMENT INSTRUCTIONS

Data movement instructions may be further classified as follows:

- MOVE ⟨ea⟩, ⟨ea⟩
  It should be noted that the two general effective addresses allow memory to memory moves. Bytes, words and longwords may be moved.
  As well as Dn and An, ⟨ea⟩ may also be used to refer to the status register SR and the condition code register CCR (the low byte of the status register as described in Chapter 5).

  MOVE SR, ⟨ea⟩
  The content of the status register is moved to ⟨ea⟩. The operand size is a word.

  MOVE ⟨ea⟩, SR
  The content of the source operand is moved to the status register. The source operand is a word and all bits of the status register are affected. It will be shown in Chapter 12 of Part 2 and in Part 3 that this instruction is privileged.

  MOVE ⟨ea⟩, CCR
  The content of the source operand is moved to the condition codes. The source operand is a word but only the low order byte is used to update the condition codes. The upper byte is ignored. If AND, OR and EOR operations are used to change the CCR then byte operations must be used.
- MOVEM, move multiple registers, see Section 7.6.1.
- MOVEA ⟨ea⟩, An   move to address register.
  This may be considered as an example of MOVE ⟨ea⟩, ⟨ea⟩. As explained in Section 1.8 however, there are restrictions on the operations that can be carried out on address registers and the use of a separate opcode mnemonic MOVEA emphasizes this. The source operand is restricted to word or longword and a word operand is sign extended to occupy the full 32-bit address register.
- LEA, load effective address.
- PEA ⟨ea⟩.
  push the effective address onto the stack using A7 as stack pointer.
- MOVEP, move peripheral data. This instruction will be explained as required in Part 2.
- MOVEQ #⟨8-bit integer⟩, Dn
  This instruction occupies one word, see Section 2.9, and moves an integer with

value in the range −128 to +127 into a data register. The integer is sign extended to 32 bits and affects the whole of the data register.

• Register Swap and Exchange

SWAP Dn   *swap words within a data register.

EXG   Dx, Dy   * exchange 32-bit register values.
EXG   Ax, Ay
EXG   Dx, Ay

It may be convenient to use the above instructions together with:

EXT.W   Dn   * byte extended to word within Dn
EXT.L   Dn   * word extended to longword within Dn

8.4   INTEGER ARITHMETIC INSTRUCTIONS

The four basic arithmetic operations add, subtract, multiply and divide are provided as well as arithmetic compare, clear and negate. Data operands may be byte, word or longword in general but some multiprecision and mixed size arithmetic instructions have been provided. Address operands may be word or longword.

The arithmetic instructions are summarized below with brief comments where appropriate and a full description of the multiply and divide instructions is then given for reference from later chapters.

Add instructions

ADD	ADD	⟨ea⟩, Dn	full range of operands
	ADD	Dn, ⟨ea⟩	
ADDA	ADDA	⟨ea⟩, An	valid address operands
ADDI	ADDI	#d, ⟨ea⟩	d may be byte, word or longword
ADDQ	ADDQ	#d, ⟨ea⟩	$1 \leq d \leq 8$

It should be noted that, unlike MOVEQ, the destination is a general effective address of which 8, 6 or 32 bits are affected as indicated in the instruction.

ADDX	ADDX	Dy, Dx	Add with extend.
	ADDX	−(Ay, −(Ax)	See Section 8.4.3

Add the source operand to the destination operand together with the extend X flag of the CCR. The size of the operation may be byte, word or longword.

Clear

CLR	CLR	⟨ea⟩	clear i.e. set 8, 16 or 32 bits to 0.

Compare instructions
Care must be taken over byte, word or longword for comparisons. In each case the

source is subtracted from the destination without affecting the destination and the condition flags are set for subsequent testing.

CMP	CMP	$\langle$ea$\rangle$, Dn	full range of operands
CMPA	CMPA	$\langle$ea$\rangle$, An	valid address operands
CMPI	CMPI	#d $\langle$ea$\rangle$	d may be byte, word or longword
CMPM	CMPM	(Ay)+, (AX)+	compare byte, word or longword of memory with memory

Examples are given in Chapter 5.

Divide instructions (see Section 8.4.2)

| DIVS | DIVS | $\langle$ea$\rangle$, Dn | signed divide |
| DIVU | DIVU | $\langle$ea$\rangle$, Dn | unsigned divide |

Sign extend

| EXT | EXT.W | Dn | byte to word within Dn |
| | EXT.L | Dn | word to longword within Dn |

Multiply instructions (see Section 8.4.1)

| MULS | MULS | $\langle$ea$\rangle$, Dn | signed multiply |
| MULU | MULU | $\langle$ea$\rangle$, Dn | unsigned multiply |

Negate instructions

NEG   NEG $\langle$ea$\rangle$ negate

The byte, word or longword operand $\langle$ea$\rangle$ is subtracted from zero and the result stored in $\langle$ea$\rangle$. It should be noted that this is a true negative, two's complement, and not a logical inversion, one's complement.

NEGX   NEGX $\langle$ea$\rangle$ negate with extend, see Section 8.4.3

The byte, word or longword operand $\langle$ea$\rangle$ together with the extend X flag in CCR are subtracted from zero and the result stored in $\langle$ea$\rangle$.

Subtract instructions

Comments on the subtract instructions are as for the corresponding add instructions.

SUB	SUB	$\langle$ea$\rangle$, Dn	
	SUB	Dn, $\langle$ea$\rangle$	
SUBA	SUBA	$\langle$ea$\rangle$, An	
SUBI	SUB	#d $\langle$ea$\rangle$	
SUBQ	SUBQ	#d, $\langle$ea$\rangle$	$1 \leq d \leq 8$
SUBX	SUBX	Dy, Dx	subtract with extend
	SUBX	−(Ay), −(Ax)	see Section 8.4.3

Test and set

TAS $\langle$ea$\rangle$

This instruction allows only a byte operand. The value of the byte operand is tested and the N and Z flags of the CCR are set accordingly. The high order bit of the operand is set. The operation is indivisible (using a read-modify-write memory cycle) to allow synchronization of several processors. This topic is explained in Part 3.

Test

   TST   ⟨ea⟩

This instruction compares the operand with zero and sets the condition codes. The operand is not affected.

8.4.1   Signed and unsigned multiply

These instructions multiply two word operands (16 bits) and return the 32-bit product in a data register. Signed and unsigned integers are described in Section 1.9.

   MULU   ⟨ea⟩, Dn   unsigned multiply

The lower word of Dn initially contains one of the operands and ⟨ea⟩ the other. The result is in Dn.

e.g.   MULU   #10,D4 (multiply by decimal 10)

	31	16 15	0
D4 before	unspecified	0000000011111111	

	31	16 15	0
D4 after	0000000000000000	0000100111110110	

e.g.   MULU   #$10,D4 (multiply by hexadecimal 10)

	31	16 15	0
D4 before	unspecified	1010101010101010	

	31	16 15	0
D4 after	0000000000001010	1010101010100000	

Fig. 8.1

The N (sign) and Z flags are set according to the result and V and C are cleared. It would be helpful if V was set to indicate whether the product could be truncated to 16 bits, as in the first example above, but this is not provided (unlike the Intel 8086). In the second example of MULU above, since unsigned integers were being multiplied the full 16 bits were used to represent positive integers as explained in Section 1.9.

If this example is repeated for signed multiplication we have:

MULS   #$10,D4 (multiply by hexadecimal 10)

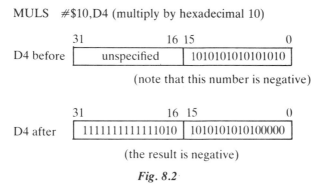

(note that this number is negative)

(the result is negative)

Fig. 8.2

Signed multiplication therefore takes account of the sign of both operands.

8.4.2   Signed and unsigned divide

DIVU   ⟨ea⟩, Dn

The 32-bit integer in Dn is divided by the 16-bit integer in ⟨ea⟩. The quotient is available in the lower 16 bits of Dn and the remainder in the upper 16 bits of Dn.

e.g.   DIVU   #10,D4

```
              31                 16 15                    0
D4 before | 0000000000000000 | 0000000000100000 | decimal 32

              31                 16 15                    0
D4 after  | 0000000000000010 | 0000000000000011 | quotient 3
                                                    remainder 2
```

Fig. 8.3

When setting up Dn for the division it is often necessary to extend a word in Dn to a longword.

EXT.L   is required for DIVS to retain the sign
AND   is required for DIVU
        e.g. ANDI.L   #$0000FFFF, D4

Divide by zero results in an automatic trap into the development system (see Chapter 12) and V is set on overflow since the quotient, for example, may exceed 16 bits.
   As described above for MULS, DIVS takes account of the sign of the operands.

8.4.3   Multi-length arithmetic

The add, subtract and negate with extend instructions, ADDX, SUBX and NEGX, provide multi precision arithmetic. As indicated in the summary in Section 8.4 the extend X flag is included in the arithmetic operation. The condition flags are normally set after each arithmetic operation. In multi-length arithmetic, the zero flag should indicate whether the whole number and not just the part generated by the last operation is zero. For this reason Z is not set for a zero result with these instructions; it is only unset for a non-zero result. The programmer must therefore set Z by software before a sequence of instructions effecting multi-length arithmetic. An example of 64-bit addition is given to illustrate this point.

```
MOVE      #4, CCR        * set Z, clear other flags
ADDX.L    –(A0), –(A1)   * add low order 32-bit word
ADDX.L    (A0), –(A1)    * add high order 32-bit word
```

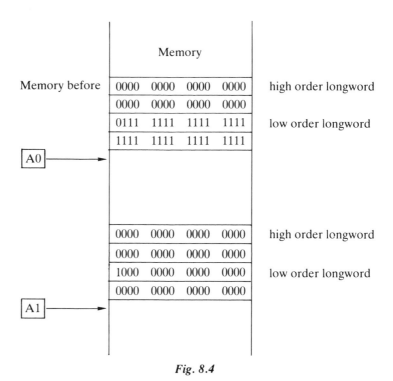

Fig. 8.4

After the first ADDX.L instruction has been executed, the Z flag is cleared. After the second ADDX.L instruction the result is zero but the Z flag is not set which is correct since the 64-bit result is not zero. After the instruction sequence, memory is as follows:

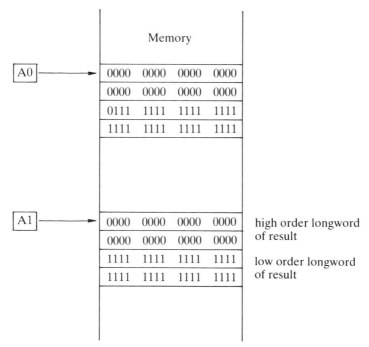

Fig. 8.5

8.5 LOGICAL INSTRUCTIONS

The logical operations AND, OR, EOR (exclusive or) and NOT (logical invert) are available for all sizes of integer data operands. The contents of an address register may not be used as an operand.

AND	AND	⟨ea⟩, Dn	
	AND	Dn, ⟨ea⟩	
ANDI	ANDI	#d, ⟨ea⟩	d may be byte, word or longword
	ANDI	#d, SR	(see Section 8.5.1)

This is a word operation; all bits of the status register are affected. It is a privileged instruction, the implications of which will be explained in Chapter 12.

ANDI #d, CCR

This is a byte operation which affects CCR, the low order byte of the status register.

EOR	EOR	Dn, ⟨ea⟩	
EORI	EORI	#d, ⟨ea⟩	d may be byte, word or longword
	EORI	#d, SR	a word operation, see also ANDI
	EORI	#d, CCR	a byte operation, see also ANDI.

NOT	NOT	⟨ea⟩	logical complement
OR	OR	⟨ea⟩, Dn	inclusive OR
	OR	Dn, ⟨ea⟩	
ORI	ORI	#d, ⟨ea⟩	defined as for ANDI and EORI.
	ORI	#d, SR	
	ORI	#d, CCR	

8.5.1   An example of ANDI

ANDI   #$F, D0

Suppose D0 before execution of the instruction is:

31		16	15				0
.anything			1011	0010	1101	1010	

The instruction forms the logical AND, bit by bit with:

$$0000 \quad 0000 \quad 0000 \quad 1111$$

giving D0 after the instruction as:

31		16	15				0
same as before			0000	0000	0000	1010	

Note that used in a program, a mnemonic might be helpful, e.g.:

MASK: EQU $000F

.

.

ANDI   #MASK, D3

8.6   SHIFT AND ROTATE INSTRUCTIONS

Shift operations to left and right are provided by arithmetic and logical shift instructions, ASL, ASR, LSL, LSR respectively. Rotate instructions, with and without inclusion of the extend X flag are also provided. All shift and rotate instructions can be performed in either data registers or memory. Register shifts and rotates support all operand sizes and allow a shift count, specified as part of the instruction, of one to eight bits or specified by a count held in a data register of 0 to 63 bits. Memory shift and rotates are for word operands only and allow only single bit shifts or rotates. There is therefore a tradeoff between repeatedly executing a one bit shift instruction on a memory location and moving the contents into a data register, shifting and moving back again. The latter is more efficient for a shift count of three or more.

Detailed examples of some of the instructions are given for those not familiar with logical operations, followed by a diagrammatic representation of all the shift and rotate instructions.

operand size

Arithmetic shift to the left

ASL	ASL Dx, Dy	8, 16, 32	shift Dy (count in Dx)
	ASL #d, Dn	8, 16, 32	$1 \leqslant d \leqslant 8$
	ASL ⟨ea⟩	16	by one bit only

Arithmetic shift to the right

	ASR Dx, Dy	8, 16, 32	shift Dy (count in Dx)
ASR	ASR #d, Dn	8, 16, 32	$1 \leqslant d \leqslant 8$
	ASR ⟨ea⟩	16	by one bit only

Logical shift to the left (and right)

LSL	as above
LSR	as above

Rotate to the left (and right), also extended

ROL	as above	
ROR	as above	
ROXL	as above	the X condition code is included
ROXR	as above	in the rotate

8.6.1   Example of a logical shift

LSR   #4, D3

LSR or LSR.W operates only on the 16 bits of D3. LSR.B operates only on the lower 8 bits whereas LSR.L operates on the full 32 bits. The instruction shifts the bit pattern four places to the right.

Fig. 8.6

The shift count may, alternatively, be set up in a data register in which case the contents of that data register specify a shift count in the range 0 to 63 where 0 produces a count of 64, e.g.:

MOVE   #4, D7

or compute the shift count dynamically in the program in D7

LSR   D7, D6   * shift D6 according to the count in D7.

8.6.2   Arithmetic shift examples

e.g. ASR #4, D3

Shift the low order word (16 bits) of D3 four places to the right preserving the *sign* of the word.

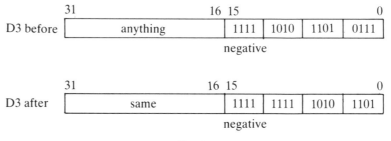

EXAMPLE 1

EXAMPLE 2

Fig. 8.7

On ASL, the sign bit is not preserved but overflow V is set if the sign bit is ever changed.

8.6.3   Shift and rotate instructions diagrammatically

The diagrams show an operand which may be of size byte, word or longword. C is the carry flag and X the extend flag (see Section 5.3). The number of positions shifted is specified in the shift count within the instructions.

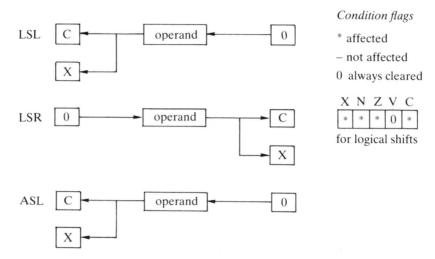

Condition flags

* affected

– not affected

0 always cleared

X	N	Z	V	C
*	*	*	0	*

for logical shifts

also, V indicates if any sign change has occurred during the shift.

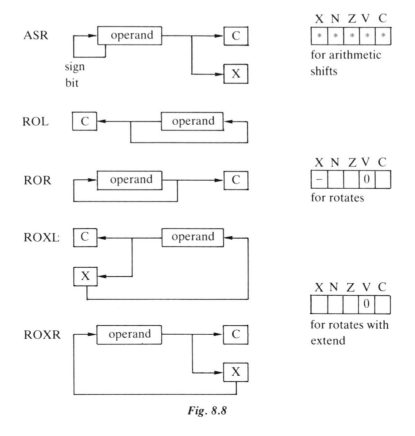

X	N	Z	V	C
*	*	*	*	*

for arithmetic shifts

X	N	Z	V	C
–			0	

for rotates

X	N	Z	V	C
			0	

for rotates with extend

Fig. 8.8

8.6.4. Shifts, multiplies and divides

The reader should verify that a shift to the left by one place of a positive or negative integer is a multiply by two and an arithmetic shift to the right is a divide by two. Multiplications and divisions by powers of two are usually implemented as shift instructions as, for example, in the hexadecimal conversion routines of Chapter 11.

8.7   BIT MANIPULATION INSTRUCTIONS

There are four instructions that test the state of any specified bit (0–31) in a data register or any specified bit (0–7) of a *byte* in memory. These instructions record the state of the specified bit in the zero (Z) condition code flag. If the bit is 0 then Z is set; if the bit is 1 then Z is cleared.

Three of these instructions also change the bit unconditionally, following the test, as follows:

BTST (bit test)	the bit is not affected
BSET (bit test and set)	the bit is set to 1
BCLR (bit test and clear)	the bit is set to 0
BCHG (bit test and change)	the state of the bit is reversed.

The bit number may be specified as the contents of a data register or as an immediate value. If a data register is being tested the bit range is 0–31. If a bit in memory is being tested, the bit range is 0–7.

The syntax for each instruction may take two forms, e.g.:

BTST	Dn, ⟨ea⟩	* the bit number is specified in Dn
BTST	#d, ⟨ea⟩	* the bit number is d.

8.8   BINARY-CODED DECIMAL INSTRUCTIONS

In binary-coded decimal, BCD. each of the decimal digits of a number is represented by four bits (see Fig. 8.9). The decimal number 72509 for example, is represented in BCD as 0111 0010 0101 0000 1001.

The 68000 provides three operations on numbers in BCD each of which operates on a *byte* only (two decimal digits) and incorporates the extend X flag:

Add decimal with extend
      ABCD   Dy, Dx
      ABCD   –(Ay), –(Ax)

decimal digit	BCD
0	0000
1	0001
2	0010
3	0011
4	0100
5	0101
6	0110
7	0111
8	1000
9	1001

Fig. 8.9

The source byte, the destination byte and X are added using BCD arithmetic and the result is stored in the destination. The operands may both be in data registers or may both be in memory, addressed via the address registers specified in the instruction using pre-decrement mode.

Subtract decimal with extend

> SBCD   Dy, Dx
> SDCS   –(Ay), –(Ax)

The source byte and X are subtracted using BCD arithmetic from the destination byte and the result is stored in the destination. Other points are as above.

Negate decimal with extend

> NBCD   ⟨ea⟩

The operand byte addressed by ⟨ea⟩ and X are subtracted from zero using BCD arithmetic and the result stored in ⟨ea⟩. This instruction produces the tens complement if X is clear and the nines complement if X is set.

Since the BCD operations operate on byte (two decimal digit) operands only, the data register versions of the instructions are limited in their usefulness and multiple digit BCD arithmetic is best organized in memory.

Suppose the decimal numbers 4036 and 2158 are stored in BCD form and are to be added and address registers A0 and A1 are initialized as shown in Fig. 8.10 (p. 124).

The instruction sequence

> ABCD   –(A0), –(A1)
> ABCD   –(A1), –(A0)

results in the following state in memory (see Fig. 8.11, p. 124).

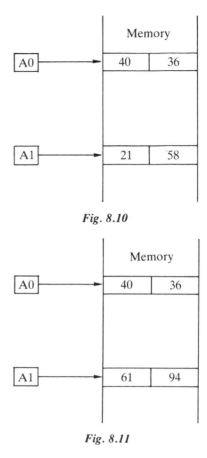

Fig. 8.10

Fig. 8.11

The Z flag is managed in the same way for BCD instructions as explained in Section 8.4.3 for multi-length binary arithmetic instructions. Z is cleared if a BCD instruction generates a non-zero result but is unaffected by a zero result. The programmer must therefore set Z before a sequence of BCD instructions, and must also clear C and X initially by MOVE #4, CCR.

8.9   PROGRAM CONTROL INSTRUCTIONS

A summary of program control instructions is given here although conditional and unconditional jump and branch instructions are described in Chapter 5 and subroutine call and return instructions are described in Chapter 7. The DBcc and Scc instructions are not described elsewhere and are explained below.

unconditional jump and branch instructions

BRA	BRA	⟨label⟩	branch always, the object code contains an 8- or 16-bit displacement
JMP	JMP	⟨ea⟩	jump

conditional branch instructions

Bcc	Bcc	⟨label⟩	branch conditional on CCR flags. The object code contains an 8- or 16-bit displacement.
DBcc	DBcc	Dn, ⟨label⟩	test condition, decrement and branch. 16-bit displacement.
Scc	Scc	⟨ea⟩	set byte according to condition: if the condition is true set all bits of the byte to 1 if the condition is false set all bits of the byte to 0.

subroutine call instructions

BSR	BSR	⟨label⟩	branch to subroutine 8- or 16-bit displacement
JSR	JSR	⟨ea⟩	jump to subroutine

return from subroutine

RTR		return and restore condition codes
RTS		return from subroutine.

8.9.1   Test condition, decrement and branch

DBcc Dn, ⟨label⟩

This is intended to be a loop control instruction. In Chapter 5 a loop skeleton was used as follows:

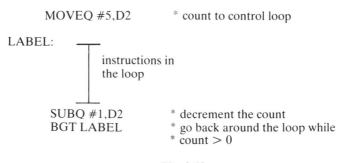

```
        MOVEQ #5,D2         * count to control loop

LABEL:  ┬
        │  instructions in
        │  the loop
        ┴
        SUBQ #1,D2          * decrement the count
        BGT LABEL           * go back around the loop while
                            * count > 0
```

Fig. 8.12

It was intended that DBcc would provide more compact and comprehensive loop control. Decrementing and testing a count are incorporated into DBcc and an additional exit condition may also be used. The effect of DBcc is as follows:

- If the condition specified in cc is true then exit from the loop is effected by PC←PC + 2.
- If the condition is false then the low word of Dn is decremented. If the resulting value is −1 then exit from the loop is effected by PC←PC + 2. If the resulting value in Dn is not −1 the loop is re-entered by PC←⟨label⟩ (coded as PC←PC + displacement).

The choice by the 68000 designers of −1 as the terminating condition is strange.

The loop shown in Fig. 8.12 may be replaced by the following:

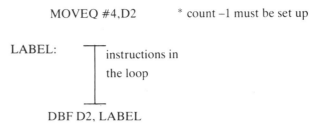

In this example, an additional terminating condition has not been included and so the false F condition is specified. Setting up count –1 rather than count in D2 makes the program less readable. The DBF instruction occupies two words and therefore takes up as much space as SUBQ and BGT in the first version. It is also complex and difficult to understand and therefore likely to lead to programming errors. So far it seems like a bad idea!

In the examples developed in subsequent chapters, DBcc will be reconsidered, in particular when two exit conditions from a loop are appropriate.

8.10   SYSTEM CONTROL INSTRUCTIONS

System control is accomplished by use of privileged instructions, trap generating instructions and instructions that use or modify the status register. Privileged instructions are described in Chapter 14.

The system control instructions are summarized below and, where appropriate at this stage, an explanation is given.

Privileged instructions

ANDI	#d, SR	see also Section 8.5
EORI	#d, SR	see also Section 8.5
MOVE	⟨ea⟩, SR	see also Section 8.3
MOVE	USP, An	move 32 bits of user stack pointer to An
MOVE	An, USP	move An to user stack pointer
ORI	#d, SR	see also Section 8.5
RESET		reset external devices
RTE		return from exception
STOP		stop program execution

Trap-generating instructions

CHK	⟨ea⟩, Dn	check register against bounds
TRAP	#n	trap
TRAPV		trap on overflow

Status register operations (other than privileged instructions)

ANDI	#d, CCR	see also Section 8.5
EORI	#d, CCR	see also Section 8.5
MOVE	⟨ea⟩, CCR	see also Section 8.3
MOVE	SR, ⟨ea⟩	see also Section 8.3
ORI	#d, CCR	see also Section 8.5

8.10.1 Trap generation

A trap is a mechanism for transferring control from a running program written by the user to a supervisor, monitor or debugging program, for example TUTOR. Use has been made of this mechanism in all the programs developed so far to exit from a program on normal termination. In the CHK and TRAPV instructions a test is made for an error condition and if the error has occurred control is transferred from the running program to a specific part of TUTOR associated with handling that error. The mechanism is described in full in Chapter 12.

TRAPV tests the overflow flag V and if it is set a trap is effected, if V is unset normal execution continues.

      CHK   ⟨ea⟩, Dn   check register against bounds.

The content of the low order word of Dn is compared with a range of values which is from 0 to the content of ⟨ea⟩. If Dn is less than zero or greater than the content of ⟨ea⟩, then a trap is generated, otherwise normal execution continues.

PART TWO

The Conventional Machine Level – Devices

Part Two, Chapters 9–15, introduces device interfacing and programming. At the end of Part Two the reader will understand how 68000 programs communicate with some external devices.

9

Connection of input and output devices

In this chapter sufficient hardware background is given for the reader to understand how devices are connected with a processor and memory to form a computer system. Subsequent chapters build on this basis to show how input and output are incorporated into 68000 programs.

Part One has introduced the idea of data transfers that take place during program execution, both within the processor and between the processor and memory. Section 9.3 explains these transfers in more detail, bringing in the use of the bus, then widens the discussion of data transfers to include input from and output to devices. The concept of device interfacing is introduced. Data communication external to the computer system is mentioned briefly to complete the picture. Important concepts are defined including synchronous, asynchronous, serial and parallel transmission of data.

Section 9.5 explains the interworking of a microprocessor IC and its bus and gives information on several widely used bus standards. Section 9.6 explains in detail how devices are interfaced to the MC68000 in a simple single board configuration.

9.1 CONNECTION TO THE MC68000

The MC68000 is an Integrated Circuit (IC) classified as Very Large Scale Integration (VLSI). This means that it has of the order of, or more than, 100,000 circuit elements within the same single circuit or chip. It is a microprocessor which connects to other devices. the outside world, via 64 metal pins encased in the edges of the plastic packaging material that contains it. Although the MC68000 has some storage (memory) within it, it needs very much more to enable it to be used as part of a micro computer system. This memory is connected to the 68000 processor by some of its 64 pins. All other external devices are connected in the same way.

The 68000 is a general purpose microprocessor which can be used in many different ways and situations. Used as the basis of a simple computer system, called a

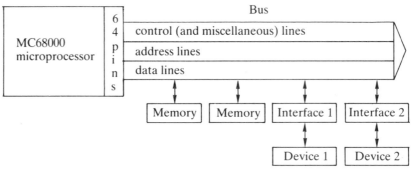

Fig. 9.1

Single-Board Computer, the memory and devices are connected directly to the 64 pins as shown in outline in Fig. 9.1.

The meaning and use of each signal on the 64 pins is called Pinout. The wires connected to these pins make a parallel channel which is called by a number of different names, for example, On-Board System Bus, Bus, Data Highway (see Section 9.5.2).

9.2   OUTLINE PROCESSOR ARCHITECTURE

In Chapter 1, processor registers visible to the programmer were described (see Fig. 1.13) and instruction execution was explained in outline. Section 1.7 described the processor's instruction cycle (or fetch–execute cycle) and Section 2.7 gave an example. In this chapter implementation of the fetch–execute cycle is described in more detail in Sections 9.3.1 and 9.3.2. This section introduces some processor components which are not visible to the programmer but which are required for a full understanding of subsequent Sections.

Fig. 9.2a shows the processor registers accessible to the programmer: the 32-bit wide Data and Address Registers (D0–D7 and A0–A7), the 16-bit Status Register (SR) and the currently 24-bit but potentially 32-bit Program Counter PC. In addition to these are the 16-bit Instruction Register (IR), which is not programmer-accessible, together with some 16-bit temporary registers named TEMP1 to TEMP4. IR is used to hold the first word (or control word) of the current instruction, when it has been fetched from memory for the duration of the execution of the instruction. When the control word is decoded, the number of extension words becomes known and these must be fetched from memory. They are held in TEMP1 to TEMP4.

Finally, the Arithmetic Logic Unit (ALU) is shown in Fig. 9.2a. This is a high speed unit for performing arithmetic and logical operations on the processor's

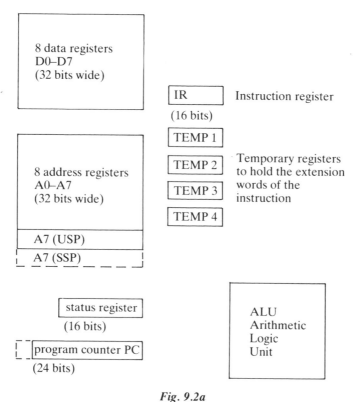

Fig. 9.2a

registers. When the PC is to be incremented, for example, the addition is performed by the ALU, represented by:

ALU←PC + 2
PC←ALU

The ALU is also used for performing the arithmetic and logical operations indicated on instruction decode, for example:

ADD   D0, D3   * add the low word of D0 to D3
LSL   #4, D1   * shift the low word of D1 by 4 binary places.

The data paths within the processor are not shown and are more appropriate to hardware-oriented texts.

Fig. 9.2a is a logical diagram of the 68000 processor and in no way represents the physical layout of the chip. A photograph of the chip is given as Fig. 9.2b and an expanded diagram as Fig. 9.2c. The components indicated in Fig. 9.2a are embedded in the IC in a complex manner which will not be described in detail.

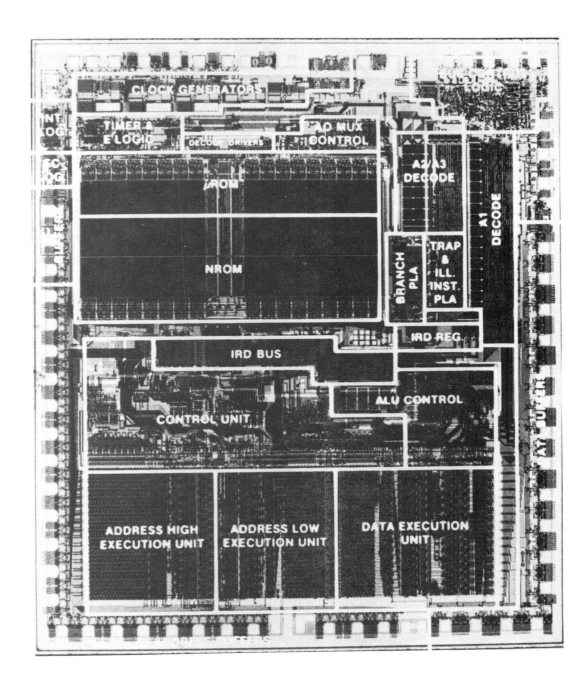

Fig. 9.2b

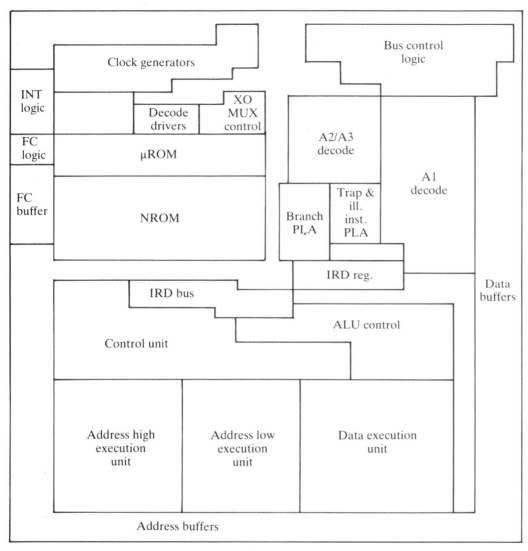

Fig. 9.2c

9.3 DATA TRANSFERS

9.3.1 Data transfers within the processor

In Chapter 1, the concept of a computer system as a hierarchy of layers was outlined (see Fig. 1.1). The Conventional Machine layer comprises binary patterns stored in selected locations in memory and coded in a form which explicitly defines the stored program as described in Chapter 2. The execution of one machine instruction is an operation described by the Instruction Fetch–Execute Cycle (see Sections 1.7 and 2.7). Implementation of the Instruction Cycle is the function of the layer below the Conventional Machine level, i.e. the *microprogramming* layer. Within this layer are defined *micro-instructions* for the processor which effect instruction execution. The micro-instructions involved in the execution of a single instruction,

MOVE.B #$35,ACIACONTROL

are now given as an example. This instruction is coded by the assembler from the form given above into machine code. It is assumed at this stage that the value of the symbol ACIACONTROL is $30061 and the reason for this is explained in detail in Chapter 10. It is also necessary to assume that the instruction is located at some specific memory addresses and an arbitrary choice is made. The machine code for the instruction is as shown in Fig. 9.3.

Location		Memory			
1064	1	3	F	C	control word
1066	0	0	3	5	first extension word $35
1068	0	0	0	3	second
106A	0	0	6	1	and third extension words holding address $30061

Fig. 9.3

The instruction is defined by the first word, or control word as explained in Section 1.5. If the program counter (PC) is set to 1064 and the machine is set running then the following sequence of events is carried out by and within the processor (refer to Fig. 9.1).

The instruction cycle for MOVEI.B $35,ACIACONTROL

FETCH

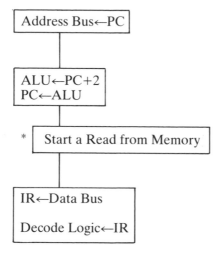

Transfer the contents of the PC to the Address lines of the Bus. (A 24-bit address is currently supported, therefore assume 24 address lines.)

Use the Arithmetic Unit to add 2 to the PC.

Fetch a 16-bit word from memory, the locations being identified by the value on the Address Bus. The result is returned via the Data lines of the Bus.

Transfer the 16-bit word to the Instruction Register.

Decode the control word of the Instruction.

The above is one way of describing the relevant transfers of data which effect the Fetch phase of the Instruction Cycle in Micro-instruction form. The first word, or control word, of the instruction has been fetched from memory. This is the same for all Machine Instructions. It is followed immediately by the Execute phase, throughout which the control word of the instruction remains in IR.

The execute phase for MOVE.B #$35, ACIACONTROL

EXECUTE

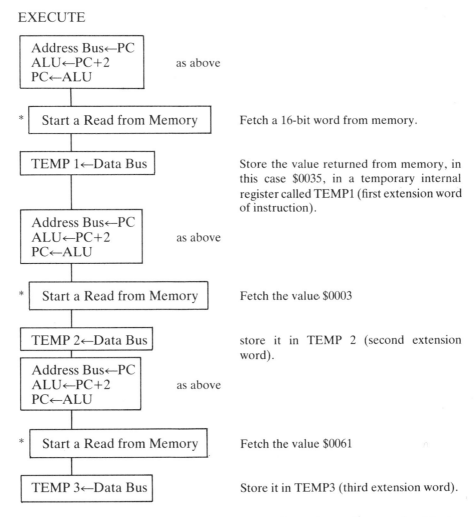

Address Bus←PC ALU←PC+2 as above PC←ALU	
* Start a Read from Memory	Fetch a 16-bit word from memory.
TEMP 1←Data Bus	Store the value returned from memory, in this case $0035, in a temporary internal register called TEMP1 (first extension word of instruction).
Address Bus←PC ALU←PC+2 as above PC←ALU	
* Start a Read from Memory	Fetch the value $0003
TEMP 2←Data Bus	store it in TEMP 2 (second extension word).
Address Bus←PC ALU←PC+2 as above PC←ALU	
* Start a Read from Memory	Fetch the value $0061
TEMP 3←Data Bus	Store it in TEMP3 (third extension word).

Decode of the instruction indicates that a byte, stored as an immediate operand in the first extension word of the instruction ($35 stored in TEMP1) is to be moved to the address stored in the next two extension words of the instruction ($0003 stored in TEMP2 and $0061 stored in TEMP3 forming the long address $30061).

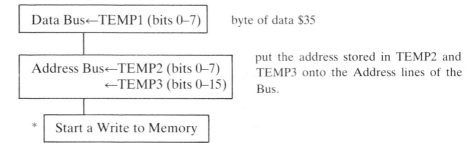

| Data Bus←TEMP1 (bits 0–7) | byte of data $35 |

| Address Bus←TEMP2 (bits 0–7)
←TEMP3 (bits 0–15) | put the address stored in TEMP2 and TEMP3 onto the Address lines of the Bus. |

* | Start a Write to Memory |

The above micro-instructions describe the data transfers carried out as the Execute phase of the instruction and complete this example. It should be noted that for this particular instruction there are five memory accesses via the bus, four reads and one write.

The execution of every machine instruction involves the Fetch–Execute Cycle which sets into operation a sequence of transfers of data both within and external to the processor IC. The Fetch phase is the same for all instructions and the Execute phase, resulting from decode of the Instruction Register, is different. All the 68000 instructions may therefore be written out in a manner similar to the above example.

In summary, each machine instruction starts the operation of a sequence of micro-instructions which essentially describe the order and flow of data and control within the processor and external to it. This topic is expanded in references 1 and 2.

9.3.2 Data transfers between the processor and memory

Memory is connected to the processor IC in the same way as any other device as shown in Fig. 9.1. A data transfer of one 16-bit word from memory to the processor always occurs in the fetch phase of the instruction cycle (to fetch the control word of the instruction). Subsequently, memory may be accessed or not according to the result of instruction decode, for example LSL #4, D0 (shift the low word of D0 4 places to the left) requires no further memory accesses. Synchronization of the processor and memory is carried out by the exchange of signals via the control lines of the bus.

In principle, memory connected to the bus may be considered as just another device although it has the following special characteristics:

- It operates at almost the same speed as the processor (unlike Input or Output devices) (see Section 9.3.3 and Chapter 10).
- It operates in a similar way to the processor, employing similar signals.
- It requires no special control signals other than the READ or WRITE signal.
- It automatically deals with data transferred to it.
- Its word length can be the same as the data bus or even the processor.
- The size of data to be transferred may be specified as byte or word. A longword must be accessed as two separate 16-bit words. See also Section 9.5.1.

9.3.3 Data transfer between the processor and devices-interfaces

Most Input and Output devices differ from memory in their characteristics, in particular with respect to their speed – or lack of it. A generally acceptable categorization of devices is as follows:

SLOW SPEED:
These are devices that change state, or produce data, in times of many hundreds of milliseconds or even seconds. Examples are switches, relays and special character displays.

MEDIUM SPEED:
Data transfers occur in the range of approximately 10 to 10,000 bits per second. Examples are keyboards, communications lines (see Section 9.3.4) and analog data acquisition.

HIGH SPEED:
Data transfers occur at rates in excess of 10,000 bits per second. Examples are magnetic discs, tapes, high speed printers, video and graphic displays and high speed communications.

Whatever category a device falls into, its connection to the 68000 Bus is via a hardware unit commonly called an *interface*. The formal definition of an interface is a set of protocols which define a boundary; the protocols specifying the rules for communication to take place across the boundary in either direction. Informally, this protocol action is carried out by a hardware unit called an interface.

There are many different types of interface. Even interfaces which apparently operate in a similar manner can have marked differences in the way they are set up and controlled. Most manufacturers offer general purpose interfaces which are capable of operating in a variety of different ways. This enables them to benefit from the reduced costs of mass production of the interface units. From the user's point of view, although there are attractions in a relatively inexpensive unit, capable of operating in many different ways, there is the major disadvantage that the interface unit is relatively complicated and difficult to control. Section 9.6 and Chapters 10, 13 and 15 deal explicitly with examples of setting up (initializing or configuring) and controlling interfaces to operate in different ways.

9.3.4 Data transfer external to the computer

In most countries it is illegal to operate public data transmission facilities except under licence from Government Communications Agencies (British Telecom in the UK, the Federal Communications Commission in the USA). British Telecom is in fact the major provider of communications facilities in the UK (Common Carrier).

To set up a communication system for connecting a (computing) device to another via the Common Carrier transmission facilities is fortunately a solved problem. The CCITT (Comité Consultatif International de Télégraphique et Téléphonique) produces recommendations which are agreed by the Government

Communications Agencies or PTTs (Post, Telegraph and Telephone Adminis-trations) and clearly define the operation of the communications.
This is shown diagrammatically in Fig. 9.4.

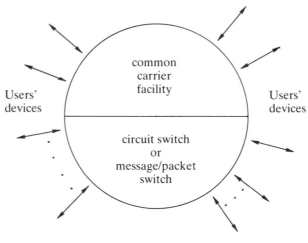

Users'
devices

common
carrier
facility

circuit switch
or
message/packet
switch

Users'
devices

Fig. 9.4

There are two major forms of switching which operate within public data networks, circuit switching and packet switching (often in the form of a datagram service). Users' devices must operate in the way prescribed by the rules (*Protocols*) of the particular public service. A good example of a protocol is X.25, a CCITT recommendation for operating in packet mode on public data transmission facilities.
Terms which are used include:

CHANNEL: A path or line for the transmission of information in the form of signals.

A channel is further classified as:

SIMPLEX: Transmission in one direction only is provided. An example of a simplex channel within a computer system is the Address part of the local MC68000 Bus (see Fig. 9.1).

HALF DUPLEX: Transmission may take place in both directions but not simultaneously. An example of a half duplex channel is the Data part of the local MC68000 Bus (see Fig. 9.1).

FULL DUPLEX: Transmission may take place in both directions simultaneously. An example is a telephone conversation on the public switched telephone network.

The major complexity of data transfer over common carrier facilities relates to the decision concerning the particular form of service to be provided. A simple circuit switch would provide users with little more than an end-to-end connection. The computer devices attached to either end (via their interfaces) would have to organise the transmission and, for example, deal with such problems as errors (corruption of the transmitted signal). A datagram service provides a more error-free path and the operations required within the attached computing device to make use of the service are totally different.

See references 3 and 6 for further reading in this area.

9.4 SERIAL AND PARALLEL DATA TRANSFER WITHIN A COMPUTER

Data is transferred both within and external to the processor in either parallel or serial form.

In the parallel mode the complete character or code is transmitted at the same time, each element of the character occupying an individual channel. This is the mode of operation of the data bus of Fig. 9.1, where the bus is sixteen separate circuits to handle a 16-bit word. Because parallel transmission employs a multiplicity of circuits it is most suited to short distance connections. One specific problem is managing the timing of the signals on each individual circuit. Variation in the speed of transmission is called *skew*, but this is easily dealt with. In general, although parallel transmission requires a more expensive and complicated channel and has the possibility of *skew* it requires only simple terminating hardware.

In the serial mode, the character or code is transmitted along a single circuit, each element of the character being transmitted in time sequence. The letter S, $53 in ASCII code, might appear as:

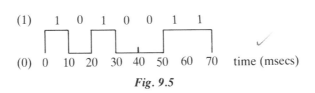

Fig. 9.5

In general, serial transmission requires a simple (single) channel but also requires complicated terminating hardware to organize the transmission and reception of characters in serial form. Clearly, it is slower than parallel mode.

With all forms of data transmission there is a problem of *synchronization*; the receiving hardware must be set up or triggered to assess the channel state for information at the appropriate time. There are a number of ways of dealing with this.

Two broad categorizations are as follows:

SYNCHRONOUS: All signals on the channel (signal events) are strictly related to a timing signal or *clock*. This clock is used by the hardware to control the message flow; it may be explicitly available as a separate signal or implicitly available by being embedded within the normal message flow.

ASYNCHRONOUS: The signal events are not related to a timing signal or clock.

Channels available to operate *synchronously* with hardware are termed *isochronous* channels. Those available to operate *asynchronously* are termed *anisochronous*.

An *isochronous* channel provides for the transmission of character information in synchronous mode i.e. with the addition of appropriate terminating hardware it provides for the explicit or implicit transmission of clock or timing signals together with the message (characters).

Serial asynchronous transmission, which is assumed in Chapters 10 and 13, is usually organized as a character (e.g. 8 bits) within two control elements, a *start* and a *stop*. This complete pattern, *start*, character, *stop*, is transmitted independently of any others. *Start* and *stop* are always of opposite polarity and *start* is of the same duration as the individual bits of the character (assuming binary representation). Thus the character S, ASCII $53, with an eighth (even) parity bit added for error detection purposes could be transmitted as:

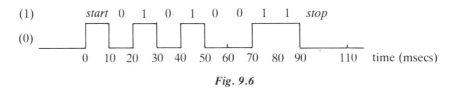

Fig. 9.6

Stop is the same state as 'line *idle*'. The receiving hardware waiting for something to arrive (*idling*) detects the transition from *idle/stop* to *start* and uses this as a reference timing point to decode the single character message which follows.

Serial transmission, in asynchronous or synchronous form, is the normal method employed when Common Carrier facilities are used. It is also most likely to be used for distances greater than about 10 metres.

Both serial and parallel device interfaces are available for use with the MC68000. The Asynchronous Communications Interface Adapter (ACIA) described in Chapters 10 and 13 is specifically for Serial, Asynchronous operation. This is appropriate for interfacing, for example, to a keyboard device because of the irregularity of its operation. Within a serial interface there is a requirement for a mechanism for serial to parallel, and parallel to serial, conversion in order to match the serial channel to the data bus. This may be represented diagrammatically as:

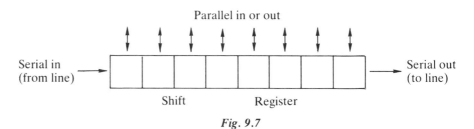

Fig. 9.7

Serial synchronous systems are more complex since they must handle the transmission of blocks of characters. The Parallel Interface Adapter (PIA) of Chapter 15 is specifically for parallel asynchronous operation.

9.5   MICROPROCESSOR INTEGRATED CIRCUITS AND BUSES

9.5.1   Handshaking

The idea of synchronization was introduced in Section 9.4. The emphasis there was on the mechanism by which receive hardware interrogates the incoming signal in order to make decisions regarding information i.e. bits comprising characters. The concept of synchronization exists at a number of logical levels. In broad terms the receive hardware needs to be synchronized with the signals arriving at it at the bit level, byte or character level and block or message level. It should also deal with errors.

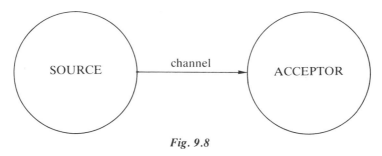

Fig. 9.8

In Fig. 9.8 the requirement is that information flows as a sequence of characters, either synchronous or asynchronous, from Source to Acceptor. In an ideal world this would be a simple task but in the real world all manner of activities may interfere with the process. Possible corruption of the signal, for example by noise, means that there are (usually) mechanisms to deal not only with the detection (recognition) of errors but also to enable recovery. In practice therefore, in order to transfer information in the form of characters *in one direction only* information associated with error detection and recovery will flow in both directions thus causing an interchange in the roles of Source and Acceptor. The Acceptor for example might signal an error state by transmitting a special message back to the Source.

The mechanism by which a message *source* and a message *acceptor* exchange signals in order to ensure the smooth and error free (within limits) transfer of information at bit, character and block levels is called *handshaking* of which there are many forms.

Handshaking can be in the form of protocols (rules) by which message sources and message acceptors organize and synchronize the flow of data. An analogy is the Public Switched Telephone Network (PSTN) where the process of setting up a full duplex channel for voice communication is preceded by a call set up phase involving dialing, answering etc. before the conversation takes place. The conversation itself may include requests to repeat mis-heard phrases. At the end of the conversation the disconnect phase is triggered by replacement of the telephone handset. A number of handshaking protocols for transferring data in the form of characters closely mirror these PSTN activities of call open and establish, call maintenance and call disconnect.

At another level handshaking can be in the form of signals on special dedicated channels or circuits. Fig. 9.9 illustrates the case where the transfer takes place between a processor IC and a peripheral.

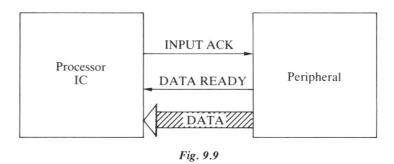

Fig. 9.9

The (time) order of events for INPUT would be:

- Data becomes available at the peripheral.
- The peripheral sets data on the data channel.
- The peripheral sets the DATA READY signal line.
- The processor reads the data.
- The processor acknowledges it has finished by setting the INPUT ACK signal line.

The principle of handshaking implemented here is:

- The peripheral signalling that data is ready.
- The processor signalling that it has completed the reading task.

Clearly, in practice, it is more complicated than this. What happens, for example, if the transferred data has an error which is detected by the processor? Double-ended handshaking involves signals for control generated at both ends. Single-ended handshaking involves any control signalling originating at one end only. For example, in Fig. 9.9 the peripheral could simply set the signal on the DATA READY line and assume that within a certain time the data had been read. If the data is not read, the effect is as if there had been an error and error recovery procedures would have to take over.

9.5.2 Bus standards

The term microprocessor usually implies a single VLSI unit which needs other units to make a computer system, thus: Microcomputer = Microprocessor + Memory + Devices. Microprocessors from different manufacturers and also different families of microprocessor from the same manufacturer have different numbers of metal pins to make connections external to them. Typical numbers are 40, 48 and 64. The MC68000 has a 64-pin system which can be connected into a Single Board Computer as shown in Fig. 9.10:

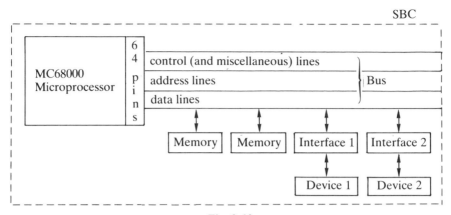

Fig. 9.10

This is a *single bus system*. Its feature is that memory appears as any other peripheral, therefore memory access may not be at optimum speed since it shares and therefore must *contend* for the bus, albeit with highest priority. But note the direct access between peripheral devices and memory.

There are many different solutions to the problem of configuring a system. More sophisticated computers invariably use several buses, normally with totally different characteristics associated with their specific function. The feature of mainframe computers is the relatively large number of buses which are used to connect the different sub-units, themselves often complete boards.

The question of *bus standards* is important since it relates to the ease with which components can be built up into a system by a user (customer) to satisfy a particular requirement. Unfortunately the IC manufacturers each have their own view of bus standards, particularly the *pinout* definitions of the single IC chip. There is some agreement however on how systems should be connected. Motorola together with the manufacturers Mostek and Philips/Signetics have agreed an architecture called VME System Architecture which appears as Fig. 9.11.

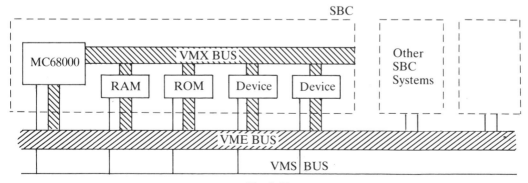

Fig. 9.11

The VMX bus is the on-board bus local to the individual processor and allows for system expansion up to the capacity of the single processor. The VME bus is fully defined and agreed and allows for the connection of many single-board sub-units to make a complete system. The VMS bus (an interesting concept) is a serial bus to allow the rapid transfer of short control messages between systems. The VME bus is thus freed from the Instruction Fetch–Execute Cycle described in Section 9.3.1.

Other manufacturers have come to similar but different solutions generally described by Fig. 9.12.

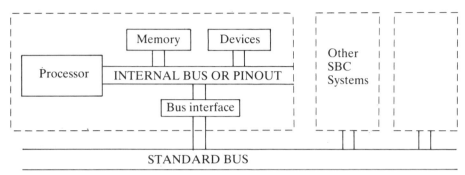

Fig. 9.12

Intel, for example, define a *triple bus* architecture where the standard bus is the well known *multibus*. The third bus in this case derives from a special device controller attached to the internal or on-board bus.

Thus the *standard* bus of Fig. 9.12 is not an agreed standard in the accepted sense. Examples of commonly used buses are:

- Motorola (+ Mostek and + Philips/Signetics) VME bus.
  This is based on the original Motorola *versabus* (1979). It is a 96-line bus and standard Eurocard format. It is fully defined and well engineered. It is defined for 16-bit data but can be extended to 32 bits by the addition of a second connector for the data and address. This is fully defined in the specification.
- Intel MULTIBUS.
  This is an 86-line bus which is fully specified and defined. It is well engineered and will support multiple processors.
- S-100.
  A 100-line bus largely used for less powerful microprocessors. It originated with the MITS Inc. home microcomputer *Altair* 8800 which used the Intel 8080 microprocessor. The bus reflects the design needs of the 8080. A special 100-pin connector is defined for S-100. It is said to be not very well engineered and has important limitations, for example, only 8 data bits. An IEEE version, IEEE 696, allows the use of 16-bit microprocessors. It has been around for a long time and is fairly common in the 'hobby' computer market.
- IEEE 488.
  It has 16 lines and is essentially an instrumentation bus developed for interfacing data acquisition equipment and microprocessors. It is fully defined.

- Texas Instruments TM990.
  A 100-line bus for the TI 9900 microprocessor family.
- Zilog MCS.
  A 100-line bus.
- UNIBUS.
  One of the DEC mini/micro buses, 56 lines, 16 for data, 18 for addresses. This is a classic double-ended synchronization bus.
- DEC LSI-11.
  A 72-line bus.
- EUROBUS.
  The Ferranti F100 bus system which is suitable for large systems plus many others.

As A. S. Tanenbaum says in his book *Computer Networks* (Prentice/Hall 1981), 'the nice thing about standards (computer network protocols in this case) is that you have so many to choose from; furthermore, if you do not like any of them you can just wait for next year's model'.

9.6 THE MC68000 SINGLE BOARD COMPUTER

9.6.1 Introduction

Fig. 9.1 shows the connection and use of the MC68000 in the classical single bus system. The major functions of the internal bus are: CONTROL
ADDRESS
DATA
pinout is the term used to describe what the signals on each pin mean and do and therefore *pinout* defines the bus. The 64 MC68000 pins are shown in Fig. 9.13 and are described in Section 9.6.2.

There are 23 lines for the Address Part of the bus named A1 . . . A23. An implied A0 which is always zero completes the normal description of the MC68000 as having 24 address lines. Since A0 (implied) is zero, addresses are always *even* therefore *words* are addressed (see Fig. 9.14, p. 148). The total addressing capacity is therefore 0 to $2^{23} - 2$ (0 to FFFFFE) or 16 Mbytes.

The MC68000 is potentially capable of dealing with address values 0 to FFFFFE and this is called the ADDRESS SPACE. Every microprocessor has an address space, almost invariably numbered 0 to $2^n - 1$, which implies that n pins are required to connect to the n address lines.

There are normally as many lines in the *data* part of the *pinout* as there are bits in a word but it is also fairly common to find the *data bus* with only half as many, for example, 8 pins for 16-bit word microcomputers.

There is some confusion about the labelling of a microprocessor as 8-, 16- or 32-bit since it is not clear whether this number should refer to the data paths internal to

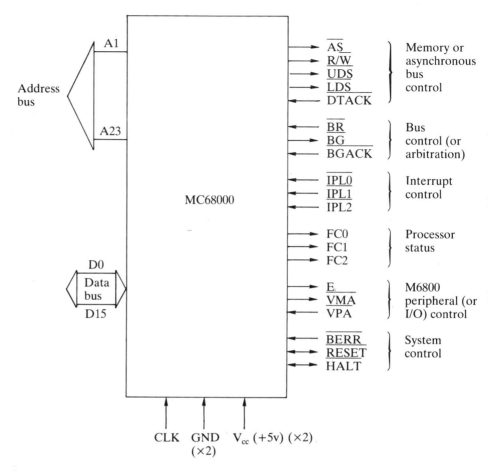

Fig. 9.13

the IC or to the *pin* data lines. For the MC68000, the data paths internal to the IC are 32 bits wide and the data bus is 16 bits. There is also variation within the 68000 family of microprocessor, for example, the MC68008 has an 8-bit data bus.

Fig. 9.14

The MC68000 *pinout* has 16 bits for data and in the conventional system used in this book is configured with 16-bit word memory. This means that one memory access is needed to fetch one word. Two memory accesses are needed to fetch longwords (32 bits).

As already explained, memory and devices are connected directly to the *pins* of the IC. Devices do not always connect to all of the *address* lines; it depends which

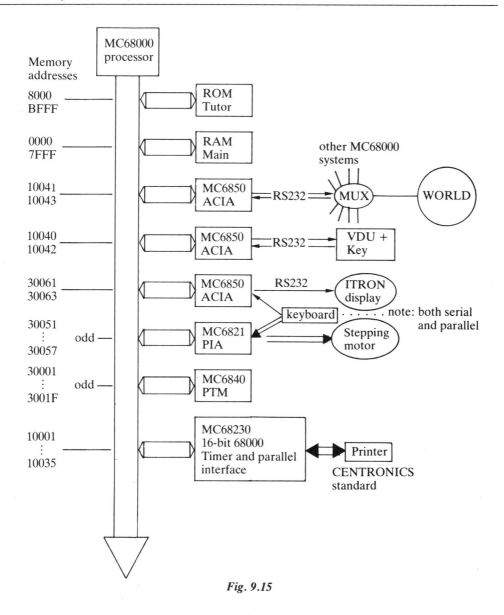

Fig. 9.15

part of the address space is needed and used. Figures 9.15 and 9.16 show a typical simple configuration together with the address space values used.

9.6.2 The MC68000 pinout

The MC68000 *pinout* is shown in Fig. 9.13. It is not intended to give a complete description of all the *pin* signals but rather to note their general function for later

MC68000 – TUTOR System

Memory map

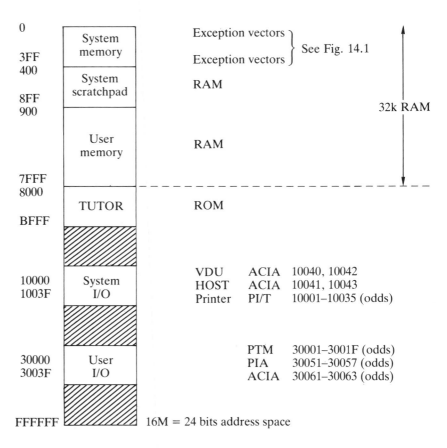

Fig. 9.16

reference. Two important general terms are as follows:

ASSERTED: means that a signal is in its *active* state. This may be *low* or *high*. The
             fact that R and W (Read and not Write) are shown in Fig. 9.13 means
             that R/W = high is the active state for Read and R/W̄ = low is the
             active state for Write.

NEGATED: is the inactive state. If R and W̄ are given as active then R̄ and W
             are the inactive states for those lines.

There are 23 (+1) pins for the Address value – *simplex* (see Section 9.6.1).
There are 16 pins for data – *half duplex*.

Data is read (Memory to Processor) with the following order of events:

- The Address value is set on the Address pins.
- The R/$\overline{\text{W}}$ line is set HIGH, i.e. R is asserted.
- The Address Strobe ($\overline{\text{AS}}$) is asserted.

The memory, taking as long as it needs, sets the word data (fetched from the address specified by the Address bus value). When this is ready:

- Data Acknowledge $\overline{\text{DTACK}}$ is asserted to indicate that the data lines can be read.

The MC68000 allows words and half words to be read by using Upper Data Strobe ($\overline{\text{UDS}}$) and Lower Data Strobe ($\overline{\text{LDS}}$). Thus the MC68000 operates *asynchronously* using *double ended handshaking*.

A data write (processor to Memory or other device) is carried out in a similar way. The major difference is that $\overline{\text{DTACK}}$ is used to signal that the peripheral has accepted the data.

These activities are specified precisely in a timing diagram which illustrates when events can or do occur. Motorola's MC68000 16/32-bit Microprocessor Programmer's Reference Manual gives such specifications.

Other *pins* are:

Bus Request ($\overline{\text{BR}}$) is used by Input and Output devices to request use of the bus.

Bus Grant ($\overline{\text{BG}}$) is used to grant the request.

Bus Grant Acknowledge ($\overline{\text{BGACK}}$) is used by the requesting device to acknowledge the Bus Grant signal.

This is another example of handshaking.

Interrupt Priority Lines ($\overline{\text{IPL0}}$, $\overline{\text{IPL1}}$, $\overline{\text{IPL2}}$) are used to encode the priority of an interrupt request. If the requesting device has a higher priority ($7 > 0$) than the current level at which the processor is executing then an interrupt is allowed to occur, otherwise it must wait (see Chapter 13).

Processor Status (FC0, FC1, FC2) are used to output status information.

MC6800 Peripheral Input or Output (E, $\overline{\text{VMA}}$, $\overline{\text{VPA}}$) are provided to allow compatibility between the MC68000 and peripherals designed for the MC6800 family of processors.

Bus Error ($\overline{\text{BERR}}$) is used to signal an error to the processor. If a device is not able to respond, the processor must not be left waiting indefinitely, for example for a data acknowledge that cannot occur for some reason. Usually, an external timer would assert $\overline{\text{BERR}}$ if there had been no activity within a reasonable time.

Reset ($\overline{\text{RESET}}$) can be used to send restart signals in either direction.

Halt ($\overline{\text{HALT}}$) can be used to indicate that the processor is halted or can be used to halt the processor (at the end of the current instruction cycle).

9.6.3   Interfacing

The concept and formal definition of an interface appears in Section 9.3.3.

There are different ways of connecting peripheral devices to a microprocessor

IC. One way is called *Memory Mapping*. The devices are then accessed using transfers broadly similar to memory transfers and the devices occupy part of the *Address Space* (see Section 9.6.1) of the IC. This is the method used by the MC68000 IC.

The term Interface is commonly used for that part of the hardware that matches the requirements and characteristics of the bus to those of the device being used. Naturally, there are interfaces for connecting to devices which operate serially and for connecting to devices which operate using parallel transmission. This book uses the Asynchronous Communications Interface Adapter (ACIA) MC6850 as an example of a serial interface (see Chapters 10 and 13) and the Peripheral or Parallel Interface Adapter (PIA) MC6821 as an example of a parallel interface (see Chapter 15). The latter is sometimes called a Generalized Peripheral Chip Interface.

These are fairly simple interfaces, originally developed for the earlier 8-bit MC6800 family. There are also a number of interface devices developed for the MC68000 family, for example:

- Enhanced Peripheral Communications Interface (EPCI) MC68661. This is capable of operating both asynchronously and synchronously.
- Parallel Interface/Timer (PI/T) MC68230.

This provides a parallel interface together with a timer. The Motorola literature should be consulted for a full and up-to-date list of Interfaces, Controllers and other special peripherals. Appendix D gives a copy of some of these.

10

Serial input and output (ACIA)

10.1 INTRODUCTION

A wide range of peripheral devices is available for the 68000. In this chapter, one interface, the ACIA or Asynchronous Communications Interface Adapter, is introduced. The Motorola MC6850 ACIA chip is a serial interface chip which was originally developed for the Motorola 6800 range of 8-bit microprocessors. The M68000 range was designed to be compatible with 6800 devices. The manufacturer's specification is included in Appendix B.

We shall assume initially that the ACIA is used to interface an ASCII keyboard for input and an ITRON alphanumeric display for output. The display is a very simple device but has been chosen for the first programs in preference to the console

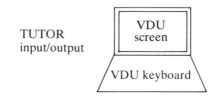

TUTOR
input/output

The console VDU is on another serial interface which is not shown

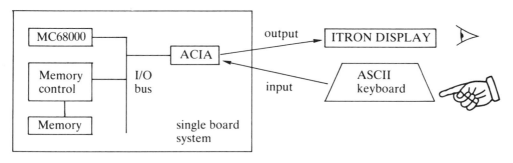

Fig. 10.1

VDU so that the effects of programs are completely separate from input and output to and from the development system.

10.2   MEMORY-MAPPED INPUT AND OUTPUT

The 68000 uses memory mapped input and output. This means that output to a device is achieved through writing to a pre-specified address in memory and input from a device is achieved through reading from an associated memory address. The address for character input and output associated with the ACIA in these examples is $30063. Assuming therefore that a character for output is in data register 0, output to the display can be achieved by

       MOVE.B   D0, $30063
or   MOVE.B   D0, ACIAOUTPUT * assuming an appropriate EQU statement

and input into D0 from the keyboard is achieved by

       MOVE.B $30063, D0
or   MOVE.B   ACIAINPUT, D0

The alternative to memory mapped input and output is to have a range of operation codes for performing input and output. The advantages of memory mapped input and output are that all the addressing modes of the MOVE instruction may be employed, including a memory to memory move, and that the instruction set design does not have to include a separate range for input and output. A disadvantage is associated with protection of devices from illegal or erroneous use and is an important issue when the operating system level is constructed (see Fig. 1.1).

10.3   PROCESSOR AND DEVICE SPEEDS

When the keyboard is used for input, a human operator must depress a key and the character is transferred (eventually) into an ACIA register and is available to the programmer, as described in Section 10.2 above, at address $30063. Input of characters must therefore take account of the speed of the human operator and the speed of the electro-mechanical components of the keyboard. The 68000 processor can execute tens of thousands of instructions while one character is being transferred from the keyboard to be available at address $30063. Similarly, on output, the rate at which characters are written to address $30063 must take account of the rate at which the display can accept them.

    To give some idea of the disparity between processor and peripheral speeds consider as an example a typical instruction execution time of a few microseconds compared with a slow peripheral which delivers a single character in 100 milliseconds

($\frac{1}{10}$ sec.). Scaling up these times:

| if 1 μs | scales to 1 second |
| 100 ms | scales to about 1 day. |

This illustrates the need for device interfaces, places where data can be buffered on its way in and out. It also illustrates the need for a mechanism to control the rate at which data is transferred and this is now discussed.

10.4   THE ACIA MOTOROLA MC6850

Because the 68000 must synchronize with the speed at which the ACIA and its associated devices can operate, control and status information must be associated with any data transfer (input or output).

The ACIA contains four registers which share two memory addresses.
- An input or receive 8-bit data register at $30063, ACIAINPUT.
- An output or transmit 8-bit data register at $30063, ACIAOUTPUT.
- A write-only 8-bit control register at $30061, ACIACONTROL.
- A read-only 8-bit status register at $30061, ACIASTATUS.

10.4.1   The status register

Details of the significance of all 8 bits of the status register are given in Appendix B. To develop programs we must be aware of at least the following:

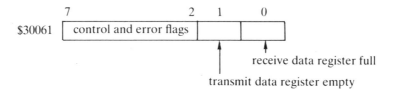

Fig. 10.2

bit 0:	receive data register full – this bit is set to 1 by the hardware when the receive data register, accessed as address, $30063, is holding a character.
bit 1:	transmit data register empty – this bit is set to 1 by the hardware when the transmit data register, accessed as address $30063, is empty and therefore available for the next character to be written.
bits 2 to 7	are used to signal error conditions, for example parity error, see Appendix B.

It should be noted that the status register is *read-only*.

10.4.2 The control register

This register is *write-only* and shares address $30061 with the read-only status register.

An important point about peripheral chips is that they can be dynamically configured by setting bits in the control register. This software configuration gives greater flexibility than the alternative method of pre-setting the hardware, but gives an additional task to the programmer. Configuration is done once at the start of a program.

Details of the significance of each bit in the control register are given in Appendix B. In outline:

	7	6	5	4	3	2	1	0
$30061 control register	receive control	transmit control		data format, parity, etc.			initialize and timing control	

For the assumed configuration and with the method of programming that will be introduced in this chapter, the required control bits are:

7	6	5	4	3	2	1	0
0	0	0	1	0	1	0	1

Fig. 10.3

In the initialization section of a program which uses the ACIA, this pattern must be set up, e.g.:

```
        MOVE.B   #$15, $30061
or      MOVE.B   #$15, ACIACONTROL
```

Initial RESET of the ACIA
According to the ACIA specification (see Appendix B), it is necessary to RESET the ACIA once and for all at the start of use (at power-on). It is therefore advisable to take this action at the start of each input or output program by:

```
        MOVE.B   #3, ACIACONTROL
```

As this instruction sets up timing controls, it is necessary to allow time for it to take effect. When ACIA programming, particularly for output, it is therefore desirable to include the following in the initialization:

```
        * RESET the ACIA
                MOVE.B   #3, ACIACONTROL
        * allow delay (about 10 ms)
                MOVE     #$400,D0              * set up delay count
```

```
DELAYLOOP:  SUBQ   #1,D0              * decrement count
            BNE    DELAYLOOP          * keep looping until
                                        count is zero
```

RESET must be performed before the ACIA control register is configured.

Fig. 10.4 shows the ACIA used for input and output.

(a) The ACIA – character input

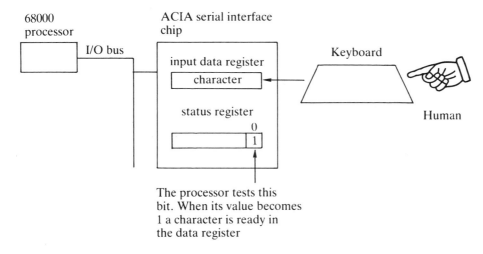

(b) The ACIA – character output

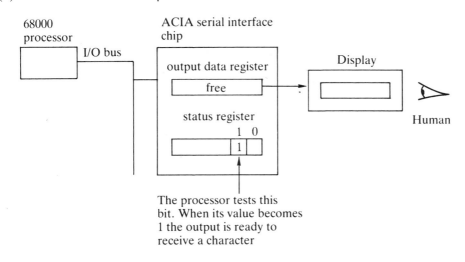

Fig. 10.4

10.5 PROGRAMMING THE ACIA

10.5.1 Initialization

It is recommended that symbolic names are used in the bodies of programs rather than hexadecimal numbers as follows:

```
* ACIA Motorola MC6850 chip
ACIASTATUS:      EQU $30061    * status register, read only
ACIACONTROL:     EQU $30061    * control register, write only
ACIAINPUT:       EQU $30063    * input data register
ACIAOUTPUT:      EQU $30063    * output data register
```

The chip must then be reset and configured as described in Section 10.4.2.

10.5.2 Subroutine to input a character into D0

```
* subroutine to input a character
* input parameters – none
* output parameter – character in low byte of D0

INCH:    EQU      *
         BTST     #0, ACIASTATUS   * test if character in data reg yet
         BEQ      INCH             * if not, go back and test again
         MOVE.B   ACIAINPUT, D0    * read character
         RTS                       * return
```

The routine tests status bit 0 and while the bit has value 0 continues to test it, possibly thousands of times. As soon as the test finds a bit 0 set to value 1, the character is read from the input data register (address $30063) into D0.

10.5.3 Subroutine to output a character from D0

```
* subroutine to output a character
* input parameter — character in low byte of D0
* output parameters — none

OUTCH:   EQU      *
         BTST #1, ACIASTATUS    * test if the data register is free
         BEQ      OUTCH         * if not, go back and test again
         MOVE.B   D0, ACIAOUTPUT * write (output) character
         RTS                     * return
```

The routine waits for bit 1 in the status register to be set to value 1 by the hardware then transfers (outputs) the character.

10.6   THE ITRON ALPHA-NUMERIC DISPLAY

The output device assumed for these examples has the following characteristics:

- A line of 20 characters can be displayed.
- When a character has been written into the display, the writing position is incremented by one position automatically.
- When the right end is reached, carriage-return occurs automatically.
- Writing the backspace character, code $08, to the display causes the writing position to move one character to the left. There is no effect if the write position is already at the left end.
- Writing the horizontal tab character, code $09, moves the writing position one place to the right. There is no effect if the write position is at the right end.
- Writing the line feed character, code $0A, overwrites all twenty character positions by spaces and moves the writing position to the left end.
- Writing the carriage-return character, code $0D, moves the write position to the left end.

10.7   A SIMPLE PROGRAM WITH INPUT AND OUTPUT

The program shown in Fig. 10.5 (pp. 160–61) achieves the following minimal task:

- clears the display,
- outputs ? followed by a space to the display,
- inputs a character from the keyboard into the low byte of D0,
- outputs this character to the display.

The components of the program are as follows:

- EQU statements including a block for the ACIA
- Initialization
  - of the stack pointer
  - configuration of the device as described in Section 10.4.2
- Main program body
  - This consists of a series of subroutine calls to effect the tasks described above followed by the exit statement.
- Subroutines for input and output
  INCH as described in Section 10.5
  OUTCH as described in Section 10.5
  CLEARDISPLAY ⎫
  PROMPT   ⎬ These routines pass the appropriate characters to the
  SPACE   ⎭ display by invoking OUTCH

In this first example, all the details of chip configuration have been shown at the top level. In later programs, configuration details will be implemented within a sub-

```
 1                              *           Figure 10.5
 2                              *
 3                              *
 4                              *
 5                              * The display is cleared and a prompt, ?, output
 6                              * The character typed at the keyboard is echoed
 7                              * on the display; busy status programming is used
 8                              *
 9          00001000           STACK:   EQU      $1000
10                              *
11                              ***********************************************************
12                              * ACIA Motorola MC6850 chip
13                              *
14          00030061           ACIASTATUS   EQU $30061  * status register read-only
15          00030061           ACIACONTROL  EQU $30061  * control register write-only
16          00030063           ACIAINPUT    EQU $30063  * data register input
17          00030063           ACIAOUTPUT   EQU $30063  * data register output
18                              *
19                              ***********************************************************
20                              *
21          00001000                    ORG      $1000
22 001000 4FF81000             INIT     LEA      STACK,SP      * load stack pointer
23                              *
24                              * RESET at power-on for the ACIA
25 001004 13FC0003
           00030061                      MOVE.B  #3,ACIACONTROL
26                              *
27                              * wait for RESET to take effect
28 00100C 303C0400                       MOVE    #$400,D0
29 001010 5340                 RESLOOP  SUBQ     #1,D0
30 001012 66FC                          BNE      RESLOOP
31
32                              * configure ACIA
33 001014 13FC0015
           00030061                      MOVE.B  #$15,ACIACONTROL
34                              *
35                              ***********************************************************
36                              * main program body
37                              *
38 00101C 4EB81032             PROG:    JSR      CLEARDISPLAY
39 001020 4EB8103C                      JSR      PROMPT
40 001024 4EB81046                      JSR      SPACE
41 001028 4EB81062                      JSR      INCH
42 00102C 4EB81050                      JSR      OUTCH
43 001030 4E40                          TRAP     #0        * exit from program
44                              *
45                              ***********************************************************
46                              * CLEARDISPLAY
47                              * subroutine to clear display
48                              *
49          00001032           CLEARDISPLAY:    EQU      *
50 001032 103C000A                      MOVE.B   #$0A,D0          * line-feed char
51 001036 4EB81050                      JSR      OUTCH
52 00103A 4E75                          RTS
53                              *
54                              ***********************************************************
```

```
55                          * PROMPT
56                          * subroutine to output prompt ?
57                          *
58          0000103C        PROMPT: EQU     *
59 00103C 103C003F                  MOVE.B  #$3F,D0         * ? char
60 001040 4EB81050                  JSR     OUTCH
61 001044 4E75                      RTS
62                          *
63                          ************************************************************
64                          * SPACE
65                          * subroutine to output a space
66                          *
67          00001046        SPACE:  EQU     *
68 001046 103C0020                  MOVE.B  #$20,D0         * space char
69 00104A 4EB81050                  JSR     OUTCH
70 00104E 4E75                      RTS
71                          *
72                          ************************************************************
73                          * OUTCH
74                          * subroutine to output a character
75                          * input parameter: character in low byte of D0
76                          *
77          00001050        OUTCH:  EQU     *
78 001050 08390001                  BTST    #1,ACIASTATUS   * test device
          00030061
79 001058 67F6                      BEQ     OUTCH           * wait until free
80 00105A 13C000030063              MOVE.B  D0,ACIAOUTPUT   * output char
81 001060 4E75                      RTS
82                          *
83                          ************************************************************
84                          * INCH
85                          * subroutine to input a character
86                          * output parameter: character in low byte of D0
87                          *
88          00001062        INCH:   EQU     *
89 001062 08390000                  BTST    #0,ACIASTATUS   * test device
          00030061
90 00106A 67F6                      BEQ     INCH            * wait for char
91 00106C 103900030063              MOVE.B  ACIAINPUT,D0    * input char into D0
92 001072 4E75                      RTS
93                          *
94                          ************************************************************
95                          *
96                                  END
```

****** TOTAL ERRORS   0--   0 -- TOTAL LINES   88

APPROX 2106 UNUSED SYMBOL TABLE ENTRIES

```
ACIACONT 030061 ACIAINPU 030063 ACIAOUTP 030063 ACIASTAT 030061 CLEARDIS 001032
INCH      001062 INIT     001000 OUTCH     001050 PROG      00101C PROMPT   00103C
RESLOOP   001010 SPACE    001046 STACK     001000
```

Fig. 10.5 Program using ACIA plus keyboard and display

routine and programs will begin, for example:

```
        ORG   $1000
INIT:   LEA   STACK, SP    * initialize stack pointer
        JSR   CONFIGURE    * configure the ACIA
```

It may be felt that the subroutines CLEARDISPLAY, PROMPT and SPACE are too small to be worth implementing as separate subroutines. When larger programs are to be developed however it is desirable that the main program section, the 'top level', should be concise, clear and give an overview of the stages involved in the program. From this point of view

```
JSR PROMPT      is preferable to      MOVE.B   #'?', D0
                                      JSR      OUTCH
                                      MOVE.B   #$20, D0
                                      JSR      OUTCH
```

A danger in using this convenient higher level is that the programmer is likely to forget that PROMPT uses D0, even if the subroutine interface documents this. To give maximum convenience and error avoidance therefore, such subroutines should save the registers they use on entry and restore them on exit, for example:

```
PROMPT   EQU      *
         MOVE     D0, -(SP)     * save D0 on the stack
         MOVE.B   #'?', D0      * parameter for OUTCH
         JSR      OUTCH
         MOVE.B   #$20, D0      * space character
         JSR      OUTCH
         MOVE     (SP)+, D0     * restore D0 from the stack
         RTS
```

This has been implemented in the subroutines shown in Fig. 10.6.

10.8   OUTPUT TO A VDU SCREEN

The output device introduced in this chapter, the ITRON 20 character display, illustrates basic principles and allows some simple programs to be developed. In some cases, however, managing the output so that only twenty characters are visible at any one time is artificial and an alternative output device is desirable. In the simple hardware configuration assumed in this text a VDU is available to the programmer, also via an ACIA MC6850 serial interface. If the EQU statements of Fig. 10.5 are changed to contain the addresses for the VDU's interface, several of the input and output routines of Section 10.5 are still appropriate, for example, INCH and OUTCH. The characteristics of the device are as follows:

- The screen size is 24 lines of 80 characters per line.
- When a character has been written to the screen, the writing position is incremented automatically.

```
*         Figure 10.6
*
* package of subroutines which will be used
* in subsequent programs
************************************************************
* ACIA Motorola MC6850
ACIASTATUS    EQU $10040    * status register read-only
ACIACONTROL   EQU $10040    * control register write-only
ACIAINPUT     EQU $10042    * data register input
ACIAOUTPUT    EQU $10042    * data register output
************************************************************
* CONFIGURE
* subroutine to configure the ACIA
* this subroutine has been "commented out" since
* TUTOR configures the VDU and an error is caused
* by a second configuration.
*
CONFIGURE       EQU     *
* first RESET the ACIA
*         MOVE.B  #3,ACIACONTROL
* wait for RESET to take effect
*         MOVE    #$400,D0
*DELAY SUBQ      #1,D0
*         BNE     DELAY
* configure
*         MOVE.B  #$15,ACIACONTROL
          RTS
*
************************************************************
* LINEFEED
* subroutine to clear display
*
LINEFEED        EQU     *
          MOVE    D0,-(SP)        * save D0 on stack
          MOVE.B  #$0A,D0         * line feed char
          JSR     OUTCH
          MOVE    (SP)+,D0        * restore D0 from stack
          RTS
*
************************************************************
* PROMPT
* subroutine to output prompt ?
*
PROMPT EQU       *
          MOVE    D0,-(SP)        * save D0 on stack
          MOVE.B  #$3F,D0         * ? char
          JSR     OUTCH
          MOVE.B  #$20,D0         * space
          JSR     OUTCH
          MOVE    (SP)+,D0        * restore D0 from stack
          RTS
```

```
****************************************************
* SPACE
* subroutine to output a space
*
SPACE   EQU     *
        MOVE    D0,-(SP)        * save D0 on stack
        MOVE.B  #$20,D0         * space char
        JSR     OUTCH
        MOVE    (SP)+,D0        * restore D0 from stack
        RTS
*
****************************************************
* NEWLINE
* subroutine to output carriage-return and line-feed
* no input or output parameters
* uses D0, calls OUTCH
*
NEWLINE EQU     *
        MOVE    D0,-(SP)        * save D0 on stack
        MOVE.B  #$0D,D0         * carriage return
        JSR     OUTCH
        MOVE.B  #$0A,D0         * line feed
        JSR     OUTCH
        MOVE    (SP)+,D0        * restore D0 from stack
        RTS
*
****************************************************
* OUTCH
* subroutine to output a character
* input parameter: character in low byte of D0
*
OUTCH   EQU     *
        BTST    #1,ACIASTATUS   * test device
        BEQ     OUTCH           * wait until free
        MOVE.B  D0,ACIAOUTPUT   * output char
        RTS
*
****************************************************
* INCH
* subroutine to input a character
* output parameter: character in low byte of D0
*
INCH    EQU     *
        BTST    #0,ACIASTATUS   * test if char ready
        BEQ     INCH            * wait for char
        MOVE.B  ACIAINPUT,D0    * input char into D0
        RTS
*
****************************************************
```

Fig. 10.6 Subroutines to control VDU

- To begin writing to a new line with the writing position at the left end, both carriage return, code $0D, and line feed, code $0A, are output.
- When the right end of a line is reached a new line occurs automatically.
- The screen is cleared by the character $1A.
- It will be assumed that the screen is used in scroll mode so that new lines are generated automatically when the screen is full.

Since a single board configuration is assumed the VDU described above is that used by TUTOR, as an operator's console, for interaction with the user. The ACIA is therefore configured as part of the system initialization procedure and this should not be repeated in a user's program. It is for this reason that the first devices introduced in this chapter were separate from the console VDU illustrating the necessity for, and flexibility of, dynamic interface configuration. For generality, the subroutine call JSR CONFIGURE has been retained in the programs which use the VDU, since a more extensive hardware configuration might well have an additional serial interface to which a separate VDU could be attached. The body of the subroutine has been 'commented out' so that the timing controls already established are not perturbed.

The subroutines which will be assumed to be available in subsequent programs and which are shown once and for all in Fig. 10.6 are:

OUTCH	output a character from D0
INCH	input a character into D0
NEWLINE	output carriage return and line feed via OUTCH. D0 is saved on entry and restored on exit in this and the following subroutines.
LINEFEED	output a linefeed character.
SPACE	output a space character.
PROMPT	output ? and a space.

This package is extended in Chapter 11 where subroutines to output a string of characters and to give the user initial instructions are developed.

11

Some example programs

11.1 INTRODUCTION

In this chapter, a selection of example programs is given, presented in order of increasing difficulty. Since all the examples make use of subroutines (Chapter 7) and input and output (Chapter 10) they are collected together at this point in the text. Many of the basic algorithms can be studied with earlier chapters and this has been indicated where appropriate.

In Chapter 10, simple input and output devices, connected to the 68000 processor via a serial interface, were introduced and a program was given in Fig. 10.5. The console VDU was then programmed for input and output in Fig. 10.6. The package of input and output subroutines developed for this latter device are more appropriate for practical use of the serial interface (as opposed to illustrating its function) and will be assumed in the programs in this chapter. In general, only the 'top level' of subroutine call for input and output will be shown in the programs. The device-dependent detail within the subroutine bodies may be examined by referring to Chapter 10.

The emphasis of the examples is towards system software since the aim of this text is to lay the foundations for illustrating how a software system is layered above the basic machine hardware. Application algorithms should, wherever possible, be programmed in a high level language. Error handling in the programs is minimal in order to keep them short and easy to follow. This topic is discussed further in Section 11.7.

11.2 A PROGRAM TO OUTPUT THE ALPHABET

Fig. 11.1 shows a program to output the alphabet, as upper case characters, on a line of the VDU screen. It illustrates that since the ASCII codes for the alphabetic characters lie in a consecutive range $41 through $5A, they may be generated 'on the fly' rather than stored in a table.

```
 1                        *          Figure 11.1
 2                        *
 3                        *
 4                        *
 5                        * The program illustrates generation of alphabetic
 6                        * characters A-Z (upper case), ASCII range $41-$5A
 7                        *
 8           00001000     STACK   EQU     $1000
 9           00001000             ORG     $1000
10 001000 4FF81000        INITIAL LEA     STACK,SP        * load stack pointer
11 001004 4EB8101E                JSR     CONFIGURE       * configure ACIA
12 001008 4EB81020                JSR     NEWLINE
13
14 00100C 721A                    MOVEQ   #26,D1          * count of letters
15 00100E 103C0041                MOVE.B  #'A',D0         * first letter
16                        * for D1:=26 downto 1 do ...
17 001012 4EB81032        ALPHOP  JSR     OUTCH           * current letter
18 001016 5240                    ADDQ    #1,D0           * form next letter
19 001018 5341                    SUBQ    #1,D1           * decrement count
20 00101A 6EF6                    BGT     ALPHOP
21 00101C 4E40                    TRAP    #0              * exit from program
22                        *
23                        ******************************************************
24                        * ACIA Motorola MC6850 - see Fig. 10.6.
31                        ******************************************************
32                        * CONFIGURE - see Fig. 10.6.
33                        * subroutine to configure the ACIA
49                        ******************************************************
50                        * NEWLINE - see Fig. 10.6.
51                        * subroutine to output a newline
62                        ******************************************************
63                        * OUTCH - see Fig. 10.6.
64                        * subroutine to output a character
73                        ******************************************************
74                        *
75                                END

****** TOTAL ERRORS    0--   0 -- TOTAL LINES    68


APPROX  2109 UNUSED SYMBOL TABLE ENTRIES

ACIACONT 010040 ACIAINPU 010042 ACIAOUTP 010042 ACIASTAT 010040 ALPHOP    001012
CONFIGUR 00101E INITIAL  001000 NEWLINE  001020 OUTCH     001032 STACK     001000
```

Fig. 11.1   Program to output the alphabet

11.3   STRING OUTPUT

Fig. 11.2 shows a program with a subroutine OUTSTRING which outputs a string of characters to the VDU screen. The program illustrates that the subroutine can be called any number of times to output different strings. The address of the string is

```
 1                        *          Figure 11.2
 2                        *
 3                        *
 4                        * This program shows how to use a subroutine to
 5                        * output a string to the VDU screen
 6                        * a switch is given to the assembler
 7                                     G
 8                        * to show strings in full
 9                        *
10        00001000        STACK        EQU  $1000
11        00000007        STERMINATOR EQU  $07      * string terminator control G
12
13        00001000                     ORG  $1000
14 001000 4FF81000                     LEA  STACK,SP        * load stack pointer
15 001004 4EB8104E                     JSR  CONFIGURE       * configure the ACIA
16
17 001008 4EB81082                     JSR  NEWLINE
18 00100C 41F81022                     LEA  ASTRING,A0       * address of string
19 001010 4EB8103C                     JSR  OUTSTRING        * call subroutine
20
21 001014 4EB81082                     JSR  NEWLINE
22 001018 41F8102E                     LEA  BSTRING,A0       * address of string
23 00101C 4EB8103C                     JSR  OUTSTRING        * call subroutine
24
25 001020 4E40                         TRAP #0               * exit from program
26                        *
27                        *************************************************************
28                        * data area
29 001022 41             ASTRING DC.B    'AAAA STRING',STERMINATOR
   001023 41
   001024 41
   001025 41
   001026 20
   001027 53
   001028 54
   001029 52
   00102A 49
   00102B 4E
   00102C 47
29 00102D 07
30 00102E 42             BSTRING DC.B    'BBBBBB STRING',STERMINATOR
   00102F 42
   001030 42
   001031 42
   001032 42
   001033 42
   001034 20
   001035 53
   001036 54
   001037 52
   001038 49
   001039 4E
   00103A 47
30 00103B 07
32
```

```
33                          * OUTSTRING
34                          * subroutine to output a string to the VDU screen
35                          * input parameters:
36                          * address of string in A0
37                          * string must be terminated by control G
38                          * named STERMINATOR
39                          * output parameters: none
40                          * ie. there are no error indications
41                          * uses D0
42                          * calls OUTCH
43                          *
44          0000103C        OUTSTRING EQU   *
45 00103C 1018                      MOVE.B  (A0)+,D0        * get one char
46 00103E 0C000007                  CMPI.B  #STERMINATOR,D0 * look for terminator
47 001042 67000008                  BEQ     OSEXIT
48 001046 4EB81098                  JSR     OUTCH           * output char
49 00104A 6EF0                      BGT     OUTSTRING
50 00104C 4E75            OSEXIT RTS
51                          *
52                          *************************************************************
53                          *
54    STANDARD SUBROUTINES ARE NOT SHOWN - see Fig. 10.6.
55                          *
154                         *************************************************************
155                         *
156                                 END
```

****** TOTAL ERRORS   0--   0 -- TOTAL LINES   147

APPROX 2102 UNUSED SYMBOL TABLE ENTRIES

```
ACIACONT 010040 ACIAINPU 010042 ACIAOUTP 010042 ACIASTAT 010040 ASTRING  001022
BSTRING  00102E CONFIGUR 00104E INCH     0010AA LINEFEED 001050 NEWLINE  001082
OSEXIT   00104C OUTCH    001098 OUTSTRIN 00103C PROMPT   00105E SPACE    001074
STACK    001000 STERMINA 000007
```

Fig. 11.2 Program to output a string

passed in A0 as an input parameter to the subroutine. Two alternative methods to control the number of characters to be output are as follows:

- The number of characters may be passed as a parameter.
- The string may be terminated by a special character.

The latter method has been chosen since it is less tedious for strings of any length and avoids using a second input parameter.

In the programs with user interaction, it is usual to output instructions to the user at the start of the program run. This will be done in a subroutine called INSTRUCT which itself calls OUTSTRING. An example is shown in Fig. 11.3 but, in subsequent programs, details of initial output to the user are not shown.

```
 1                              *           Figure 11.3
 2                              *
 3                              *
 4                              * This program illustrates how a range of alphabetic
 5                              * characters may be generated
 6                              * Valid inputs are F, B or a terminator (control D)
 7                              * Other characters are ignored
 8                              * Outputs the alphabet forwards (F) or backwards (B)
 9                              *
10          00001000           STACK       EQU  $1000
11          00000004           PTERMINATOR EQU  $04      * program terminator control D
12          00000007           STERMINATOR EQU  $07      * string terminator control G
13
14          00001000                       ORG  $1000
15 001000 4FF81000             INIT    LEA     STACK,SP        * load stack pointer
16 001004 4EB810CC                     JSR     CONFIGURE       * configure the ACIA
17 001008 4EB810B0                     JSR     INSTRUCT        * instructions to user
18
19                              * while input char <> terminator do....
20 00100C 4EB81100             INLOOP  JSR     NEWLINE
21 001010 4EB810DC                     JSR     PROMPT
22 001014 4EB81128                     JSR     INCH            * input into D0
23 001018 4EB81116                     JSR     OUTCH           * echo to display
24 00101C 0C000004                     CMPI.B  #PTERMINATOR,D0 * test input char
25 001020 67000028                     BEQ     EXIT            * terminator found
26 001024 0C000046                     CMPI.B  #'F',D0         * test input char
27 001028 6700000C                     BEQ     FFOUND
28 00102C 0C000042                     CMPI.B  #'B',D0
29 001030 6700000E                     BEQ     BFOUND
30 001034 60D6                         BRA     INLOOP          * ignore other chars
31
32 001036 4EB810F2             FFOUND  JSR     SPACE
33 00103A 4EB8104C                     JSR     FORWARDS        * to output A to Z
34 00103E 60CC                         BRA     INLOOP
35
36 001040 4EB810F2             BFOUND  JSR     SPACE
37 001044 4EB81060                     JSR     BACKWARDS       * to output Z to A
38 001048 60C2                         BRA     INLOOP
39
40 00104A 4E40               EXIT    TRAP    #0              * exit from program
41                              *
42                              ****************************************************
43                              * FORWARDS
44                              * subroutine to output A to Z
45                              * no input or output parameters
46                              * uses D0, D1
47                              * calls OUTCH
48                              *
49          0000104C           FORWARDS EQU     *
50 00104C 103C0041                     MOVE.B  #'A',D0         * initial letter
51 001050 323C001A                     MOVE    #26,D1          * count
52 001054 4EB81116             ATOZ    JSR     OUTCH
53 001058 5200                         ADDQ.B  #1,D0           * form next letter
54 00105A 5341                         SUBQ    #1,D1           * decrement count
55 00105C 6EF6                         BGT     ATOZ
56 00105E 4E75                         RTS
57
```

```
59                              * BACKWARDS
60                              * subroutine to output Z to A
61                              * no input or output parameters
62                              * uses D0,D1
63                              * calls OUTCH
64                              *
65          00001060       BACKWARDS EQU    *
66 001060 103C005A              MOVE.B  #'Z',D0      * initial letter
67 001064 323C001A              MOVE    #26,D1       * count
68 001068 4EB81116       ZTOA   JSR     OUTCH
69 00106C 5300                  SUBQ.B  #1,D0        * form next letter
70 00106E 5341                  SUBQ    #1,D1        * decrement count
71 001070 6EF6                  BGT     ZTOA
72 001072 4E75                  RTS
73                              *
74                              **********************************************************
75                              * INSTRUCT
76                              * subroutine to output instructions to the user
77                              * no input or output parameters
78                              * uses D0,A0
79                              * calls OUTSTRING
80                              *
81                              * data area
82 001074 57             INITMESS DC.B 'When ? is output type in F, B  or the'
83 001092 20                    DC.B ' terminator, control D ',STERMINATOR
84
85          000010B0       INSTRUCT       EQU    *
86 0010B0 41F81074              LEA     INITMESS,A0  * address parameter
87 0010B4 4EB810BA              JSR     OUTSTRING
88 0010B8 4E75                  RTS
89                              *
90                              **********************************************************
91                              * OUTSTRING - see Fig. 11.2.
92                              * subroutine to output a string to the VDU screen
110                             **********************************************************
111                             *
112     STANDARD SUBROUTINES ARE NOT SHOWN - see Fig. 10.6.
113                             *
212                             **********************************************************
213                             *
214                                       END
```

****** TOTAL ERRORS   0--   0 -- TOTAL LINES 205

APPROX 2094 UNUSED SYMBOL TABLE ENTRIES

```
ACIACONT 010040 ACIAINPU 010042 ACIAOUTP 010042 ACIASTAT 010040 ATOZ      001054
BACKWARD 001060 BFOUND   001040 CONFIGUR 0010CC EXIT     00104A FFOUND    001036
FORWARDS 00104C INCH     001128 INITMESS 001074 INIT     001000 INLOOP    00100C
INSTRUCT 0010B0 LINEFEED 0010EA NEWLINE  001100 OSEXIT   0010CA OUTCH     001116
OUTSTRIN 0010BA PROMPT   0010DC PTERMINA 000004 SPACE    0010F2 STACK     001000
STERMINA 000007· ZTOA     001068
```

Fig. 11.3   Alphabet forwards or backwards

The implementation of the subroutine OUTSTRING employs the addressing mode 'address register indirect with postincrement', for example:

OSLOOP: MOVE.B   (A0)+, D0

extracts one character from the string to be output, initially the first character. Each time, A0 is incremented by one byte, thus pointing to the next character in the string. Characters are output in sequence until the terminator is found when return to the calling level is effected.

In this one example, the complete strings are shown in the assembly listing. This is requested by a directive to the assembler. The default is that only the first character of a string is shown in the listing in order to keep the listing compact and relatively easy to follow. A general point to note when data and code are interleaved, as with local data within subroutines or global data inserted at the end of a main program segment, is that a data structure of bytes may end at an odd address and any subsequent word or longword data or instructions must start at an even address, for example:

```
                 ORG   $2000
STERMINATOR:     EQU   $07        * control G
STRING:          DC.B  'AAAA', STERMINATOR
CODE:            EQU   *
                 LEA   STRING, A0
```

Consider the memory map of the above:

```
2000 | $41  $41 | 2001
2002 | $41  $41 | 2003
2004 | $07       | 2005
```

It is reasonable to expect the assembler to work out on behalf of the programmer that the symbol CODE may not have value $2005 since it labels an instruction which must start at an even address. Some assembler implementations do not perform this service and output error messages. If the programmer wishes to avoid counting the characters in long messages such error messages may be treated as routine and an extra byte inserted where necessary to correct the errors.

11.4   A PROGRAM TO OUTPUT THE ALPHABET FORWARDS OR BACKWARDS

Fig. 11.3 shows an extension of the basic idea presented in Fig. 11.1 incorporating some user interaction.

- Instructions are output to the user JSR INSTRUCT.
- The user is prompted for input with ?.
- If control D is input, the program terminates.
- If F is input, the alphabet is output forwards.
- If B is input, the alphabet is output backwards.

- If any other character is input, it is ignored.
- The program cycles, allowing the user to input characters, until the terminator is typed.

It should be noted that the terminator is declared in an EQU statement instead of being embedded in the program text:

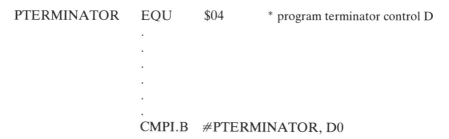

```
PTERMINATOR    EQU      $04        * program terminator control D
               .
               .
               .
               .
               .

               .
               CMPI.B   #PTERMINATOR, D0
```

This is easier to read and easier to change.

It should also be noted that the subroutine call instructions JSR or BSR are unconditional; for example, the following must be used:

```
               .
               .
               CMPI,B   #'F', D0   * was the input char F?
               BEQ      FFOUND
               .
               .
               .
               .
               .

               .
FFOUND         JSR   FORWARDS
               BRA   INLOOP
```

11.5   A PROGRAM TO TEST THE TYPE OF A CHARACTER

Fig. 11.4 shows a program which analyses whether a character typed in by a user is alphabetic, numeric or 'other'. This illustrates the ASCII ranges of character types and makes use of the subroutine OUTSTRING to output a variety of messages.

The subroutine ALPHTEST for example is used to test whether the character, passed as an input parameter in D0, lies in the ranges 'A' to 'Z' ($41 to $5A) or 'a' to 'z' ($61 to $7A) and if so outputs the string 'alphabetic'. On return from the subroutine, the calling level needs to know whether the character was alphabetic and this is achieved by means of an output parameter. If, on return from the subroutine, the low byte of D0 contains zero, the character was alphabetic and the string

```
 1                              *          Figure 11.4
 2                              *
 3                              *
 4                              * This program illustrates character types and ranges
 5                              * A character is input and, if not the terminator,
 6                              * is analyzed as alphabetic, numeric or other
 7                              *
 8           00001000           STACK       EQU $1000
 9           00000004           PTERMINATOR EQU  $04     * program terminator  control D
10           00000007           STERMINATOR EQU  $07     * string terminator control G
11
12           00001000                       ORG    $1000
13
14 001000 4FF81000              INIT   LEA      STACK,SP        * load stack pointer
15 001004 4EB81104                     JSR      CONFIGURE       * configure the ACIA
16 001008 4EB810E8                     JSR      INSTRUCT        * instruct user
17
18                              * while input char <> terminator do.....
19
20 00100C 4EB81138              INLOOP JSR      NEWLINE
21 001010 4EB81114                     JSR      PROMPT
22 001014 4EB81160                     JSR      INCH            * char into D0
23 001018 4EB8114E                     JSR      OUTCH           * echo to display
24 00101C 0C000004                     CMPI.B   #PTERMINATOR,D0
25 001020 67000018                     BEQ      EXIT            * terminator found
26 001024 4EB81048                     JSR      ALPHTEST        * test char in D0
27 001028 4A00                         TST.B    D0              * if D0=0
28 00102A 67E0                         BEQ      INLOOP          * char was alphabetic
29 00102C 4EB81072                     JSR      NUMTEST         * char still in D0
30 001030 4A00                         TST.B    D0              * if D0=0
31 001032 67D8                         BEQ      INLOOP          * char was numeric
32 001034 4EB8109A                     JSR      OTHER           * char still in D0
33 001038 60D2                         BRA      INLOOP          * repeat
34
35 00103A 4E40                  EXIT   TRAP     #0              * exit from program
36                              *
37                              ********************************************************
38                              * ALPHTEST
39                              * subroutine to test if a char is alphabetic
40                              * and if so to output a message
41                              * input parameters char in D0 (low byte)
42                              * output parameters:
43                              * 0 in D0 (low byte) if char was alphabetic
44                              * char still in D0 if char was not alphabetic
45                              * uses D1,A0
46                              * calls OUTSTRING
47                              *
48                              * data area:
49                              *
50 00103C 41                    ASTRING DC.B     'ALPHABETIC ',STERMINATOR
51                              *
52                              * subroutine code:
53           00001048           ALPHTEST EQU      *
54 001048 0C000041                      CMPI.B   #'A',D0
55 00104C 6D00001A                      BLT      NOTALPH
```

```
56 001050 0C00005A              CMPI.B  #´Z´,D0
57 001054 6E000012              BGT     NOTALPH
58 001058 4EB8112A    ALPH      JSR     SPACE
59 00105C 41F8103C              LEA     ASTRING,A0      * address parameter
60 001060 4EB810F2              JSR     OUTSTRING       * call subroutine
61 001064 4200                  CLR.B   D0              * output parameter
62 001066 4E75                  RTS
63 001068 4E75      NOTALPH RTS                         * char is still in D0
64                  *
65                  ******************************************************
66                  * NUMTEST
67                  * subroutine to test if a char is numeric
68                  * and if so to output a message
69                  * input parameters char in D0 (low byte)
70                  * output parameters:
71                  * 0 in D0 (low byte) if char was numeric
72                  * char still in D0 if char was not numeric
73                  * uses D1,A0
74                  * calls OUTSTRING
75                  *
76                  * data area:
77 00106A 4E        NSTRING DC.B    ´NUMERIC´,STERMINATOR
78                  *
79                  * subroutine code:
80         00001072 NUMTEST EQU     *
81 001072 0C000030              CMPI.B  #´0´,D0
82 001076 6D00001A              BLT     NOTNUM
83 00107A 0C000039              CMPI.B  #´9´,D0
84 00107E 6E000012              BGT     NOTNUM
85 001082 4EB8112A    NUM       JSR     SPACE
86 001086 41F8106A              LEA     NSTRING,A0      * address parameter
87 00108A 4EB810F2              JSR     OUTSTRING       * call subroutine
88 00108E 4200                  CLR.B   D0              * output parameter
89 001090 4E75                  RTS
90 001092 4E75      NOTNUM  RTS                         * char is still in D0
93                  * OTHER
94                  * subroutine to output message "other"
95                  * since char was not alphabetic or numeric
96                  * uses D1,A0
97                  * calls OUTSTRING
98                  *
99                  * data area:
100 001094 4F       OSTRING DC.B    ´OTHER´,STERMINATOR
101                 *
102                 * subroutine code:
103        0000109A OTHER   EQU     *
104 00109A 4EB8112A              JSR     SPACE
105 00109E 41F81094              LEA     OSTRING,A0      * address parameter
106 0010A2 4EB810F2              JSR     OUTSTRING       * call subroutine
107 0010A6 4E75                  RTS
108                 *
109                 ******************************************************
110                 * INSTRUCT
111                 * subroutine to output instructions to user
```

```
112                          * no input or output parameters
113                          * uses DO,AO
114                          * calls OUTSTRING
115                          *
116                          * data area:
117 0010A8 57               INITMESS DC.B 'When ? is output type any character'
118 0010CB 20                        DC.B ' to terminate type ctrl D',STERMINATOR
119         000010E8        INSTRUCT EQU   *
120 0010E8 41F810A8                  LEA     INITMESS,AO    * address of string
121 0010EC 4EB810F2                  JSR     OUTSTRING
122 0010FO 4E75                      RTS
123                          *
124                          ****************************************************
12.5                         * OUTSTRING - see Fig. 11.2.
126                          * subroutine to output a string to the VDU screen
144                          ****************************************************
145                          *
146          STANDARD SUBROUTINES ARE NOT SHOWN - see Fig. 10.6.
146                          *
245                          ****************************************************
246                          *
247                                      END
```

****** TOTAL ERRORS   0--   0 -- TOTAL LINES 240

APPROX 2090 UNUSED SYMBOL TABLE ENTRIES

ACIACONT 010040	ACIAINPU 010042	ACIAOUTP 010042	ACIASTAT 010040	ALPHTEST 001048	
ALPH 001058	ASTRING 00103C	CONFIGUR 001104	EXIT 00103A	INCH 001160	
INITMESS 0010A8	INIT 001000	INLOOP 00100C	INSTRUCT 0010E8	LINEFEED 00111E	
NEWLINE 001138	NOTALPH 001068	NOTNUM 001092	NSTRING 00106A	NUM 001082	
NUMTEST 001072	OSEXIT 001102	OSTRING 001094	OTHER 00109A	OUTCH 00114E	
OUTSTRIN 0010F2	PROMPT 001114	PTERMINA 000004	SPACE 00112A	STACK 001000	
STERMINA 000007					

Fig. 11.4 Character type test program

'alphabetic' was therefore output. If not, D0 still contains the character to be tested and further tests must be made.

JSR	ALPHTEST	* test if char in D0 is alphabetic
		* and if so output 'alphabetic'
TST.B	D0	* test return parameter
BEQ	INLOOP	* if 0 char was alphabetic

This illustrates a simple use of the general concept of setting a flag in a subroutine to indicate a range of alternatives so that the calling level can test the flag on return to analyze what happened within the subroutine and decide on subsequent action.

11.6   PROGRAM TO MATCH A CHARACTER AGAINST A STORED TABLE

Fig. 11.5 shows a program which matches a single character key input by the user
against a table of keys and if a match is found outputs an associated message. It is
assumed that each alphabetic character key has one associated message only. In more
detail:

1. Output instructions to the user.
2. Prompt for a character.
3. Input a character and echo to the screen.
4. Test for the terminator and, if found, exit.
5. Validate the character as alphabetic. If not alphabetic, return to 2.
6. Compare the character against characters stored in a table of keys.
7. If no match is found, output the message 'no match' and return to step 2.
8. If a match is found, a (variable-length) message associated with the matched
   character is output, for example:

   A   AMERICA
   C   CANADA
   B   NO MATCH
   then return to step 2.

The messages are variable-length and are terminated by the special character
detected by OUTSTRING, #07, control G. The essential problem in this example is

```
1                          *          Figure 11.5
2                          *
3                          *
4                          *
5                          * This program illustrates matching an input key
6                          * and selecting an associated message for output
7                          *
8          00001000        STACK      EQU $1000
9          00000004        PTERMINATOR EQU $04    * program terminator control D
10         00000007        STERMINATOR EQU $07    * string terminator control G
11
12         00001000                   ORG   $1000
13 001000 4FF81000         INIT   LEA     STACK,SP       * load stack pointer
14 001004 4EB81162                JSR     CONFIGURE      * configure ACIA
15 001008 4EB81146                JSR     INSTRUCT       * instruct user
16
17                         * while input char <> terminator do....
18 00100C 4EB81196         INLOOP JSR     NEWLINE
19 001010 4EB81172                JSR     PROMPT
20 001014 4EB811BE                JSR     INCH           * input into D0
21 001018 4EB8.11AC               JSR     OUTCH          * echo to display
22 00101C 0C000004                CMPI.B  #PTERMINATOR,D0 * test input char
23 001020 67000010                BEQ     EXIT           * terminator found
```

```
24 001024 4EB81034          JSR    VALIDATE         * is char alphabetic
25 001028 4A00              TST.B  D0               * if D0=0
26 00102A 67E0              BEQ    INLOOP           * char not alphabetic
27 00102C 4EB81098          JSR    KEYMAT           * match & o/p message
28 001030 60DA              BRA    INLOOP
29
30 001032 4E40       EXIT   TRAP   #0               * exit from program
31                          *
32                          **********************************************************
33                          * VALIDATE
34                          * subroutine to test if a char is alphabetic
35                          * input parameter: char in D0
36                          * output parameter:
37                          * 0 in D0 if char not alphabetic
38                          * char still in D0 if alphabetic
39                          *
40         00001034  VALIDATE EQU   *
41 001034 0C000041          CMPI.B #'A',D0
42 001038 6D00000C          BLT    NOTALPH
43 00103C 0C00005A          CMPI.B #'Z',D0
44 001040 6E000004          BGT    NOTALPH
45 001044 4E75              RTS                     * char still in D0
46 001046 4200       NOTALPH CLR.B D0
47 001048 4E75              RTS
48                          *
49                          **********************************************************
50                          * KEYMAT
51                          * subroutine to match a single character key
52                          * against a table of keys
53                          * an associated message is output if matched
54                          * "no match" is output if not matched
55                          * input parameter: char in D0 (low byte)
56                          * uses D1,A0
57                          * calls OUTSTRING
58                          *
59                          * data area:
60         00000006  TABLENGTH EQU  6
61 00104A 41         KEYTABLE DC.B  'ACFIPS'
62 001050 105C       ADDTABLE DC.W ASTRING,CSTRING,FSTRING,ISTRING,PSTRING
63 00105C 20         ASTRING DC.B   ' AMERICA',STERMINATOR
64 001065 20         CSTRING DC.B   ' CANADA',STERMINATOR
65 00106D 20         FSTRING DC.B   ' FRANCE',STERMINATOR
66 001075 20         ISTRING DC.B   ' ITALY',STERMINATOR
67 00107C 20         PSTRING DC.B   ' PORTUGAL',STERMINATOR
68 001086 20         SSTRING DC.B   ' SPAIN',STERMINATOR
69 00108D 20         NOMATSTRING DC.B        ' NO MATCH ',STERMINATOR
70                          *
71                          * subroutine code:
72         00001098  KEYMAT EQU *
73 001098 41F8104A          LEA    KEYTABLE,A0      * initialize pointer
74 00109C 323C0006          MOVE   #TABLENGTH,D1    * number of keys
75 0010A0 4242              CLR    D2
76 0010A2 B018       MATLOOP CMP.B (A0)+,D0         * compare D0 with key
77 0010A4 67000016          BEQ    MATCH            * match found
78 0010A8 6D000008          BLT    NOMATCH          * alphabetical order
79 0010AC 5442              ADDQ   #2,D2            * increment for word
```

```
80 0010AE 5341                SUBQ     #1,D1              * decrement count
81 0010B0 6EF0                BGT      MATLOOP
82
83 0010B2 41F8108D   NOMATCH  LEA      NOMATSTRING,A0
84 0010B6 4EB81150             JSR      OUTSTRING
85 0010BA 4E75                RTS
86
87 0010BC 41F81050   MATCH    LEA      ADDTABLE,A0
88 0010C0 30702000             MOVE     0(A0,D2),A0        * address parameter
89 0010C4 4EB81150             JSR      OUTSTRING
90 0010C8 4E75                RTS
91                   *
92                   ****************************************************
93                   * INSTRUCT
94                   * subroutine to output instructions to the user
95                   * no input or output parameters
96                   * uses D0,A0
97                   * calls OUTSTRING
98                   *
99                   * data area:
100 0010CA 57        INITMESS DC.B     'When ? is output type in an alphabetic'
101 0010F1 63                 DC.B     'char. An associated message or'
102 001118 20                 DC.B     ' no match will be output. '
103 001129 54                 DC.B     'The terminator is ctrl D ',STERMINATOR
104
105        00001146  INSTRUCT EQU      *
106 001146 41F810CA            LEA      INITMESS,A0        * address parameter
107 00114A 4EB81150            JSR      OUTSTRING
108 00114E 4E75                RTS
109                  *
110                  ****************************************************  ********
111                  * OUTSTRING - see Fig. 11.2.
112                  * subroutine to output a string to the VDU screen
130                  ****************************************************
131                  *
132          STANDARD SUBROUTINES ARE NOT SHOWN - see Fig. 10.6.
133                  *
231                  ****************************************************
232                  *
233                           END
```

****** TOTAL ERRORS   0--   0 -- TOTAL LINES 226

APPROX 2085 UNUSED SYMBOL TABLE ENTRIES

```
ACIACONT 010040 ACIAINPU 010042 ACIAOUTP 010042 ACIASTAT 010040 ADDTABLE 001050
ASTRING  00105C CONFIGUR 001162 CSTRING  001065 EXIT     001032 FSTRING  00106D
INCH     0011BE INITMESS 0010CA INIT     001000 INLOOP   00100C INSTRUCT 001146
ISTRING  001075 KEYMAT   001098 KEYTABLE 00104A LINEFEED 001164 MATCH    0010BC
MATLOOP  0010A2 NEWLINE  001196 NOMATCH  0010B2 NOMATSTR 00108D NOTALPH  001046
OSEXIT   001160 OUTCH    0011AC OUTSTRIN 001150 PROMPT   001172 PSTRING  00107C
PTERMINA 000004 SPACE    001188 SSTRING  001086 STACK    001000 STERMINA 000007
TABLENGT 000006 VALIDATE 001034
```

Fig. 11.5 Key matching program

associated with organization of the data:

- Storage of the keys.
- Storage of the address of strings.
- Use of addressing modes to handle the tables.

In the implementation shown in Fig. 11.5, the keys are stored as a table of bytes:

      ADDTABLE: DC.B   'ACFIPS'

The addresses of the strings associated with the keys are stored as a table of words:

    ADDTABLE: DC.W ASTRING, CSTRING, FSTRING, ISTRING,   PSTRING, SSTRING

The messages then follow:

    ASTRING: DC.B 'AMERICA', 07
    CSTRING: DC.B 'CANADA', 07
    etc.

In the KEYMAT subroutine, the character in D0 is compared with each of the characters in turn in KEYTABLE. Since KEYTABLE contains the keys in alphabetical order, the search can be stopped when the character in D0 has a code less than those being accessed in the table. The loop is controlled by a count initialized to the length of the table.

```
                LEA      KEYTABLE, A0        * table base into A0
                MOVE     #TABLELENGTH, D1    * length into D1
                CLR      D2
MATLOOP:        CMP.B    (A0)+, D0           * compare with a key
                BEQ      MATCH
                BLT      NOMATCH             * past the point in the
                                               alphabet
                ADDQ     #2, D2              * record the position in
                                               the table
                SUBQ     #1, D1              * decrement count
                BGT      MATLOOP
NOMATCH:        .
                .
                .
```

If no match is found, the 'NO MATCH' string is output.
If a match is found, the address of the string corresponding to the matched key must be located in ADDTABLE as follows:

```
MATCH:     MULU    #2, D2        * adjust D2 to word count
                                   (LSL #2, D2 could be used)
           LEA     ADDTABLE, A0  * table base into A0
           MOVE    0(A0, D2), A0 * select address from table
           JSR     OUTSTRING     * output the string at that address
```

The rest of the program does not introduce new concepts.

An alternative approach is to combine the two tables into a single table of records, each record containing a key and an associated address. Since the key occupies a byte and the address a word, a byte must be left empty in each record, for example:

KEYADDTAB: DC.W ASTRING,'A', CSTRING,'C', etc.

The table entries then have the form:

Since each entry occupies only a longword, automatic postincrement mode could still be employed, for example:

```
                 LEA         KEYADDTAB,A0
                 MOVEQ       #TABLELENGTH,D1
    MATLOOP:     MOVE.L      (A0)+,D2
                 CMP.B       D2,D0
                 BEQ         MATCH
                 BLT         NOMATCH
                 SUBQ        #1,D1
                 BGT         MATLOOP
    NOMATCH:     .
                 .
                 .
                 .
```

When MATCH is reached, D2 contains

address	0	char

```
    MATCH     MOVE.L     D2,A0
              LSR.L      #16,A0        * shift address to low word of A0
              JSR        OUTSTRING
```

11.6.1 Extensions of the matching program

The idea of the basic program could be extended in the following ways:

- The matching could be of more than a single character. Consider, for example, an application associated with one function of an assembler. A table of user defined symbols is constructed during a first pass through the code. Translation into object code is carried out by pass two. One aspect of this task is to replace a symbol by its value, for example, in:

MOVE LABEL, D0

the symbol (character string) LABEL must be matched in the symbol table and the associated value extracted.

- Another similar application is the storage of an on-line dictionary. A character string is matched and the corresponding definition is extracted. The strings to be matched are of variable length.
- Some applications involving the storage of multi-field records may require a key for each record which must be matched in order that the associated information may be accessed, for example:

SURNAME INITIALS
DATE OF BIRTH
SALARY
DATE OF EMPLOYMENT etc.

The surnames in alphabetical order may be used as keys.

11.7   SUMMARY

Although the programs developed in this chapter are relatively short and simple, some general problem areas may be selected:

1. Keeping track of the use of registers by subroutines
The method of documenting the subroutine interfaces has been employed. When longer programs are developed in which there may be a high degree of nesting of subroutine calls, a more satisfactory method is to save the contents of all the registers that will be used by the subroutine on entry and restore them on exit. A convenient instruction for this purpose MOVEM, move multiple registers, is illustrated in Section 7.6.1.

2. Parameter passing
Since the programs are short and simple, the efficient and convenient method of using registers has been employed. A full discussion of the more general case is given in Section 7.6.

3. Location of data
In a very short program it may make sense to put all of the data in one place, i.e. to use global data. When a program listing becomes longer than two or three pages, it is inconvenient to search around for the data area. More important, however, is that if global data can be accessed in an uncontrolled way by subroutines it becomes increasingly difficult to debug programs as they grow in size. It is not sufficient to look at the subroutine interfaces to keep track of what is happening to the data but one must delve inside the subroutine body and examine the instructions there. For this reason, any access to global data should be via parameters. If a data structure is used by one subroutine only, it should be implemented as local data for that subroutine. It

may be the case that only two or three subroutines access a data structure, for example, to initialize it, manipulate it and print it out. In such a case, a modular structure could be devised. An example is given in Fig. 12.16 and this is also discussed in Section 7.7.

4. Error handling

The programs developed in this chapter contain minimal error handling in order to keep them as short and simple to follow as possible. Error handling is an important part of any piece of robust, practical software, particularly when interaction with a user is involved, and a decision must be taken over the degree of assistance to be given.

When typing a command in response to a debugging program or development system, a slight syntax error could be made, for example:

TUTOR 1.X>BR 2000;5 2020:6 3060 3100

The response could be

WHAT?
TUTOR 1.X>

or assistance could be attempted

TUTOR 1.X>BR 2000;5 2020:6 3060 3100
ILLEGAL SYNTAX ------*
TUTOR 1.X>

A tradeoff is involved, since providing a convenient user interface requires a large amount of code and data. Supervisory software may be located in read-only memory to protect it from corruption by erroneous user programs and a design aim may well be that it should be as small as possible.

In general, error handling during user input could be provided at several levels, for example:

- An error message is output and the user is prompted to retype all of the characters.
- An error message is output and the user is told to retype the invalid character and continue from that point.
- An error message is output, the correct characters are output on a new line and the user continues typing the rest of the characters. This requires that the input characters are stored in a buffer to be available for output.
- A general input package including error handling is developed which allows the user the normal line editing facilities of deleting characters and restarting a line.

12

Character input and output conversion routines

12.1 INTRODUCTION

In Chapter 1, the representation of numeric data in the memory was described in Sections 1.4.1 and 1.9. Appendix A covers this topic in detail. In Chapter 10, input and output was described. The initial sections of this chapter are concerned with conversion between the internal binary representation of numeric data and the sequence of characters input from or output to the user. Fig. 12.1 shows a word of memory containing the binary pattern 1010101100010011. As a convenient shorthand, this is written in hexadecimal as $AB13. Also in Fig. 12.1, the user input is shown to be a sequence of characters obtained by depressing the appropriate keys and user output is again a row of characters. In the interface registers, the ASCII code for the character 3, $33 is shown in the output register and for the character SP, $20 in the input register.

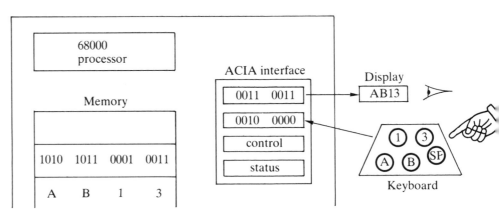

Fig. 12.1

As a further example consider the following 16-bit word:

	15			0
location \$1000 contents	0001	0010	0011	0100
hex	1	2	3	4

Fig. 12.2

Suppose the contents of this word are to be output for a user to read on a display as described in Section 10.6, on a VDU screen or printed on paper. For example, when the MD command is given to TUTOR, the output on the console VDU screen is in hexadecimal

TUTOR > MD 1000 (user input is underlined)
1000 12 34 etc.

The output to the VDU screen of the contents of location \$1000 takes the form of four hexadecimal characters:

character 1	has code	\$31	(see Fig. 1.16)
2		\$32	
3		\$33	
4		\$34	

Formatting characters such as the space which has code \$20 are also output and the characters comprising the address \$1000 input by the user are repeated in the output. To effect the output, the internal representation must be converted to a sequence of characters which are written to the screen in the correct order.

Algorithms to convert a word of binary to four hexadecimal characters for output and to perform the reverse conversion on input are developed in Sections 12.2 to 12.4.

As a final example, consider a program written in a high level language and containing statements such as:

read (N) where N is an integer
print (N)
read (X) where X is a real number
print (X)

The user interacting with such a program expects to be able to type a sequence of characters, for example, +532 or –2734 as values for N or +30.32 or –0.631 as values for X perhaps followed by a space, a comma or a carriage-return and line-feed.

In this case, it is assumed that the characters represent a decimal number and that the correct binary internal representation will be produced by some piece of system software. Algorithms for performing conversion to and from decimal are developed in Sections 12.5 and 12.6.

12.2   HEXADECIMAL NUMBERS AND CHARACTER CODES

Input and output as a sequence of characters which are the hexadecimal representation of the binary number will first be considered. Fig. 12.3 shows the printed
characters, their ASCII codes and the numbers they represent in decimal and binary.

Character as printed	ASCII code	Decimal number	Binary number
0	$30	0	0000
1	$31	1	0001
.	.	.	.
.	.	.	.
.	.	.	.
9	$39	9	1001
A	$41	10	1010
B	$42	11	1011
.	.	.	.
.	.	.	.
F	$46	15	1111

Fig. 12.3

It should be noted that the printed hex characters 0–9, A–F do not lie in a
continuous range. $3A, $3B . . . . $40 print as : ; . . . @ (see Fig. 1.16).

Suppose a character has been input, is to be validated as hexadecimal and
converted to the corresponding number in the range 0 to 15. The following ranges of
codes must be tested and conversions made as indicated:

char < $30	error – not hex
$30 ≤ char ≤ $39	subtract $30 to form the corresponding number
$3A ≤ char ≤ $40	error – not hex
$41 ≤ char ≤ $46	subtract $41 – $A (=$37) to form the corresponding number
$47 ≤ char	error – not hex

The full range of compare and branch instructions is available for convenient
validation of the input characters.

12.3   HEXADECIMAL INPUT OF ONE WORD

Four characters in the hexadecimal range are to be input in response to a prompt and
the 16-bit binary representation of the corresponding four hex-digit number is to

be formed, for example:

At the display/keyboard	Internally
? 1234	0001 0010 0011 0100
? AF0D	1010 1111 0000 1101
? Z	error

Fig. 12.4

To achieve this, the following algorithm, given in outline, is used:

Clear a register to hold the answer, say D5 (the low word)
Output a prompt, say ? to the display
Four times ⌐ Input a character from the keyboard
Output(echo) to the display as confirmation to the user
Validate as hex (take error action if not hex)
Convert to a number
Shift D5 left by four binary places
⌐ Add on the new hex number (four binary digits)

The contents of the low word of D5 as the characters are input are as follows:

?	0000 0000 0000 0000
?1	0000 0000 0000 0001
?12	0000 0000 0001 0010
?123	0000 0001 0010 0011
?1234	0001 0010 0011 0100

Fig. 12.5

As specified here, the algorithm inputs exactly four characters. It is easily modified to input eight characters to form a longword or two characters to form a byte.

If such a program was to be used in a realistic environment, a user would expect to be able to input one, two, three or four characters to represent a word; for example, to be able to type 1 and not 0001. The basic algorithm outlined above could again easily be modified to look for a terminating character (or a set of terminating characters such as , space or return) and to exit from the loop before four characters are input. This is because D5 is cleared initially and shifted left each time a new character is input as shown in Fig. 12.5. If the user types a terminator after 1, 12 or 123 have been typed, the resulting word in D5 is correct.

12.3.1 The hexadecimal input program

The aim of the program in Fig. 12.6 is to show an implementation of the hexadecimal input algorithm described above. If hexadecimal input is to be incorporated into practical working software, it is likely to be required in the form of a subroutine as shown in Fig. 12.10. It is also necessary to include error handling. In Fig. 12.6, error handling is not included. If the user types an invalid character the program stops.

```
 1                        *          Figure 12.6
 2                        *
 3                        *
 4                        *
 5                        * The program inputs four hexadecimal characters
 6                        * validates them as hex, converts them to binary
 7                        * and stores them in a single word (in D5)
 8                        *
 9          00001000      STACK    EQU     $1000
10
11          00001000               ORG     $1000
12
13 001000 4FF81000       START    LEA     STACK,SP        * load stack pointer
14 001004 4EB81066                JSR     CONFIGURE       * configure ACIA
15
16 001008 7804                    MOVEQ   #4,D4           * number of chars
17 00100A 4285                    CLR.L   D5              * to hold answer
18 00100C 4EB8109A                JSR     NEWLINE
19 001010 4EB81076                JSR     PROMPT          * output ? to user
20
21                        * for D4:=4 downto 1 do ....
22 001014 4EB810C2       IPLOOP   JSR     INCH            * input char into D0
23 001018 4EB810B0                JSR     OUTCH           * echo
24 00101C 4EB81034                JSR     HEXTOBIN        * validate & convert
25 001020 0C00FFFF                CMPI.B  #-1,D0          * test error code
26 001024 6700000C                BEQ     IPERROR
27 001028 E94D                    LSL     #4,D5           * shift answer so far
28 00102A DA00                    ADD.B   D0,D5           * add on new number
29 00102C 5344                    SUBQ    #1,D4           * for loop control
30 00102E 66E4                    BNE     IPLOOP
31 001030 4E40                    TRAP    #0              * exit from program
32
33 001032 4E40           IPERROR  TRAP    #0              * error exit
34                        * error handling is needed for practical software
35                        *
36                        ********************************************************
37                        * HEXTOBIN
38                        * subroutine to validate a character as hex
39                        * and to convert to the corresponding number
40                        * input parameter: character in low byte of D0
41                        * output parameters:
42                        * corresponding number in D0 if hex character input
43                        * -1 in D0 if input character is not hex
44                        *
45          00001034      HEXTOBIN EQU     *
46 001034 0C000030                CMPI.B  #'0',D0
47 001038 6D000026                BLT     NOTHEX
48 00103C 0C000039                CMPI.B  #'9',D0
49 001040 6E000008                BGT     ATOFTST
50 001044 04000030                SUBI.B  #$30,D0         * convert to number
51 001048 4E75                    RTS
52 00104A 0C000041       ATOFTST  CMPI.B  #'A',D0
53 00104E 6D000010                BLT     NOTHEX
54 001052 0C000046                CMPI.B  #'F',D0
55 001056 6E000008                BGT     NOTHEX
```

```
56 00105A 04000037          SUBI.B  #$37,D0     * convert to number
57 00105E 4E75              RTS
58 001060 103CFFFF  NOTHEX  MOVE.B  #-1,D0      * indicate invalid
59 001064 4E75              RTS
60                       *
61                       *********************************************************
                         *
6.2        STANDARD SUBROUTINES NOT SHOWN - see Fig. 10.6.
                         *
159                      *********************************************************
160                      *
161                          END

****** TOTAL ERRORS    0--    0 -- TOTAL LINES   153


APPROX  2102 UNUSED SYMBOL TABLE ENTRIES

ACIACONT 010040 ACIAINPU 010042 ACIAOUTP 010042 ACIASTAT 010040 ATOFTST  00104A
CONFIGUR 001066 HEXTOBIN 001034 INCH     0010C2 IPERROR  001032 IPLOOP   001014
LINEFEED 001068 NEWLINE  00109A NOTHEX   001060 OUTCH    0010B0 PROMPT   001076
SPACE    00108C STACK    001000 START    001000
```

Fig. 12.6 Hex input

In Fig. 12.10 error handling is indicated by a subroutine call:

    IPERROR: EQU   *

                JSR   INPUTERROR   * call error handling routine

                RTS

and details of error handling within the subroutine body are not shown. An assumption must be made about how to continue after error and in this case D0 is set to 0 in HEXINPUT to indicate an input error, the calling level tests D0 and re-prompts the user. Alternative actions are possible, for example a jump within HEXINPUT to re-type the character.

12.4   HEXADECIMAL OUTPUT OF ONE WORD

Again a simple specification, to output one word as four hexadecimal characters, is considered, for example:

Internally	*At the display*
1010 1111 0000 1101	AF0D

Fig. 12.7

As no hexadecimal validation is required on output, a table lookup may be used for conversion from number to code:

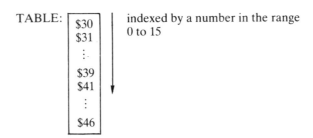

Fig. 12.8

This table could be set up as a byte array of characters as follows:

TABLE   DC.B '0 1 2 3 4 5 6 7 8 9 A B C D E F'

The assembler will set up the ASCII codes and this is equivalent to

TABLE   DC.B $30,$31,$32, ... etc.

An addressing mode which will allow a displacement or index into the table from the base at location TABLE is required; for example, the following fragment of code achieves the desired effect:

```
*  assume D0 contains the index into the table (range 0 to 15)
      LEA        TABLE, A0       * put the table base address in A0
      MOVE.B    0(A0, D0), D0    * extract the byte from the table

   (no further      (contains              (contains the index into the table)
   displacement)    the base)
```

The *algorithm in outline* is as follows:
(Assuming that the 16-bit word to be output is in D5)

four times | Rotate the low order 16 bits of D5 by four binary places to the left
Extract a copy of the least significant four binary digits
Convert to the corresponding character code using the table
Output the character

Initially, D5 contains:

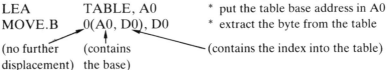

Each time round the loop after the rotate has been executed, D5 and the output to the display are shown in Fig. 12.9.

Fig. 12.9 shows that the four binary digit number to be converted to a hexadecimal character is moved to the low end of D5 each time round the loop. It remains to extract these four bits leaving the 16 bits in D5 intact and this may be achieved by the

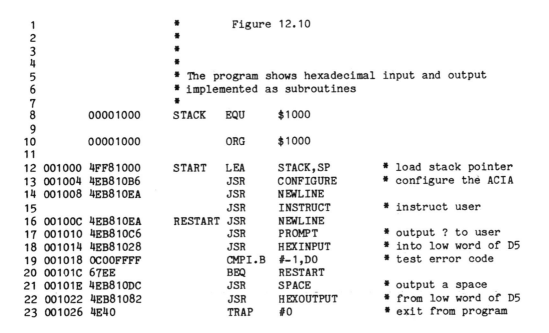

Fig. 12.9

following fragment of code:

```
ROL    #4, D5        * rotate D5 to the left by 4 bits
MOVE   D5, D0        * copy D5 to D0
ANDI   #$F, D0       * AND D0 with four binary 1's
```

It should be noted that all these instructions are word instructions and operate on the low-order 16 bits of the specified registers. Shift, rotate and logical instruction are introduced in Chapter 8. After these instructions, D0 contains the required displacement into the code conversion table and the corresponding code may be obtained by table lookup as shown above.

A program which has the basic hexadecimal input and output algorithms provided as subroutines in given as Fig. 12.10.

```
 1                      *          Figure 12.10
 2                      *
 3                      *
 4                      *
 5                      * The program shows hexadecimal input and output
 6                      * implemented as subroutines
 7                      *
 8        00001000      STACK   EQU     $1000
 9
10        00001000              ORG     $1000
11
12 001000 4FF81000      START   LEA     STACK,SP        * load stack pointer
13 001004 4EB810B6              JSR     CONFIGURE       * configure the ACIA
14 001008 4EB810EA              JSR     NEWLINE
15                              JSR     INSTRUCT        * instruct user
16 00100C 4EB810EA      RESTART JSR     NEWLINE
17 001010 4EB810C6              JSR     PROMPT          * output ? to user
18 001014 4EB81028              JSR     HEXINPUT        * into low word of D5
19 001018 0C00FFFF              CMPI.B  #-1,D0          * test error code
20 00101C 67EE                  BEQ     RESTART
21 00101E 4EB810DC              JSR     SPACE           * output a space
22 001022 4EB81082              JSR     HEXOUTPUT       * from low word of D5
23 001026 4E40                  TRAP    #0              * exit from program
```

```
24              *
25              ********************************************************
26              * HEXINPUT
27              * subroutine to input a word as four hex characters
28              * output parameters: number in low word of D5
29              *        D0 (low byte) cleared on input error
30              * uses D4 and D0
31              * calls INCH and HEXTOBIN
32              * called by main program
33              *
34      00001028     HEXINPUT EQU    *
35 001028 7804                MOVEQ   #4,D4              * number of chars
36 00102A 4285                CLR.L   D5                 * to hold answer
37
38              * for D4:=4 downto 1 do ....
39 00102C 4EB81112    IPLOOP  JSR     INCH               * input char into D0
40 001030 4EB81100            JSR     OUTCH              * echo
41 001034 4EB81050            JSR     HEXTOBIN           * validate & convert
42 001038 0C00FFFF            CMPI.B  #-1,D0             * test error code
43 00103C 6700000C            BEQ     IPERROR
44 001040 E94D                LSL     #4,D5              * shift current answer
45 001042 DA40                ADD     D0,D5              * add on new number
46 001044 5344                SUBQ    #1,D4              * decrement count
47 001046 66E4                BNE     IPLOOP
48 001048 4E75                RTS
49
50      0000104A     IPERROR EQU    *
51              *       JSR     INPUTERROR         * error handling
52              * commented out in this program
53 00104A 103CFFFF            MOVE.B  #-1,D0             * indicate error
54 00104E 4E75                RTS
55
56
57              * HEXTOBIN
58              * subroutine to validate a character as hex
59              * and to convert to the corresponding number
60              * input parameter: character in low byte of D0
61              * output parameters:
62              * corresponding number in D0 if hex character input
63              * -1 in D0 if input character is not hex
64              * called by HEXINPUT
65              *
66      00001050     HEXTOBIN EQU *
67 001050 0C000030            CMPI.B  #'0',D0
68 001054 6D000026            BLT     NOTHEX
69 001058 0C000039            CMPI.B  #'9',D0
70 00105C 6E000008            BGT     ATOFTST
71 001060 04000030            SUB.B   #$30,D0            * convert to number
72 001064 4E75                RTS
73 001066 0C000041    ATOFTST CMPI.B  #'A',D0
74 00106A 6D000010            BLT     NOTHEX
75 00106E 0C000046            CMPI.B  #'F',D0
76 001072 6E000008            BGT     NOTHEX
77 001076 04000037            SUB.B   #$37,D0            * convert to number
78 00107A 4E75                RTS
79 00107C 103CFFFF    NOTHEX  MOVE.B  #-1,D0             * indicate error
80 001080 4E75                RTS
```

```
 81                              *
 82                              ********************************************************
 83                              * HEXOUTPUT
 84                              * subroutine to output a word as four hex characters
 85                              * input parameter: number in low word of D5
 86                              * uses D4 and D0
 87                              * calls OUTCH and BINTOHEX
 88                              * called by main program
 89                              *
 90           00001082           HEXOUTPUT EQU   *
 91 001082 383C0004                        MOVE    #4,D4           * count
 92
 93                              * for D4:=4 downto 1 do ....
 94 001086 E95D                  OPLOOP  ROL     #4,D5           * rotate 4 bits
 95 001088 3005                          MOVE    D5,D0           * make a copy
 96 00108A 0240000F                      ANDI    #$F,D0          * mask off hex digit
 97 00108E 4EB810AC                      JSR     BINTOHEX        * convert to char
 98 001092 4EB81100                      JSR     OUTCH           * both subs use D0
 99 001096 5344                          SUBQ    #1,D4           * decrement count
100 001098 6EEC                          BGT     OPLOOP
101 00109A 4E75                          RTS
102                              *
103                              ********************************************************
104                              * BINTOHEX
105                              * subroutine to convert a hex number to an ASCII char
106                              * input parameter: number in range 0-15 in D0
107                              * output parameter: corresponding ASCII code in D0
108                              * called by HEXOUTPUT
109                              * the input parameter is used to index into a table
110                              * to extract the corresponding ASCII character
111                              *
112 00109C 30                    BHTABLE DC.B    '0123456789ABCDEF'
113
114           000010AC           BINTOHEX EQU    *
115 0010AC 41F8109C                       LEA     BHTABLE,A0      * base of table
116 0010B0 10300000                       MOVE.B  0(A0,D0),D0     * index table
117 0010B4 4E75                           RTS
118                              *
119                              ********************************************************
120                              *
121       STANDARD SUBROUTINES ARE NOT SHOWN - see Fig. 10.6.
216                              *
217                              ********************************************************
218                              *
219                                      END
```

****** TOTAL ERRORS   0--   0 -- TOTAL LINES 212

APPROX 2096 UNUSED SYMBOL TABLE ENTRIES

```
ACIACONT 010040 ACIAINPU 010042 ACIAOUTP 010042 ACIASTAT 010040 ATOFTST  001066
BINTOHEX 0010AC CONFIGUR 0010B6 HEXINPUT 001028 HEXOUTPU 001082 HEXTOBIN 001050
INCH     001112 IPERROR  00104A IPLOOP   00102C LINEFEED 0010B8 NEWLINE  0010EA
NOTHEX   00107C OPLOOP   001086 OUTCH    001100 PROMPT   0010C6 RESTART  00100C
SPACE    0010DC STACK    001000 START    001000 BHTABLE  00109C
```

Fig. 12.10 Hex input and output as subs

12.5   DECIMAL INPUT

In this section, the characters input by the user represents a decimal integer and each character may therefore be in the range 0–9 (ASCII code $30 to $39). The decimal number is to be converted to a 16-bit word of binary, for example:

At the keyboard/display	*Internally*
? 1024	0000 0100 0000 0000
? 2053	0000 1000 0000 0101
? A	error – not a decimal character
? 32767	0111 1111 1111 1111
? 35	0000 0000 0010 0011

Fig. 12.11

Assuming word input (into 16 bits), the maximum positive unsigned integer that can be stored is $2^{16}-1$, the maximum positive signed integer is $2^{15}-1$ (see Section 1.9).

$$2^{16}-1 = 65535$$
$$2^{15}-1 = 32767$$

In the case of a positive decimal integer to be stored in unsigned form in a single word, therefore, a sequence of five decimal characters is valid if the first is less than 6, is invalid (too large) if the first character is greater than 6 and may or may not be valid if the first character is 6. It is suggested therefore that the number is formed in a 32-bit register, and the final word result is compared against 65535. It is also suggested that a terminating character is chosen so that the user may input 1, 2, 3, 4 or 5 characters.

A basic algorithm to input a positive decimal integer is as follows:

prompt the user
clear a register (32 bits) to accumulate the answer, say D5

Input a character
Output (echo) the character
Is it the terminator ? → YES, exit from loop

NO
Validate the character, as decimal 0–9.
Convert the character to a number (subtract $30)
Multiply the answer so far (in D5) by 10 (see Section 8.4)
Add on the new number
Check the number of characters input; if less than 5 repeat the loop.

A multiply by 10 is needed for decimal (base 10) input whereas, in hexadecimal input, a left shift by four places was used, being equivalent to a multiply by 16. Multiply instructions are explained in Chapter 8.

Following the algorithms through for input of 35, for example:

?   D5 | 0000 0000 0000 0000 | 0000 0000 0000 0000 |

?3   D5 | 0011 |

?35   when the second character is input, D5 is multiplied by 10 giving decimal 30.

       D5 | 0001 1110 |

then the number 5 is added to give decimal 35.

       D5 | 0010 0011 |

Fig. 12.12

If the terminator, for example a space, is then input, D5 contains the correct result. If this basic algorithm is to be developed into a realistic subroutine, decisions must be taken over its precise specification. So far, the discussion has assumed a positive decimal integer to be stored in unsigned form terminated by a space. It is easy to modify the basic algorithm to accept positive or negative integers and a range of terminating characters. If the algorithm is developed as a subroutine, the heading should document the specification.

Fig. 12.13 is a program which includes subroutines to implement the algorithm for the simplest case of positive decimal integers to be converted into unsigned binary representation.

```
 1                        *         Figure 12.13
 2                        *
 3                        *
 4                        *
 5                        * The program shows decimal input and output
 6                        * implemented as subroutines
 7                        *
 8          00001000      STACK    EQU      $1000
 9
10          00001000               ORG      $1000
11
12 001000 4FF81000        START    LEA      STACK,SP        * load stack pointer
13 001004 4EB810B0                 JSR      CONFIGURE       * configure the ACIA
14 001008 4EB810E4                 JSR      NEWLINE
15                                 JSR      INSTRUCT        * instruct user
16 00100C 4EB810E4                 JSR      NEWLINE
17 001010 4EB810C0        RESTART  JSR      PROMPT          * output ? to user
18 001014 4EB81028                 JSR      DECINPUT        * into D5 low word
19 001018 0C00FFFF                 CMPI.B   #-1,D0          * test error code
20 00101C 67F2                     BEQ      RESTART
21 00101E 4EB810D6                 JSR      SPACE
22 001022 4EB81080                 JSR      DECOUTPUT       * from D5
23 001026 4E40                     TRAP     #0              * exit from program
24                        *
```

```
25                      ***********************************************************
26                      * DECINPUT
27                      * subroutine to input ASCII characters,
28                      * validate as decimal 0-9 and convert to binary
29                      * maximum number is 65535
30                      * output parameter: number in D5 low word
31                      * calls DECTOBIN
32                      * called by main program
33                      * uses D0,D1
34                      *
35        00000020      ITERMINATOR    EQU     $20      * space is terminator
36                      *
37        00001028      DECINPUT       EQU     *
38 001028 7205                MOVEQ   #5,D1             * max number of chars
39 00102A 4285                CLR.L   D5                * to hold number
40
41                      * for D1:=5 downto 1 do ....
42 00102C 4EB8110C      DECLOOP JSR     INCH
43 001030 4EB810FA              JSR     OUTCH           * echo
44                      * while input-char <> terminator do ....
45 001034 0C000020              CMPI.B  #ITERMINATOR,D0
46 001038 67000018              BEQ     DECEND
47 00103C 4EB8105E              JSR     DECTOBIN        * validate & convert
48 001040 0C00FFFF              CMPI.B  #-1,D0          * test error code
49 001044 67000016              BEQ     DECERROR
50 001048 CAFC000A              MULU    #10,D5          * answer so far *10
51 00104C DA00                  ADD.B   D0,D5           * add on new number
52 00104E 5341                  SUBQ    #1,D1           * decrement count
53 001050 6EDA                  BGT     DECLOOP
54 001052 0C45007F      DECEND  CMPI    #$7F,D5         * maximum number
55 001056 6E000004              BGT     DECERROR
56 00105A 4E75                  RTS
57
58        0000105C      DECERROR   EQU    *
59                      *       JSR     DECINERROR      * error handling
60                      * commented out in this program
61 00105C 4E75                  RTS
62                      *
63                      ***********************************************************
64                      * DECTOBIN
65                      * subroutine to validate a character as decimal
66                      * and to convert to the corresponding number
67                      * input parameter: character in low byte of D0
68                      * output parameters:
69                      * corresponding number in D0 if char is decimal
70                      * -1 in D0 if input character is not decimal
71                      * called by DECINPUT
72                      *
73        0000105E      DECTOBIN EQU *
74 00105E 0C000030              CMPI.B  #'0',D0
75 001062 6D000010              BLT     NOTDEC
76 001066 0C000039              CMPI.B  #'9',D0
77 00106A 6E000008              BGT     NOTDEC
78 00106E 04000030              SUBI.B  #$30,D0         * convert to number
79 001072 4E75                  RTS
80 001074 103CFFFF      NOTDEC  MOVE.B  #-1,D0          * indicate invalid
```

```
81 001078 4E75                    RTS
82                          *
83                          ********************************************************
84                          * DECOUTPUT
85                          * subroutine to output a word as decimal characters
86                          * input parameter: number in low word of D5
87                          * uses D0,D1,D4 and A6
88                          * calls OUTCH
89                          * called by main program
90                          * data area:
91 00107A 0006              DECHARS DS.B   6                   * to hold numbers
92                          *
93         00001080         DECOUTPUT  EQU  *
94 001080 4281                    CLR.L  D1
95 001082 4DF8107F                LEA    DECHARS+5,A6          * for stack pointer
96
97                          * for D1:=0 to 4 do ....
98 001086 8AFC000A          OLOOP   DIVU   #10,D5
99 00108A 4845                      SWAP   D5                  * quotient & remaindr
100 00108C 1D05                     MOVE.B D5,-(A6)            * stack remainder
101 00108E E08D                     LSR.L  #8,D5               * shift down quotient
102 001090 E08D                     LSR.L  #8,D5               * 8 is max immediate
103 001092 5241                     ADDQ   #1,D1
104                         * while quotient <> 0 do ....
105 001094 4A45                     TST    D5                  * zero quotient?
106 001096 67000008                 BEQ    DECPRINT            * no more chars
107 00109A 0C410005                 CMPI   #5,D1               * maximum of 5 chars
108 00109E 6DE6                     BLT    OLOOP
109
110 0010A0 101E             DECPRINT MOVE.B (A6)+,D0           * unstack a number
111 0010A2 06400030                 ADDI   #$30,D0            * convert to char
112 0010A6 4EB810FA                 JSR    OUTCH
113 0010AA 5341                     SUBQ   #1,D1
114 0010AC 6EF2                     BGT    DECPRINT
115 0010AE 4E75                     RTS
116                         *
117                         ********************************************************
118                         *
119     STANDARD SUBROUTINES NOT SHOWN - see Fig. 10.6.
214                         *
215                         ********************************************************
216                         *
217                                 END
```

****** TOTAL ERRORS   0--   0 -- TOTAL LINES 210

APPROX 2095 UNUSED SYMBOL TABLE ENTRIES

```
ACIACONT 010040 ACIAINPU 010042 ACIAOUTP 010042 ACIASTAT 010040 CONFIGUR 0010B0
DECEND   001052 DECERROR 00105C DECHARS  00107A DECINPUT 001028 DECLOOP  00102C
DECOUTPU 001080 DECPRINT 0010A0 DECTOBIN 00105E INCH     00110C ITERMINA 000020
LINEFEED 0010B2 NEWLINE  0010E4 NOTDEC   001074 OLOOP    001086 OUTCH    0010FA
PROMPT   0010C0 RESTART  001010 SPACE    0010D6 STACK    001000 START    001000
```

Fig. 12.13   Decimal input and output as subs

12.6   DECIMAL OUTPUT

In this Section, it will be assumed that a 16-bit word contains an unsigned integer representing a decimal number and an output routine will be developed. The largest possible number is $2^{16}-1 = 65535$ and in the basic algorithm five characters will always be output. The modification of suppressing leading zeros is discussed later.

One possible algorithm is to use the following approach, assuming 65535 is the value to be output:

$$65535 \div 10^4 \text{ gives quotient } 6 \text{ remainder } 5535$$
$$5535 \div 10^3 \text{ gives quotient } 5 \text{ remainder } 535$$
$$535 \div 10^2 \text{ gives quotient } 5 \text{ remainder } 35$$
$$35 \div 10^1 \text{ gives quotient } 3 \text{ remainder } 5$$
$$5 \div 10^0 \text{ gives quotient } 5 \text{ remainder } 0$$

This is not the most efficient algorithm but it is easy to understand. The divide instructions are described in Chapter 8. A 32-bit data register must be set up, for example:

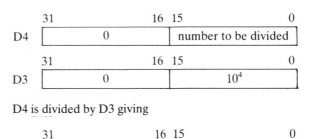

D4 is divided by D3 giving

Fig. 12.14

The quotient may be extracted (copied into another register), converted to an ASCII character by adding $30 and output. The remainder may be shifted into the low order word of D4 ready for the next division and the process repeated five times.

If suppression of leading zeros is required, the quotient may be tested for zero after each division and printing of the character suppressed until the first non-zero quotient is found for example:

$$306 \div 10^4 \text{ gives quotient } 0 \text{ remainder } 306 \text{ (suppress output)}$$
$$306 \div 10^3 \text{ gives quotient } 0 \text{ remainder } 306 \text{ (suppress output)}$$
$$306 \div 10^2 \text{ gives quotient } 3 \text{ remainder } 6 \text{ (print 3)}$$
$$6 \div 10^1 \text{ gives quotient } 0 \text{ remainder } 6 \text{ (print 0)}$$
$$6 \div 10^0 \text{ gives quotient } 6 \text{ remainder } 0 \text{ (print 6)}$$

An alternative algorithm is to repeatedly divide by 10 and to stack the remainder after each division, for example:

$$65535 \div 10 \text{ gives quotient } 6553 \text{ remainder } 5 \text{ (stack 5)}$$
$$6553 \div 10 \text{ gives quotient } 655 \text{ remainder } 3 \text{ (stack 3)}$$
$$655 \div 10 \text{ gives quotient } 65 \text{ remainder } 5 \text{ (stack 5)}$$
$$65 \div 10 \text{ gives quotient } 6 \text{ remainder } 5 \text{ (stack 5)}$$
$$6 \div 10 \text{ gives quotient } 0 \text{ remainder } 6 \text{ (stack 6)}$$

The numbers are then unstacked, thus reversing the order, converted to characters and printed. As soon as the quotient becomes zero there are no more characters so that suppression of leading zeros is easy to manage.

Fig. 12.13 is a program which provides decimal input and output as subroutines. The approach of dividing by ten and stacking the remainder is used as the output algorithm.

12.7 A PROGRAM TO DISPLAY MEMORY IN SELECTED MODES

The program in Fig. 12.15 shows the implementation of one function of a debugging facility, that of memory display. The user is instructed to input four hexadecimal characters representing an address, followed by a / and a mode key which may be H (hexadecimal), B (Binary) or A (ASCII). The contents of the specified address are output in the mode indicated. Suppose location $2001 has the following contents (expressed in binary):

$2000 [   ] [01000001] $2001

Interaction with the user is as follows:

```
? 2001/H 41
? 2001/B 01000001
? 2001/A A
```

```
 1                          *           Figure 12.15
 2                          *
 3                          *
 4                          *
 5                          * This program inputs an address as four hex chars
 6                          * and outputs the contents (a byte) in the selected
 7                          * mode, binary (/B), hexadecimal (/H) or ASCII (/A)
 8                          *
 9          00001000        STACK        EQU $1000
10          00000004        PTERMINATOR  EQU $04  * program terminator control D
11          00000007        STERMINATOR  EQU $07  * string terminator control G
12
13          00001000                     ORG    $1000

14 001000  4FF81000         INIT   LEA   STACK,SP      * load stack pointer
15 001004  4EB81204                JSR   CONFIGURE     * configure ACIA
```

```
16 001008 4EB811E8              JSR     INSTRUCT        * instruct user
17
18 00100C 4EB81238    RESTART JSR     NEWLINE
19 001010 4EB81214            JSR     PROMPT
20 001014 4EB81046            JSR     ADDRESSIN       * into D5
21 001018 0C00FFFF            CMPI.B  #-1,D0          * test error code
22 00101C 67EE               BEQ     RESTART
23 00101E 0C000004            CMPI.B  #PTERMINATOR,D0
24 001022 6700001E            BEQ     EXIT            * program terminator
25 001026 31C51044            MOVE    D5,ADDRESS      * save address
26 00102A 4EB810B0            JSR     MODEIN
27 00102E 0C00FFFF            CMPI.B  #-1,D0          * test error code
28 001032 67D8               BEQ     RESTART
29 001034 4EB8122A            JSR     SPACE
30 001038 3A381044            MOVE    ADDRESS,D5      * parameter
31 00103C 4EB810D6            JSR     CONTENTOUT      * mode still in D0
32 001040 60CA               BRA     RESTART
33 001042 4E40       EXIT    TRAP    #0              * program exit
34                   *
35                   * data area
36 001044 0002       ADDRESS DS      1
37                   *
38                   ****************************************************************
39                   * ADDRESSIN
40                   * subroutine to input a word as four hex characters
41                   * output parameters: number in low word of D5
42                   *       D0 (low byte) set to -1 on input error
43                   * uses D4 and D0
44                   * calls INCH and HEXTOBIN
45                   * called by main program
46                   *
47         00001046  ADDRESSIN EQU   *
48 001046 7805               MOVEQ   #5,D4           * max number of chars
49 001048 4285               CLR.L   D5              * to hold answer
50
51                   * for D4:=5 downto 1 do ....
52 00104A 4EB81260   IPLOOP  JSR     INCH            * input char into D0
53 00104E 4EB8124E            JSR     OUTCH           * echo
54 001052 0C00002F            CMPI.B  #'/',D0         * address terminator?
55 001056 6700001E            BEQ     IPEXIT
56 00105A 0C000004            CMPI.B  #PTERMINATOR,D0
57 00105E 67000016            BEQ     IPEXIT          * program terminator
58 001062 4EB8107E            JSR     HEXTOBIN        * validate & convert
59 001066 0C00FFFF            CMPI.B  #-1,D0          * test error code
60 00106A 6700000C            BEQ     IPERROR
61 00106E E94D               LSL     #4,D5           * shift answer so far
62 001070 DA00               ADD.B   D0,D5           * add on new number
63 001072 5344               SUBQ    #1,D4           * decrement count
64 001074 66D4               BNE     IPLOOP
65 001076 4E75       IPEXIT  RTS
66
67         00001078  IPERROR EQU     *
68                   *       JSR     INPUTERROR      * error handling
69                   * commented out in this program
70 001078 103CFFFF            MOVE.B  #-1,D0          * indicate error
71 00107C 4E75               RTS
```

```
72                        *
73                        ****************************************************
74                        * HEXTOBIN
75                        * subroutine to validate a character as hex
76                        * and to convert to the corresponding number
77                        * input parameter: character in low byte of D0
78                        * output parameters:
79                        * corresponding number in D0 if hex character input
80                        * -1 in D0 if input character is not hex
81                        * called by ADDRESSIN
82                        *
83          0000107E      HEXTOBIN EQU *
84  00107E 0C000030                CMPI.B  #´0´,D0
85  001082 6D000026                BLT     NOTHEX
86  001086 0C000039                CMPI.B  #´9´,D0
87  00108A 6E000008                BGT     ATOFTST
88  00108E 04000030                SUB.B   #$30,D0         * convert to number
89  001092 4E75                    RTS
90  001094 0C000041      ATOFTST CMPI.B  #´A´,D0
91  001098 6D000010                BLT     NOTHEX
92  00109C 0C000046                CMPI.B  #´F´,D0
93  0010A0 6E000008                BGT     NOTHEX
94  0010A4 04000037                SUB.B   #$37,D0         * convert to number
95  0010A8 4E75                    RTS
96  0010AA 103CFFFF      NOTHEX  MOVE.B  #-1,D0          * indicate invalid
97  0010AE 4E75                    RTS
100                       * MODEIN
101                       * subroutine to input and validate the output mode
102                       * required, ASCII(A), Binary(B) or Hex(H)
103                       * uses D0
104                       * calls OUTCH
105                       * called by main program
106                       *
107         000010B0      MODEIN  EQU     *
108 0010B0 4EB81260                JSR     INCH
109 0010B4 4EB8124E                JSR     OUTCH           * echo
110 0010B8 0C000041                CMPI.B  #´A´,D0
111 0010BC 67000016                BEQ     MODEXIT
112 0010C0 0C000042                CMPI.B  #´B´,D0
113 0010C4 6700000E                BEQ     MODEXIT
114 0010C8 0C000048                CMPI.B  #´H´,D0
115 0010CC 67000006                BEQ     MODEXIT
116 0010D0 103CFFFF                MOVE.B  #-1,D0          * indicate invalid
117 0010D4 4E75          MODEXIT RTS
118                       *
119                       ****************************************************
120                       * CONTENTOUT
121                       * subroutine to output the contents of an address
122                       * in a selected mode binary(B), hex(H) or ASCII(A)
123                       * input parameters: address in D5 low word
124                       *                   mode in D0 low byte
125                       * uses D0,A0
126                       * calls HEXOUT, BINOUT, ASCIIOUT
127                       * called by main program
128                       *
129         000010D6      CONTENTOUT      EQU     *
```

```
130 0010D6 3045                    MOVEA    D5,A0
131 0010D8 1A10                    MOVE.B   (A0),D5        * get contents
132 0010DA 0C000048                CMPI.B   #'H',DO
133 0010DE 67000014                BEQ      HMODE
134 0010E2 0C000042                CMPI.B   #'B',DO
135 0010E6 67000012                BEQ      BMODE
136 0010EA 0C000041                CMPI.B   #'A',DO
137 0010EE 67000010                BEQ      AMODE
138 0010F2 4E75                    RTS
139 0010F4 4EB81138    HMODE       JSR      HEXOUT
140 0010F8 4E75                    RTS
141 0010FA 4EB81106    BMODE       JSR      BINOUT
142 0010FE 4E75                    RTS
143 001100 4EB8111E    AMODE       JSR      ASCIIOUT
144 001104 4E75                    RTS
145
146
147                                * BINOUT
148                                * subroutine to output 8 bits as 8 chars (0 or 1)
149                                * input parameter: byte for output in D5
150                                * uses D0,D1
151                                * calls OUTCH
152                                * called by CONTENTOUT
153         00001106    BINOUT  EQU      *
154 001106 7208                   MOVEQ    #8,D1          * number of chars
155                                * for D1:=8 downto 1 do ....
156 001108 E31D        BINLOOP ROL.B    #1,D5
157 00110A 1005                   MOVE.B   D5,D0          * make a copy
158 00110C 02000001               ANDI.B   #$1,D0         * mask off a bit
159 001110 06000030               ADDI.B   #$30,D0        * convert to char
160 001114 4EB8124E               JSR      OUTCH
161 001118 5341                   SUBQ     #1,D1          * decrement count
162 00111A 6EEC                   BGT      BINLOOP
163 00111C 4E75                   RTS
164                                *
165                                ********************************************************
166                                * ASCIIOUT
167                                * subroutine to output a byte as an ASCII char
168                                * input parameter: byte in D5
169                                * uses D0
170                                * called by CONTENTOUT
171                                * calls OUTCH
172                                * action on non-printing character is not shown
173                                *
174         0000111E    ASCIIOUT        EQU      *
175 00111E 0C050020               CMPI.B   #$20,D5
176 001122 6D000012               BLT      NONPRINTING
177 001126 0C05007F               CMPI.B   #$7F,D5
178 00112A 6E00000A               BGT      NONPRINTING
179 00112E 1005                   MOVE.B   D5,D0
180 001130 4EB8124E               JSR      OUTCH
181 001134 4E75                   RTS
182         00001136    NONPRINTING     EQU      *
183                                *       JSR      NONPRINTACTION
184                                * not implemented, commented out in this program
185 001136 4E75                   RTS
```

```
188                            * HEXOUT
189                            * subroutine to output a byte as two hex characters
190                            * input parameter: number in low byte of D5
191                            * uses D4 and D0
192                            * calls OUTCH and BINTOHEX
193                            * called by CONTENTOUT
194                            *
195          00001138          HEXOUT EQU     *
196 001138 383C0002                   MOVE    #2,D4               * count
197                            * for D4:=2 downto 1 do ...
198 00113C E91D               OPLOOP ROL.B    #4,D5               * rotate 4 bits
199 00113E 1005                       MOVE.B  D5,D0               * make a copy
200 001140 0200000F                   ANDI.B  #$F,D0              * mask off hex digit
201 001144 4EB81162                   JSR     BINTOHEX            * call sub to convert
202 001148 4EB8124E                   JSR     OUTCH               * both subs use D0
203 00114C 5344                       SUBQ    #1,D4               * decrement count
204 00114E 6EEC                       BGT     OPLOOP
205 001150 4E75                       RTS
206                            *
207                            *******************************************************
208                            * BINTOHEX
209                            * subroutine to convert a hex number to ASCII
210                            * input parameter: number in range 0-15 in D0
211                            * output parameter: corresponding ASCII code in D0
212                            * called by HEXOUT
213                            * the input parameter is used to index into a table
214                            * to extract the corresponding ASCII character
215                            *
216 001152 30                 BHTABLE DC.B    '0123456789ABCDEF'
217
218          00001162          BINTOHEX EQU    *
219 001162 41F81152                   LEA     BHTABLE,A0          * base of table
220 001166 10300000                   MOVE.B  0(A0,D0),D0         * index table
221 00116A 4E75                       RTS
222                            *
223                            *******************************************************
224                            *
225      STANDARD SUBROUTINES NOT SHOWN - see Fig. 10.6.
358                            *
359                            *******************************************************
361                                    END
```

****** TOTAL ERRORS   0--   0 -- TOTAL LINES 353

APPROX 2079 UNUSED SYMBOL TABLE ENTRIES

```
ACIACONT 010040 ACIAINPU 010042 ACIAOUTP 010042 ACIASTAT 010040 ADDRESS  001044
ADDRESSI 001046 AMODE    001100 ASCIIOUT 00111E ATOFTST  001094 BHTABLE  001152
BINLOOP  001108 BINOUT   001106 BINTOHEX 001162 BMODE    0010FA CONFIGUR 001204
CONTENTO 0010D6 EXIT     001042 HEXOUT   001138 HEXTOBIN 00107E HMODE    0010F4
INCH     001260 INITMESS 00116C INIT     001000 INSTRUCT 0011E8 IPERROR  001078
IPEXIT   001076 IPLOOP   00104A LINEFEED 001206 MODEIN   0010B0 MODEXIT  0010D4
NEWLINE  001238 NONPRINT 001136 NOTHEX   0010AA OPLOOP   00113C OSEXIT   001202
OUTCH    00124E OUTSTRIN 0011F2 PROMPT   001214 PTERMINA 000004 RESTART  00100C
SPACE    00122A STACK    001000 STERMINA 000007
```

Fig. 12.15 Debug program

The basic program may be extended:

- To allow an additional switch to request byte, word or longword display. A check must then be made that word and longword display is requested at an even address.
- To allow an extended range of modes, for example:
  D (decimal)
  I (instruction).
  The latter is a complex facility requiring an inverse translation from a binary pattern to a mnemonic instruction (disassembly).
- To allow display of a sequence of locations, for example, if the user presses 'return', the contents of the next location in sequence are output. An escape character, for example '.' is required.
- To allow update after display as provided in the memory modify MM facility of TUTOR, see Section 3.4.

12.8   A PROGRAM TO PERFORM TEXT ANALYSIS

The program in Fig. 12.16 instructs the user to type in a piece of text with a specified terminator. A table of frequency of occurrence of alphabetic characters is then output. Upper and lower case alphabets are combined.

```
1                        *          Figure 12.16
2                        *
3                        *
4                        *
5                        * The program inputs a piece of text terminated by
6                        * control G and outputs a frequency analysis of the
7                        * alphabetic characters, both upper and lower case
8                        *
9           00001000     STACK        EQU     $1000
10          00000004     PTERMINATOR  EQU     $04  * program terminator control D
11          00000007     STERMINATOR  EQU     $07  * string terminator control G
12
13          00001000                  ORG     $1000
14 001000 4FF81000       START  LEA    STACK,SP       * load stack pointer
15 001004 4EB811CA              JSR    CONFIGURE      * configure ACIA
16 001008 4EB8106C              JSR    INITTAB        * clear table
17 00100C 4EB811AE              JSR    INSTRUCT       * instructions to user
18 001010 4EB811DA              JSR    PROMPT
19
20                      * while input-char <> terminator do ....
21 001014 4EB81226       INLOOP JSR    INCH
22 001018 4EB81214              JSR    OUTCH          * echo to screen
23 00101C 0C000004              CMPI.B #PTERMINATOR,D0
24 001020 67000010              BEQ    OUT            * input finished
25 001024 4EB810EA              JSR    VALIDATE       * alphabetic?
26 001028 4A00                  TST.B  D0             * test error code
```

```
27 00102A 67E8              BEQ     INLOOP      * ignore invalid char
28 00102C 4EB8107C          JSR     COUNTALPH   * add to frequency
29 001030 60E2              BRA     INLOOP
30 001032 4EB8108E  OUT     JSR     PRINTTAB    * output frequencies
31 001036 4E40      EXIT    TRAP    #0          * exit from program
32                          *
33                          **********************************************************
34                          * MODULE TO MANAGE FREQUENCY TABLE
35                          **********************************************************
36                          *
37                          * module data area
38 001038 0034      FREQTAB DS.W    26       * not initialized to 0
39                          *
40                          **********************************************************
41                          * INITTAB
42                          * subroutine to clear frequency table
43                          * no input or output parameters
44                          * called from main program (initialization)
45                          * uses D1,A0
46                          *
47        0000106C  INITTAB EQU     *
48 00106C 323C001A          MOVE    #26,D1      * length of table
49 001070 41F81038          LEA     FREQTAB,A0  * base of table
50 001074 4258      INITLOOP CLR    (A0)+       * clear table
51 001076 5341              SUBQ    #1,D1
52 001078 6EFA              BGT     INITLOOP
53 00107A 4E75              RTS
54                          *
55                          **********************************************************
56                          * COUNTALPH
57                          * subroutine to count frequency of letters
58                          * by adding to FREQUTAB
59                          * input parameter: char in D0
60                          * no output parameters
61                          * uses A0
62        0000107C  COUNTALPH EQU   *
63 00107C 41F81038          LEA     FREQTAB,A0  * table base
64 001080 04400041          SUB     #$41,D0     * convert to number
65 001084 C0FC0002          MULU    #2,D0       * word table
66 001088 52700000          ADDQ    #1,0(A0,D0) * count in table
67 00108C 4E75              RTS
68                          *
69                          **********************************************************
70                          * PRINTTAB
71                          * subroutine to print out frequency table with
72                          * format: letter followed by frequency
73                          * no input or output parameters
74                          * called from main program
75                          * calls DECOUT
76                          * uses  D1,D2,D5,A0
77                          *
78        0000108E  PRINTTAB EQU    *
79 00108E 41F81038          LEA     FREQTAB,A0  * table base
80 001092 721A              MOVEQ   #26,D1      * count
81 001094 143C0041          MOVE.B  #´A´,D2
82                          * for D1:=26 downto 1 do ....
```

```
 83 001098 4EB811FE   PRINTLOOP JSR    NEWLINE
 84 00109C 1002                 MOVE.B D2,D0        * letter to D0
 85 00109E 4EB81214             JSR    OUTCH
 86 0010A2 5242                 ADDQ   #1,D2        * form next letter
 87 0010A4 4EB811F0             JSR    SPACE
 88 0010A8 3A18                 MOVE   (A0)+,D5     * get frequency
 89 0010AA 4EB810BA             JSR    DECOUT       * convert to decimal
 90 0010AE 5341                 SUBQ   #1,D1        * decrement count
 91 0010B0 6EE6                 BGT    PRINTLOOP
 92 0010B2 4E75                 RTS
 93                    *
 94                    ********************************************************
 95                    * END OF MODULE
 96                    ********************************************************
 97                    * DECOUT
 98                    * subroutine to output a word as decimal characters
 99                    * input parameter: number in low word of D5
100                    * uses D0, D4 and A6
101                    * calls OUTCH
102                    * called by main program
103                    * data area:
104 0010B4 0006       DECHARS DS.B    6            * to hold numbers
105                    *
106        000010BA   DECOUT  EQU     *
107 0010BA 4284               CLR.L   D4
108 0010BC 4DF810B9           LEA     DECHARS+5,A6 * for stack pointer
109 0010C0 8AFC000A   OLOOP   DIVU    #10,D5
110 0010C4 4845               SWAP    D5           * quotient & remaindr
111 0010C6 1D05               MOVE.B  D5,-(A6)     * stack remainder
112 0010C8 E08D               LSR.L   #8,D5        * shift down quotient
113 0010CA E08D               LSR.L   #8,D5        * 8 is max immediate
114 0010CC 5244               ADDQ    #1,D4
115 0010CE 4A45               TST     D5           * zero quotient?
116 0010D0 67000008           BEQ     DECPRINT     * no more chars
117 0010D4 0C440005           CMPI    #5,D4        * maximum of 5 chars
118 0010D8 6DE6               BLT     OLOOP
119
120 0010DA 101E       DECPRINT MOVE.B (A6)+,D0     * unstack a number
121 0010DC 06400030            ADDI   #$30,D0      * convert to char
122 0010E0 4EB81214            JSR    OUTCH
123 0010E4 5344                SUBQ   #1,D4
124 0010E6 6EF2                BGT    DECPRINT
125 0010E8 4E75                RTS
126                    *
127                    ********************************************************
128                    * VALIDATE
129                    * subroutine to test if a char is alphabetic
130                    * input parameter: char in D0
131                    * output parameter:
132                    * 0 in D0 if char not alphabetic
133                    * char still in D0 if u.c. alphabetic
134                    * corresponding u.c. char in D0 if l.c.
135                    *
136        000010EA   VALIDATE EQU    *
137 0010EA 0C000041            CMPI.B #'A',D0
138 0010EE 6D00000C            BLT    NOTUCALPH
```

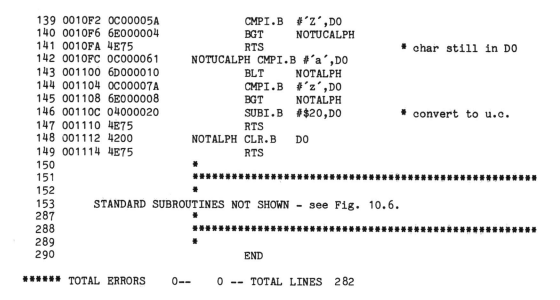

```
139 0010F2 0C00005A          CMPI.B  #'Z',DO
140 0010F6 6E000004          BGT     NOTUCALPH
141 0010FA 4E75              RTS              * char still in DO
142 0010FC 0C000061 NOTUCALPH CMPI.B #'a',DO
143 001100 6D000010          BLT     NOTALPH
144 001104 0C00007A          CMPI.B  #'z',DO
145 001108 6E000008          BGT     NOTALPH
146 00110C 04000020          SUBI.B  #$20,DO  * convert to u.c.
147 001110 4E75              RTS
148 001112 4200     NOTALPH  CLR.B   DO
149 001114 4E75              RTS
150                     *
151                     ********************************************************
152                     *
153      STANDARD SUBROUTINES NOT SHOWN - see Fig. 10.6.
287                     *
288                     ********************************************************
289                     *
290                          END

****** TOTAL ERRORS   0--   0 -- TOTAL LINES  282


APPROX  2086 UNUSED SYMBOL TABLE ENTRIES

ACIACONT 010040 ACIAINPU 010042 ACIAOUTP 010042 ACIASTAT 010040 CONFIGUR 0011CA
COUNTALP 00107C DECHARS  0010B4 DECOUT   0010BA DECPRINT 0010DA EXIT     001036
FREQTAB  001038 INCH     001226 INITLOOP 001074 INITMESS 001116 INITTAB  00106C
INLOOP   001014 INSTRUCT 0011AE LINEFEED 0011CC NEWLINE  0011FE NOTALPH  001112
NOTUCALP 0010FC OLOOP    0010C0 OSEXIT   0011C8 OUT      001032 OUTCH    001214
OUTSTRIN 0011B8 PRINTLOO 001098 PRINTTAB 00108E PROMPT   0011DA PTERMINA 000004
SPACE    0011F0 STACK    001000 START    001000 STERMINA 000007 VALIDATE 0010EA
```

Fig. 12.16 Frequency analysis of text

Since the table (of 26 words) in which the frequencies of the letters are accumulated is accessed by three subroutines INITTAB, COUNTTAB and PRINT-TAB, a module has been used, encapsulating the three subroutines with the table. In some high level languages (Simula 67, Modula 1, Modula 2, Concurrent Pascal, etc.) this kind of structure is supported and enforced by the compiler.

In assembly language programs, disciplined use of data must be self imposed but the commenting of the program can make the intended structure clear. Modular structure is also discussed in Section 7.7.

The program could be extended to represent the frequencies of the letters in the form of a histogram. This is a simple task for a short piece of text but in a more realistic application, where, for example, input is taken from a file, problems of scaling would arise.

13

Device interrupt programming

13.1   INTRODUCTION

In Chapter 10 it was shown that, when the 68000 is executing a program which interacts frequently with peripherals, it spends most of its time idle, waiting for the peripheral to input or output. The analogy given there was that if the times involved are scaled up by $10 \uparrow 6$ the processor will spend a few seconds executing a few instructions which access the memory but will have to wait for a day for one input or output instruction to complete. The method of programming used, called busy status programming, was for the processor to loop, testing a status bit and waiting for it to be changed by the hardware from 0 (device busy) to 1 (device free).

On input, the *device busy* status indicates that a character is not yet available in the input data register in the interface. On output, 'device busy' indicates that the output data register is not yet free for a new character to be sent to it since its previous contents are still in the process of being output.

In this chapter, a method of device programming called interrupt programming is introduced. Mechanisms are provided in the hardware to allow use to be made of the waiting time described above and interrupt programming is the style of device programming which makes use of these mechanisms.

The essential new mechanism is that the device interface must tell the processor, by sending an *interrupt signal*, that it has a character ready in its input data register on input or that its output data register is ready for a new character on output. If this is done, the processor no longer has to 'busy wait' in a loop which repeatedly tests the appropriate bit in the status register in the interface. Instead, it can make use of what was previously idle time by executing some other program in parallel.

In summary:

Busy status programming: the processor loops, testing a register in the device interface (see Fig. 13.1).

Interrupt programming: the processor starts the device doing input or output, gets on with executing some other program in parallel until the device signals to the processor (sends an interrupt signal) that it has done the assigned task. The

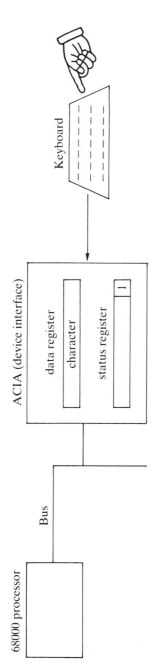

(a) *Busy status* – the device interface sits passively with the receive status bit set; the processor must test this bit to find out if a character is ready in the data register

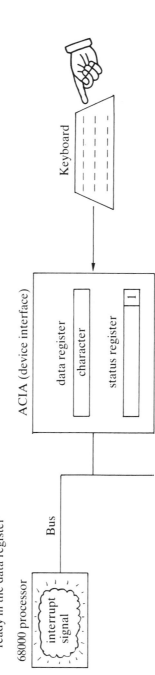

(b) *With receive interrupts enabled* – the device interface actively sends an interrupt signal to the processor to tell it that a character is ready in the data register

Fig. 13.1

processor then leaves the parallel program temporarily (i.e. is interrupted), services and possibly restarts the device then returns to the interrupted parallel program (see Fig. 13.1).

In the programs that have been developed so far, there would be no point in using interrupt programming since within any one of these programs there is little or no processing that could be carried out in parallel with input and output. It must be emphasized that interrupt programming is more complex than busy status programming and it should therefore only be used when a real advantage is to be gained.

The kind of software that requires interrupt programming is:

- Process control or real-time systems – a large number of devices must be handled and there may be time constraints, i.e. a given device must be serviced in a specified time or data will be lost.
- Operating systems – even in an operating system which supports only a single user, activities such as printing a file, reading from disc, performing VDU input or output and program execution may be carried out in parallel. In operating systems which support more than one simultaneous user, it is essential that while one user's program waits for input or output another program is run in parallel.

In this chapter the hardware mechanisms to support interrupt programming are explained and some simple interrupt programs are developed. Chapter 14 discusses the general topic of exceptions and exception-handling and device interrupt programming is then shown in a more general context.

It will be assumed in the example programs developed here that there is in fact some parallel program the CPU can execute. A dummy WORK program will be used which never terminates and counts forever in a register. By examining this register the user can see that WORK has been executed in parallel with the input and output.

Interrupt programs will have at least three components:

- Initialization.
- WORK that is always available for execution.
- An Interrupt Service Routine to program a device.

In these initial examples, input from and output to a single device are programmed under interrupt control in order to illustrate the basic concepts. Before the programs can be developed further the hardware support for interrupt programming is explained.

13.2   THE 68000 PROCESSOR STATUS REGISTER

In Section 5.3 the user byte of the status register, containing condition codes, was described. The system byte must now be considered.

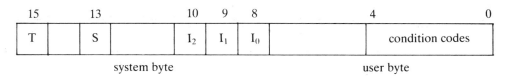

Fig. 13.2

bit 15: T   T = 1 indicates that trace mode is on
bit 13: S   If S = 1 the processor is executing in supervisor state
                 If S = 0 the processor is executing in user state
bits 10 – 8: $I_2 I_1 I_0$ A 3-bit field with value range 000 to 111 (0 to 7 decimal) called the 'interrupt mask'

13.2.1 The interrupt mask

The value in this field indicates the level of priority at which the processor is executing ranging from 0 (lowest) to 7 (highest). The value set in this field on initial RESET is 7 and it may be changed by program using, for example, ANDI #F8FF,SR which sets the interrupt mask to 0 and leaves the rest of the status register unchanged. The MOVE,ORI and EORI instructions may also be used. Each device interface is assigned an interrupt level, for example, the ACIA is assigned to level 4. If the processor is executing at level 4 or higher it will ignore an interrupt signal from the ACIA. If it is executing at levels 0, 1, 2 or 3 it will service the device, temporarily leaving its current program, i.e. an interrupt takes place. How this is effected is explained in the rest of this chapter.

   ABORT is assigned the highest priority and pressing this button always causes the processor to abandon its current program (see also Section 13.9).

13.2.2 System and user state

When the processor is executing in system state, the full capability of the hardware is available to it. Every instruction in the instruction set may be executed and every programmable register may be read or written. This is the initial state of the processor and deliberate action has to be taken to move into user state, i.e. the S bit in the processor status register must be changed from 1 to 0. This may be effected by ANDI #DFFF,SR.

   When the processor is executing in user state, some instructions may not be executed and some registers may not be written to. In particular, a program executing in user state must be prevented from writing to the system byte of the processor status register or it could put itself into system state with full privileges. The mechanism for enforcing this is explained in Chapter 14 and the set of restrictions comprising the lower privilege of user state are listed there.

The fact that the 68000 processor can execute in two states, supervisor state with full privileges and user state with restricted privileges, makes it suitable for building the operating system level of Fig. 1.1. The 8-bit microprocessors lack this facility and their operating systems are therefore comparatively unprotected. This topic is discussed further in Chapter 14.

The main emphasis at this point is to explain how devices are programmed under interrupt control.

13.2.3 System and user stack pointers

The use of A7 or SP as a stack pointer for implementing a control stack for subroutine call and return was explained in Chapter 7. All the subsequent example programs have made liberal use of subroutines as a structuring tool.

In fact there are two control stack pointers in the 68000 processor, the system stack pointer SSP and the user stack pointer USP. Both are accessed by program as A7 or SP. If the processor is executing in supervisor state, SSP is used by the hardware and, if in user state, USP is selected. This allows the construction of a system stack and one or more user stacks. One of the privileges of supervisor state is to be allowed access to USP through specific instructions which explicitly name USP. User programs must be prevented from accessing the system stack or SSP.

13.3 KEYBOARD INPUT USING INTERRUPTS – INTRODUCTION

As an introduction to interrupt programming, a single task, keyboard input, is programmed under interrupt control. A program is developed which contains:

- Initialization.
- A WORK routine which executes at level 0.
- An interrupt service routine for the ACIA which interrupts at level 4.

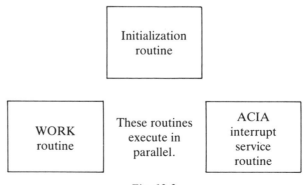

Fig. 13.3

The complete program is given in Fig. 13.10. The task is to input a string of characters of maximum length 100 terminated by control D into a buffer area. This is of course carried out in parallel with execution of the WORK routine as shown in Fig. 13.3.

13.4 INITIALIZATION – THE ACIA CONTROL REGISTER

This register was introduced in Section 10.4.2. It is accessed at address $30061 in the example configuration used in this text. Fields of the control register which have not yet been described are required for interrupt programming as shown in Fig. 13.4:

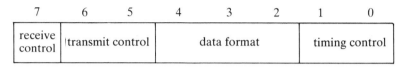

Fig. 13.4

and the register was configured for busy status programming to:

$$\boxed{0 \mid 0 \quad 0 \mid 1 \quad 0 \quad 1 \mid 0 \mid 1}$$

Fig. 13.5

Configuring this register with bits 7, 6, and 5 cleared, disables receive and transmit interrupts from the ACIA, i.e. no interrupt signals are sent to the processor.

If a program is to be written in which receive interrupt signals are sent from the ACIA and effect an interrupt, bit 7 must be set to 1 to 'enable receive interrupts'. Configuration is now achieved by:

MOVE.B   #$95, ACIACONTROL

This ensures that if a program is executing at a level less than 4 then a receive interrupt signal from the ACIA will cause the 68000 processor to leave the program (i.e. be interrupted) and attend to the device, i.e. read the character. Note that transmit interrupts are still disabled.

The ACIA also requires initial RESET as described in Chapter 10.

13.5 INTERRUPT VECTORS

We must now focus on how the processor is interrupted from fetching and executing instructions from the WORK routine and starts fetching and executing instructions from a level 4 interrupt service routine. There must clearly be some hardware assistance as interrupts occur in 'real time', i.e. at unpredictable or random times. It can be seen from Fig. 13.6 that the flow of control is the same as for a subroutine call even though there is no JSR instruction in the WORK routine.

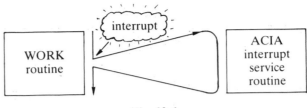

Fig. 13.6

The convention used is that the addresses of the various interrupt service routines must be put in a fixed, pre-arranged place in the memory. When an interrupt signal arrives, the processor can pick up the value to put in the program counter (the service routine address) from the agreed place in memory. The full list of interrupt vectors is given as Fig. 14.1. Those of interest to the device programmer are shown in Fig. 13.7.

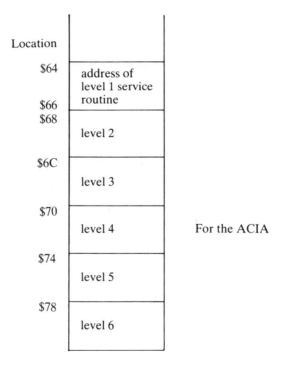

Fig. 13.7

If the level 4 interrupt service routine is called LEV4ISR this address must be put in location $70.

MOVE.L   #LEV4ISR, $70

A long move is required since 32 bits are allocated to each level. This gives full generality of where the service routines can be located in memory.

13.5.1 The keyboard input program in outline

More detail can now be filled in in the modules of the program to input a string of characters from the keyboard under interrupt control. The complete program is given in Fig. 13.8.

```
Initialization
  • Configure the Device Interface including
    interrupt enabling (of receive interrupts)
  • Set up the Interrupt Vector
  • Set the processor status register (SR) to
    level 0
  • Pass control to WORK
```

```
Work routine
Count forever
in a register
```

```
Level 4 interrupt service routine
  • Check the ACIASTATUS bit
  • Transfer character (unset interrupt)
  • Exit (return to WORK)
```

Fig. 13.8

13.6 PROCESSOR ACTION TO EFFECT AN INTERRUPT

When a device interface sends an interrupt signal to the processor, the information supplied is as shown in Fig. 13.9.

In detail, the device interface makes an initial interrupt request and supplies its priority level. This is left pending until execution of the current instruction is complete. The processor then compares the priority level of the interrupt request with the interrupt mask in its status register SR and, if the level of the interrupt signal is higher than that of the current program, an interrupt is effected. The processor then acknowledges the interrupt and requests the interrupt vector number from the device interface. This is supplied by the interface and the processor computes the vector address by multiplying by four.

The processor must save the state of the interrupted program so that it can be resumed when interrupt service is complete. In practice SR and PC are saved on the

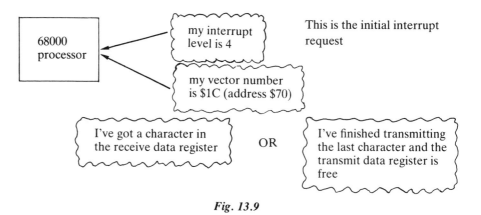

Fig. 13.9

system stack. The new context may then be set up in SR and PC. The steps taken are as follows:

- The processor status register SR is copied into a 68000 internal register.
- In SR, the status bit is set to 1 (supervisor state) and the trace bit T is set to 0 (trace mode disabled).
- The processor gets the interrupt level of the device and sets it in the interrupt mask in SR.
- The processor gets the interrupt vector number from the device and computes the interrupt vector location (4 × vector number).
- The program counter PC is stacked (SSP is used since S = 1). The saved SR is stacked.
- The PC is set up from the interrupt vector location.
- Fetch and execute continues (now from the interrupt service routine).

Returning to the interrupted program
The instruction RTE, return from exception, sets up the program counter and status register from the stack thus effecting a return to the interrupted program.

An interrupt service routine has similarities with a subroutine. It is entered by hardware as described above, the interrupted PC being stacked by hardware (comparable with hardware stacking of the link address on subroutine call). The differences are lack of an explicit call and automatic stacking of SR in addition to PC. Return from subroutine, RTS, causes PC to be set up from the stack, RTE causes PC and SR to be set up from the stack, to summarize:

Subroutine call and return	*Interrupt service*
• explicit call by JSR or BSR	• automatic entry by hardware
• PC stacked on entry	• PC and SR stacked on entry
• SR unchanged	• SR set to a new context
	– supervisor state
	– trace disabled
	– interrupt level
• exit by RTS (unstacks into PC)	• exit by RTE
	(unstacks into PC and SR)

The sequence of events described above is modified slightly to accommodate peripherals that were designed for the 6800 processor. In this case the peripheral, instead of supplying the vector number, requests that the processor should compute the vector number corresponding to the interrupt level. Details and further references are given in the 68000 processor reference manual, ref. 4.

13.7   THE KEYBOARD INPUT PROGRAM

All aspects of the program in Fig. 13.10 have now been covered. The program is structured as an initialization module followed by a WORK module then an interrupt service module. The details shown in the initialization module would, in more realistic programs, be provided in subroutines. At this stage the detail is of interest and is given at the top level.

```
 1                          *
 2                          *
 3                          *
 4                          *
 5                          * this program illustrates interrupt programming
 6                          * for input from the keyboard
 7
 8                          ********************
 9                          * INITIALIZATION  *
10                          ********************
11
12          00001000        STACK   EQU     $1000
13
14          00001000                ORG     $1000
15
16 001000 4FF81000          INITIAL LEA     STACK,SP       * load stack pointer
17                          * set up interrupt vectors:
18 001004 21FC0000111A
          0064              VECTINIT        MOVE.L  #INT1,$64       * level 1
19 00100C 21FC0000111C
          0068                              MOVE.L  #INT2,$68       * level 2
20 001014 21FC0000111E
          006C                              MOVE.L  #INT3,$6C       * level 3
21 00101C 21FC000010DA
          0070                              MOVE.L  #ACIAISR,$70    * level 4
22 001024 21FC00001120
          0074                              MOVE.L  #INT5,$74       * level 5
23 00102C 21FC00001122
          0078                              MOVE.L  #INT6,$78       * level 6
24
25 001034 4EB810B2                  JSR     RESET           * ACIA initial RESET
26 001038 4EB810C4                  JSR     CONFIGURE       * configure & enable
27 00103C 4EB810CE                  JSR     INITINPUT       * initialize data
28
29                          * set the 68000 status register to level 0:
30 001040 027CF8FF                  ANDI    #$F8FF,SR
32                          * end of initialization section
```

```
33                              ********************************************************
34                              * WORK MODULE *
35                              ***************
36                              *
37          00001044            WORK     EQU     *
38 001044 4286                           CLR.L   D6
39 001046 5286                  WLOOP    ADDQ.L  #1,D6
40 001048 60FC                           BRA     WLOOP   * loop forever incrementing D
41                              *
42                              ********************************************************
43                              * INPUT MODULE - INITIALIZATION AND INTERRUPT SERVICE
44                              ********************************************************
45                              *
46          00000004            TERMINATOR EQU   $04     * control D
47          00030061            ACIASTATUS EQU   $30061  * status register read only
48          00030061            ACIACONTROL EQU  $30061  * control register write only
49          00030063            ACIAINPUT EQU    $30063  * input data register
50          00030063            ACIAOUTPUT EQU   $30063  * output data register
51                              *
52                              * data area
53 00104A 0064                  INBUFF   DS.B    100     * input buffer area
54 0010AE 0002                  IBUFFPTR DS.W    1       * working pointer
55 0010B0 0002                  ICHARCOUNT DS.W  1       * number of chars input
56                              *
57                              ********************************************************
58                              * RESET
59                              * subroutine for initial RESET of ACIA
60                              *
61          000010B2            RESET    EQU     *
62 0010B2 13FC0003
          00030061                       MOVE.B  #3,ACIACONTROL
63                              * wait for RESET to take effect
64 0010BA 303C0400                        MOVE    #$400,D0
65 0010BE 5340                  RLOOP    SUBQ    #1,D0
66 0010C0 66FC                           BNE     RLOOP
67 0010C2 4E75                           RTS
68                              *
69                              ********************************************************
70                              * CONFIGURE
71                              * subroutine for initial configuration
72                              * also enables receive interrupts
73                              *
74          000010C4            CONFIGURE EQU    *
75 0010C4 13FC0095
          00030061                       MOVE.B  #$95,ACIACONTROL
76 0010CC 4E75                           RTS
77                              *
78                              ********************************************************
79                              * INITINPUT
80                              * subroutine to initialize data
81                              *
82          000010CE            INITINPUT EQU    *
83 0010CE 427810B0                        CLR     ICHARCOUNT
84                              * move address of buffer into buffer pointer
85 0010D2 31FC104A10AE                    MOVE    #INBUFF,IBUFFPTR
```

```
86 0010D8 4E75                       RTS
87                          *
88                          ****************************************************
89                          * ACIAISR
90                          * interrupt service routine for ACIA
91                          * registers used are saved on stack and restored
92                          *
93         000010DA         ACIAISR EQU  *
94 0010DA 2F00                      MOVE.L  D0,-(SP)        * save D0 on stack
95 0010DC 2F08                      MOVE.L  A0,-(SP)        * save A0 on stack
96 0010DE 08390000
           00030061                 BTST    #0,ACIASTATUS   * check rx interrupt
97 0010E6 6700002E                  BEQ     ERROR           * shouldn't be here
98
99 0010EA 103900030063             MOVE.B  ACIAINPUT,D0    * read char into D0
100 0010F0 0C000004                 CMPI.B  #TERMINATOR,D0
101 0010F4 67000022                 BEQ     FINISH          * terminator found
102
103 0010F8 307810AE                 MOVE    IBUFFPTR,A0
104 0010FC 10C0                     MOVE.B  D0,(A0)+        * store in buffer
105 0010FE 31C810AE                 MOVE    A0,IBUFFPTR     * save buffer pointer
106
107 001102 527810B0                 ADDQ    #1,ICHARCOUNT
108 001106 0C78006410B0             CMPI    #100,ICHARCOUNT
109 00110C 6700000A                 BEQ     FINISH          * buffer full
110
111 001110 205F                     MOVE.L  (SP)+,A0        * restore A0
112 001112 201F                     MOVE.L  (SP)+,D0        * restore D0
113 001114 4E73                     RTE                     * return
114
115 001116 4E40             ERROR   TRAP    #0              * exit from program
116
117 001118 4E40             FINISH  TRAP    #0              * exit from program
118                          ****************************************************
119                          * interrupts should not occur at levels 1,2,3,5,6
120                          * the service routines cause a clean exit
121 00111A 4E40             INT1    TRAP    #0              * exit from program
122 00111C 4E40             INT2    TRAP    #0
123 00111E 4E40             INT3    TRAP    #0
124 001120 4E40             INT5    TRAP    #0
125 001122 4E40             INT6    TRAP    #0
126
127                          ****************************************************
128                                  END

****** TOTAL ERRORS   0--    0 -- TOTAL LINES  117


APPROX  2096 UNUSED SYMBOL TABLE ENTRIES

ACIACONT 030061 ACIAINPU 030063 ACIAISR  0010DA ACIAOUTP 030063 ACIASTAT 030061
CONFIGUR 0010C4 ERROR    001116 FINISH   001118 IBUFFPTR 0010AE ICHARCOU 0010B0
INBUFF   00104A INITIAL  001000 INITINPU 0010CE INT1     00111A INT2     00111C
INT3     00111E INT5     001120 INT6     001122 RESET    0010B2 RLOOP    0010BE
STACK    001000 TERMINAT 000004 VECTINIT 001004 WLOOP    001046 WORK     001044
```

Fig. 13.10   Keyboard input under interrupt control

Initialization

- The stack pointer is loaded.
- The device interrupt vectors are set up. In this program, the only device to be programmed is at level 4. Interrupt service routines have been provided for levels 1, 2, 3, 4, 5, and 6 which merely exit into TUTOR since something is seriously wrong if interrupts occur at these levels. The initialization of the vectors for these routines and the routines themselves provide a skeleton for development of more realistic interrupt programs.
- The ACIA is configured.
  RESET is as for busy status programming. The control register is set up to enable receive interrupts.
- A pointer is initialized to a buffer area for storing the string of characters which are to be input and a count of the number of characters input is initialized to zero.
- The processor status register SR is changed to execute at interrupt level 0 by setting 0 in the interrupt mask field.
- Control is transferred to the WORK module.

The WORK module

D6 is cleared and is then incremented in a never-ending loop.

The interrupt service module

- The name TERMINATOR is given to the control D character.
- An input buffer with space for 100 characters is set up with associated pointer and count.
- Subroutines to RESET and configure the ACIA and initialize the data area are included.
- The Service routine for the ACIA.
  First, a check is made that a character is indeed waiting in the ACIA input data register by testing the appropriate bit of the status register. If not, an error exit is made. This test may appear to be unnecessary since the only reason for entering the service routine is that the device has signaled. The test should be included, however, as a fail-safe device since, in general, programmers may not foresee in advance every circumstance that might arise. Also, in more realistic interrupt programs, several devices may interrupt at the same level and a test must be made by software to find out which one is currently interrupting. If a small extension is made to this program so that it can handle both input and output via the ACIA, it is essential to test by software whether input or output has caused the interrupt so that the correct service code can be executed.

In the rest of the service routine, the character is transferred from the ACIA input data register and tested against the terminator. If the terminator is found, exit occurs from the program. An alternative is to pass control back to WORK and to allow it to execute indefinitely, which is perhaps a little more realistic for interrupt-driven software, but not so easy for the user running this first interrupt program to follow at run-time. If the terminator is not found the count is incremented to make sure that the input buffer is not about to overflow and thus overwrite the code of the service routine. In this case the error exit is taken otherwise the character is stored in the buffer and control returns to the work routine through RTE.

13.8 OUTPUT TO THE DISPLAY UNDER INTERRUPT CONTROL

A minimal output program is now developed which clears the display and outputs twenty characters under interrupt control. Fig. 13.12 gives a listing of the program. It is necessary to enable transmit interrupts in the ACIA control register as shown in Fig. 13.11. A transmit interrupt signal indicates that the ACIA data output register, accessed as location $30063, is empty and ready for the next character to be transmitted.

An interrupt signal therefore occurs immediately transmit interrupts are enabled.

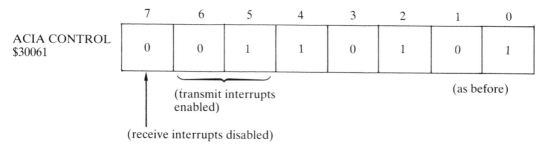

Fig. 13.11

```
 1                          *
 2                          *
 3                          *
 4                          *
 5                          * this program illustrates interrupt programming
 6                          * for output to the display
 7
 8                          ********************
 9                          * INITIALIZATION *
10                          ********************
11
12          00001000    STACK   EQU     $1000
13
14          00001000            ORG     $1000
15
16 001000 4FF81000     INITIAL LEA     STACK,SP     * load stack pointer
17 001004 4EB8108E             JSR     VECTINIT     * set up vectors
18 001008 4EB810C0             JSR     RESET        * ACIA initial RESET
19 00100C 4EB810D2             JSR     CONFIGURE    * configure
20 001010 4EB81038             JSR     INITOUTPUT   * initialise data
21
```

```
22                             * set the 68000 status register to level 0:
23 001014 027CF8FF                   ANDI    #$F8FF,SR
24
25                             * end of initialization section
26                             ****************************************************
27                             * WORK MODULE *
28                             ***************
29                             *
30         00001018            WORK    EQU     *
31 001018 4286                         CLR.L   D6
32 00101A 5286                WLOOP    ADDQ.L  #1,D6
33 00101C 60FC                         BRA     WLOOP   * loop forever incrementing D
34                             *
35                             ****************************************************
36                             * INPUT MODULE - INITIALIZATION AND INTERRUPT SERVICE
37                             ****************************************************
38                             *
39         00000004            TERMINATOR  EQU $04     * control D
40         00030061            ACIASTATUS  EQU $30061  * status register read only
41         00030061            ACIACONTROL EQU $30061  * control register write only
42         00030063            ACIAINPUT   EQU $30063  * input data register
43         00030063            ACIAOUTPUT  EQU $30063  * output data register
44                             *
45                             * data area
46 00101E 0A                  OUTBUFF DC.B   $0A,'0123456789ABCDEFGHIJ',0
47 001034 0002                OBUFFPTR    DS.W 1         * working pointer
48 001036 0002                OCHARCOUNT  DS.W 1         * number of chars output
49                             *
50                             ****************************************************
51                             * INITOUTPUT
52                             * subroutine to initialize data
53                             *
54         00001038            INITOUTPUT EQU  *
55                             * set up count of tx interrupts (no of chars+1):
56 001038 31FC00161036                MOVE    #22,OCHARCOUNT
57                             * move address of buffer into buffer pointer:
58 00103E 31FC101E1034                MOVE    #OUTBUFF,OBUFFPTR
59 001044 13FC0035
         00030061                     MOVE.B  #$35,ACIACONTROL   * enable transmit
60 00104C 4E75                        RTS
61                             *
62                             ****************************************************
63                             * ACIAISR
64                             * interrupt service routine for ACIA
65                             * registers used are saved on stack and restored
66                             *
67         0000104E            ACIAISR EQU  *
68 00104E 2F08                        MOVE.L  A0,-(SP)       * save A0 on stack
69 001050 08390001
         00030061                     BTST    #1,ACIASTATUS  * check tx interrupt
70 001058 6700001C                    BEQ     ERROR          * shouldn't be here
71
72 00105C 53781036                    SUBQ    #1,OCHARCOUNT  * decrement count
73 001060 67000016                    BEQ     FINISH         * output complete
74
75 001064 30781034                    MOVE    OBUFFPTR,A0
```

```
76 001068 13D800030063          MOVE.B  (A0)+,ACIAOUTPUT  * output char
77 00106E 31C81034              MOVE    A0,OBUFFPTR       * save buffer pointer
78
79 001072 205F                  MOVE.L  (SP)+,A0          * restore A0
80 001074 4E73                  RTE                       * return
81
82 001076 4E40          ERROR   TRAP    #0                * exit from program
83
84 001078 13FC0015
         00030061 FINISH MOVE.B  #$15,ACIACONTROL  * disable transmit
85 001080 205F                  MOVE.L  (SP)+,A0          * restore A0
86 001082 4E73                  RTE                       * return to WORK
87                      *********************************************************
88                      * interrupts should not occur at levels 1,2,3,5,6
89                      * the service routines cause a clean exit
90 001084 4E40          INT1    TRAP    #0
91 001086 4E40          INT2    TRAP    #0
92 001088 4E40          INT3    TRAP    #0
93 00108A 4E40          INT5    TRAP    #0
94 00108C 4E40          INT6    TRAP    #0
95
96                      *********************************************************
97                      * VECTINIT
98                      * subroutine to set up interrupt vectors
99                      *
100        0000108E     VECTINIT          EQU     *
101 00108E 21FC00001084
           0064                 MOVE.L  #INT1,$64         * level 1
102 001096 21FC00001086
           0068                 MOVE.L  #INT2,$68         * level 2
103 00109E 21FC00001088
           006C                 MOVE.L  #INT3,$6C         * level 3
104 0010A6 21FC0000104E
           0070                 MOVE.L  #ACIAISR,$70      * level 4
105 0010AE 21FC0000108A
           0074                 MOVE.L  #INT5,$74         * level 5
106 0010B6 21FC0000108C
           0078                 MOVE.L  #INT6,$78         * level 6
107 0010BE 4E75                 RTS
108                      *
109                      *********************************************************
110                      * RESET
111                      * subroutine for initial RESET of ACIA
112                      *
113        000010C0     RESET   EQU     *
114 0010C0 13FC0003
           00030061             MOVE.B  #3,ACIACONTROL
115                      * wait for RESET to take effect
116 0010C8 303C0400             MOVE    #$400,D0
117 0010CC 5340         RLOOP   SUBQ    #1,D0
118 0010CE 66FC                 BNE     RLOOP
119 0010D0 4E75                 RTS
120                      *
121                      *********************************************************
122                      * CONFIGURE
123                      * subroutine for initial configuration
```

```
124                              *
125              000010D2        CONFIGURE  EQU  *
126 0010D2 13FC0015
             00030061              MOVE.B  #$15,ACIACONTROL
127 0010DA 4E75                    RTS
128                              *
129                              ********************************************************
130                              *
131                                END
```

****** TOTAL ERRORS   0--   0 -- TOTAL LINES   120

APPROX   2096 UNUSED SYMBOL TABLE ENTRIES

```
ACIACONT 030061 ACIAINPU 030063 ACIAISR  00104E ACIAOUTP 030063 ACIASTAT 030061
CONFIGUR 0010D2 ERROR    001076 FINISH   001078 INITIAL  001000 INITOUTP 001038
INT1     001084 INT2     001086 INT3     001088 INT5     00108A INT6     00108C
OBUFFPTR 001034 OCHARCOU 001036 OUTBUFF  00101E RESET    0010C0 RLOOP    0010CC
STACK    001000 TERMINAT 000004 VECTINIT 00108E WLOOP    00108E WORK     001018
```

Fig. 13.12   Display output under interrupt control

The only way to unset a transmit interrupt is to transmit a character after which another transmit interrupt arrives (when the data register is free again). It is therefore not possible, as with receive interrupts, to enable transmit interrupts in advance and output later. Transmit interrupts are enabled immediately prior to outputting the first character and must be disabled after the last character has been output. Apart from this point, the output program is very similar to the keyboard input program, containing an initialization module, a work module and an interrupt module including the interrupt service routine at level 4 to control the output.

13.9   AN INTERRUPT PROGRAM WITH BOTH INPUT AND OUTPUT

Fig. 13.13 shows an interrupt program in which a piece of text of arbitrary length is output to the display twenty characters at a time. Output of the text is controlled by the user from the keyboard as follows:

- Output does not commence until any character is input.
- Each display full of text is held until the user inputs any character. The display is then cleared.
- When output of the text is complete, subsequent inputs are ignored.
- Any input while the display is not full is ignored.

The program illustrates the need for software analysis of the cause of an interrupt since both input and output can cause entry to the level 4 service routine. It also illustrates the management of transmit interrupts. When a full display is being held or on completion of output of the text, transmit interrupts are disabled.

Although the specific character input by the user is of no interest, the character is however read from the input buffer in order to unset the receive interrupt.

```
 1                           *
 2                           *
 3                           *
 4                           *
 5                           * this program illustrates interrupt programming
 6                           * output of text to the display is controlled
 7                           * by input from the keyboard
 8                           * any char input causes output to commence
 9                           * each full display is held until a char is input
10                           * after all output complete, input is ignored
11
12                           ********************
13                           * INITIALIZATION  *
14                           ********************
15
16           00001000        STACK   EQU     $1000
17
18           00001000                ORG     $1000
19
20 001000 4FF81000           INITIAL LEA     STACK,SP        * load stack pointer
21 001004 4EB81110                   JSR     VECTINIT        * set up vectors
22 001008 4EB81142                   JSR     RESET           * ACIA initial RESET
23 00100C 4EB81154                   JSR     CONFIGURE       * configure & enable
24 001010 4EB8104C                   JSR     INITIO          * initialize data
25
26                           * set the 68000 status register to level 0:
27 001014 027CF8FF                   ANDI    #$F8FF,SR
28
29                           * end of initialization section
30                           ********************************************************
31                           * WORK MODULE *
32                           ***************
33                           *
34           00001018        WORK    EQU     *
35 001018 4286                       CLR.L   D6
36 00101A 5286               WLOOP   ADDQ.L  #1,D6
37 00101C 60FC                       BRA     WLOOP   * loop forever incrementing D
38                           *
39                           ********************************************************
40                           * INPUT MODULE - INITIALIZATION AND INTERRUPT SERVICE
41                           ********************************************************
42                           *
43           00000004        TERMINATOR   EQU $04    * control D
44           00030061        ACIASTATUS   EQU $30061 * status register read only
45           00030061        ACIACONTROL  EQU $30061 * control register write only
46           00030063        ACIAINPUT    EQU $30063 * input data register
47           00030063        ACIAOUTPUT   EQU $30063 * output data register
48                           *
49                           * data area:
50 00101E 51                 OTEXT   DC.B    'QWERTYUIOPASDFGHJKLZ'
51 001032 30                         DC.B    '012345678901234567890',TERMINATOR
52 001048 0002               OTEXTPTR    DS.W 1     * working pointer
53 00104A 0001               OCHARCOUNT  DS.B 1     * working count
54 00104B 0001               TERMFLAG    DS.B 1     * terminator found?
55                           *
```

```
57                           * INITIO
58                           * subroutine to initialize data
59                           *
60          0000104C         INITIO  EQU    *
61                           * set count of chars to be output to 0
62 00104C 4238104A                   CLR.B   OCHARCOUNT
63                           * set flag to indicate terminator not found
64 001050 4238104B                   CLR.B   TERMFLAG
65                           * put address of output text into text pointer
66 001054 31FC101E1048               MOVE    #OTEXT,OTEXTPTR
67 00105A 4E75                       RTS
68                           *
69                           ****************************************************
70                           * ACIAISR
71                           * interrupt service routine for ACIA
72                           * registers used are saved on stack and restored
73                           *
74          0000105C         ACIAISR EQU  *
75 00105C 2F00                       MOVE.L  D0,-(SP)        * save D0 on stack
76 00105E 2F08                       MOVE.L  A0,-(SP)        * save A0 on stack
77 001060 08390000
       00030061                      BTST.B  #0,ACIASTATUS   * test rx interrupt
78 001068 66000012                   BNE     INPUT           * rx bit set
79 00106C 08390001
       00030061                      BTST    #1,ACIASTATUS   * test tx interrupt
80 001074 6600002E                   BNE     OUTPUT          * tx bit set
81 001078 60000088                   BRA     LEVEL4ERROR     * neither rx nor tx
82
83          0000107C         INPUT   EQU    *
84                           * char is read to unset rx but is not used
85 00107C 103900030063               MOVE.B  ACIAINPUT,D0    * read char
86 001082 4A38104B                   TST.B   TERMFLAG        * output finished?
87 001086 66000074                   BNE     ACIAEXIT        * yes
88                           * input is ignored after all text is output
89
90 00108A 4A38104A                   TST.B   OCHARCOUNT
91 00108E 6600006C                   BNE     ACIAEXIT           * ignore if not full
92                           * input only noted when count at 0 (display full)
93
94                           * when count is at 0 output new display
95                           * set up count of tx interrupts (no of chars+1):
96 001092 11FC0016104A               MOVE.B  #22,OCHARCOUNT
97 001098 13FC00B5
       00030061                      MOVE.B  #$B5,ACIACONTROL * enable rx & tx
98 0010A0 6000005A                   BRA     ACIAEXIT
99
100         000010A4         OUTPUT  EQU    *
101                          * check if start of a new display (count at 22):
102 0010A4 0C380016104A               CMPI.B  #22,OCHARCOUNT
103 0010AA 67000040                   BEQ     CLEARDISPLAY
104
105                          * get a char from the output text into D0:
106 0010AE 30781048                   MOVEA   OTEXTPTR,A0
107 0010B2 1018                       MOVE.B  (A0)+,D0
108 0010B4 31C81048                   MOVE    A0,OTEXTPTR     * save pointer
109
```

```
110                             * check if text output complete (terminator fetched):
111 0010B8 0C000004                    CMPI.B   #TERMINATOR,D0
112 0010BC 6700001C                    BEQ      TERMFOUND
113
114 0010C0 13C000030063               MOVE.B   D0,ACIAOUTPUT     * output char
115 0010C6 5338104A                   SUBQ.B   #1,OCHARCOUNT     * decrement count
116                             * check if display is full (count at 0):
117 0010CA 66000030                   BNE      ACIAEXIT          * not full
118                             * if display full, disable tx:
119 0010CE 13FC0095
           00030061                   MOVE.B   #$95,ACIACONTROL        * rx only
120 0010D6 60000024                   BRA      ACIAEXIT
121
122         000010DA        TERMFOUND EQU      *
123                             * set flag to indicate text output is complete:
124 0010DA 11FCFFFF104B               MOVE.B   #-1,TERMFLAG
125 0010E0 13FC0095
           00030061                   MOVE.B   #$95,ACIACONTROL        * rx only
126 0010E8 60000012                   BRA      ACIAEXIT
127
128         000010EC        CLEARDISPLAY      EQU      *
129 0010EC 13FC000A
           00030063                   MOVE.B   #$0A,ACIAOUTPUT * clear display
130 0010F4 5338104A                   SUBQ.B   #1,OCHARCOUNT     * decrement count
131 0010F8 60000002                   BRA      ACIAEXIT
132
133         000010FC        ACIAEXIT  EQU      *
134 0010FC 205F                       MOVE.L   (SP)+,A0          * restore A0
135 0010FE 201F                       MOVE.L   (SP)+,D0          * restore D0
136 001100 4E73                       RTE                       * return
137
138 001102 4E40            LEVEL4ERROR TRAP #0      * exit from program
139
140 001104 4E40            FINISH   TRAP     #0     * exit from program
141                        ****************************************************
142                             * interrupts should not occur at levels 1,2,3,5,6
143                             * the service routines cause a clean exit
144 001106 4E40            INT1     TRAP     #0
145 001108 4E40            INT2     TRAP     #0
146 00110A 4E40            INT3     TRAP     #0
147 00110C 4E40            INT5     TRAP     #0
148 00110E 4E40            INT6     TRAP     #0
149
150                        ****************************************************
151                             * VECTINIT
152                             * subroutine to set up interrupt vectors
153                             *
154         00001110        VECTINIT EQU      *
155 001110 21FC00001106
           0064                       MOVE.L   #INT1,$64         * level 1
156 001118 21FC00001108
           0068                       MOVE.L   #INT2,$68         * level 2
157 001120 21FC0000110A
           006C                       MOVE.L   #INT3,$6C         * level 3
158 001128 21FC0000105C
           0070                       MOVE.L   #ACIAISR,$70      * level 4
```

```
159 001130 21FC0000110C
           0074                   MOVE.L  #INT5,$74      * level 5
160 001138 21FC0000110E
           0078                   MOVE.L  #INT6,$78      * level 6
161 001140 4E75                   RTS
162                        *
163                        ************************************************************
164                        * RESET
165                        * subroutine for initial RESET of ACIA
166                        *
167        00001142  RESET     EQU     *
168 001142 13FC0003
           00030061             MOVE.B  #3,ACIACONTROL
169                        * wait for RESET to take effect
170 00114A 303C0400             MOVE    #$400,D0
171 00114E 5340      RLOOP     SUBQ    #1,D0
172 001150 66FC                 BNE     RLOOP
173 001152 4E75                 RTS
174                        *
175                        ************************************************************
176                        * CONFIGURE
177                        * subroutine for initial configuration
178                        * also enables receive interrupts
179                        *
180        00001154  CONFIGURE EQU     *
181 001154 13FC0095
           00030061             MOVE.B  #$95,ACIACONTROL
182 00115C 4E75                 RTS
183                        *
184                        *
185                                  END
```

****** TOTAL ERRORS   0--   0 -- TOTAL LINES   170

APPROX   2090 UNUSED SYMBOL TABLE ENTRIES

```
ACIACONT 030061 ACIAEXIT 0010FC ACIAINPU 030063 ACIAISR   00105C ACIAOUTP 030063
ACIASTAT 030061 CLEARDIS 0010EC CONFIGUR 001154 FINISH    001104 INITIAL  001000
INITIO   00104C INPUT    00107C INT1     001106 INT2      001108 INT3     00110A
INT5     00110C INT6     00110E LEVEL4ER 001102 OCHARCOU  00104A OTEXT    00101E
OTEXTPTR 001048 OUTPUT   0010A4 RESET    001142 RLOOP     00114E STACK    001000
TERMFLAG 00104B TERMFOUN 0010DA TERMINAT 000004 VECTINIT  001110 WLOOP    00101A
WORK     001018
```

Fig. 13.13   Input and output under interrupt control

14
Exceptions

14.1 INTRODUCTION

In Chapter 13, device interrupt programming was introduced as an alternative to busy status programming. The hardware mechanisms necessary to support interrupt programming were explained and programs were developed. In this Chapter a general discussion of exceptions is given. Exceptions include device interrupts as a subset.

The use of the interrupt mechanism may be generalized to handle a wide range of conditions in a computer system. If, because of a logical error, a programmer attempts to divide by zero, the mechanism used to stop the execution of the program and to transfer control to a system routine to handle the error is the interrupt, or more generally the *exception* mechanism. In more detail, the hardware in the arithmetic logic unit, on sensing a zero divisor, raises an exception and an exception handling routine is entered by means of the address in the exception vector. Other examples of exceptions are RESET and ABORT which are caused by the corresponding keys being pressed by the operator.

It should be noted that exception handling routines are always executed with the processor in supervisor or privileged state, i.e. with the supervisor bit S = 1 in the processor status register SR. The two states or modes, supervisor and user state, were discussed in Section 13.2 when the system byte of SR was first considered. The association of a 'user stack pointer' USP with user state was also described.

In Chapter 13, the device interrupt service routines (or device exception handling routines) were written by the programmer and their addresses were set up in the appropriate vector locations during the initialization section of the program. In most cases of exceptions, the exception handling routines are part of the supervisory software. In the configuration assumed for the practical aspects of this text, a simple monitor or debugging program, TUTOR, has been assumed and the exception-handling routines are part of TUTOR.

The aim of this text is not to show how application software is developed but rather to show how a software system may be layered on top of the basic machine hardware. The concepts of exception handling and supervisor and user state are fundamental to this.

Fig. 14.1 shows the complete range of exception vectors and Section 14.2 gives a brief explanation of the cause of each one and the action taken in general terms. Section 14.3 explains exception processing, i.e. how the processor causes the execution of one program to be suspended (temporarily or permanently) and a new program, the exception handling routine, to be entered. Fig. 14.3 summarizes exception processing for all types of exception. Section 14.4 considers multiple exceptions and explains the action of the processor when two exceptions occur 'simultaneously' or within the same instruction cycle. Section 14.5 points out the distinction between the normal processing state of the 68000 when instructions are being fetched and executed and the exception processing state when a context switch between 'interrupted' context and the exception handling context is being made.

14.2 THE 68000 RANGE OF EXCEPTIONS

Fig. 14.1 shows the exceptions provided in the 68000, their vector numbers and associated locations in memory (four times the vector number). The device interrupt vectors and locations which were used in Chapter 13 can be seen as a subset of the complete range.

A short explanation is now given of the cause of each exception and the action taken when it occurs. In later sections, the hardware mechanisms to support exception-handling are covered.

Vector   *RESET*

0   One method of effecting RESET is to depress the RESET button.

(and 1)   RESET is also asserted by the hardware as a result of some catastrophic failure such as loss of power. The RESET input to the processor is allocated the highest priority since it indicates that any current processing should be aborted. Unlike device interrupts, there is no concept of saving the interrupt state for later restoration. The most common use of RESET is for system initialization.

2   *Bus Error*

This is a system-generated control signal to indicate that a problem has arisen within the hardware such as:

- an attempt to write to read-only memory
- a spurious (unanticipated) interrupt has occurred
- an expected hardware signal has not arrived in the expected time.

The action of the service routine, from the programmer's point of view, is

Vector address (hex)		Vector number
00	SSP	0
	RESET	
	PC	1
08	Bus Error	2
0C	Illegal Address	3
10	Illegal Instruction	4
14	Divide by zero	5
18	CHK instruction	6
1C	TRAPV instruction	7
20	Privilege Violation	8
24	TRACE	9
28	1010 Emulator	A
2C	1011 Emulator	B
30		C
	Unassigned/Reserved	
5C		17
60	Spurious Interrupt	18
64	Level 1 autovector	19
68	Level 2 autovector	1A
6C	Level 3 autovector	1B
70	Level 4 autovector ACIA	1C
74	Level 5 autovector	1D
78	Level 6 autovector	1E
7C	Level 7 autovector Abort	1F
80		20
	Trap instructions	
BC		2F
C0		30
	Unassigned/Reserved	
FC		3F
100		40
	User Interrupts	
3FC		FF

Fig. 14.1   Address assignments for exceptions

to output a 'BUS ERROR' message to the VDU and to give the full display of register contents.

3   *Illegal Address*
This exception is caused by an attempt to fetch a word or longword from an odd address in memory. An error message is output.

4   *Illegal Instruction*
This exception is generated when the first word, the control word, of an instruction has been fetched into the processor's instruction register and the bit pattern there does not constitute a legal instruction.
An error message is output.

5   *Divide by Zero*
A division instruction DIVS or DIVU in a program has been executed with a divisor of zero.

6   *CHK Instruction*
The definition of the check against bounds instruction is given in Chapter 8. If the bounds are exceeded an exception is generated.

7   *TRAPV Instruction*
Execution of this instruction causes the overflow flag V to be tested and an exception to be generated if the flag is set.

8   *Privilege Violation*
In Section 13.2.2, supervisor state (with full privilege) and user state (with restricted privilege) were introduced. The exception mechanism is used to enforce the restricted privilege of user state. If a program executing in user state attempts any privileged action, an exception is generated.
The privileged instructions are as follows:

> RESET
> STOP
> RTE
> those instructions which write to the system byte of SR, i.e word operations with ANDI, ORI, EORI and MOVE
> MOVE USP, An
> MOVE An, USP

The last two instructions are provided for a supervisor to access the stack pointer of the program which most recently executed in user mode. A program running in user mode names its control stack pointer SP or A7.

9   *TRACE*
Trace mode is entered by giving a command to a debugging program such

as TUTOR as described in Chapter 3. This sets bit 15 (T = 1) of SR as described in Section 13.2. When a program is executing in trace mode, an exception is generated after each instruction is executed allowing the debugging program to be entered. Typically, a full register dump is output to the screen and control is passed to the user. By this means the user can monitor the effect of each instruction.

A	1010 Emulator
and B	1011 Emulator

If bits 15 through 12 of the first word of an instruction contain these patterns, an exception is generated. The provision of two exception vectors separate from the illegal instruction vector allows efficient emulation of unimplemented instructions by software. For example, a processor may not have a floating point hardware unit and floating point arithmetic operations may be provided by software. This facility also allows emulation of one processor by another.

18   *Spurious Interrupt*
This is invoked as a result of a bus error exception when a spurious interrupt signal has been detected.

19   *Levels 1 through 7 autovectors*
through   These exceptions are caused by external device interrupts as explained in
1F   Sections 13.1 through 13.8. An interrupt is effected only when the interrupt signal from the device interface is at a higher level of priority than that at which the processor is executing, indicated by the interrupt mask in the processor status register SR. An exception to this rule is that interrupts at the highest priority, level 7, are 'non-maskable', i.e. they are not inhibited by the interrupt mask. The abort button, for example, is at level 7. The service routine for this interrupt outputs the state of the processor on abort for debugging purposes. A typical occasion for its use is when the user suspects that the program being run has gone into an infinite loop.

20   *TRAP instructions*
through   TRAP instructions are used specifically for the purpose of generating
2F   exceptions in order to transfer control from the executing program to the 'system'. This type of instruction is called a 'software interrupt' by some manufacturers. The 'system' assumed so far in this text is the simple monitor or debugging program TUTOR. The TRAP #0 instruction has been used in all the example programs as an EXIT instruction. The sixteen TRAP instructions may be used to implement a range of system calls when both system and user level software is to be developed.

14.3   EXCEPTION PROCESSING

In general, exception processing consists of making a context switch from the state in which the processor was executing when the exception occurred to a new state in which the exception is handled. The two major tasks involved in exception processing are therefore:

- Saving the current context. In practice, only SR and PC are saved automatically by hardware.
- Setting up a new context (SR and PC for the exception-handling routine).

The context before the exception is saved for two reasons:

- It can be restored when exception processing is complete. This is appropriate, for example, in the case of an external device interrupting an executing program. When the device has been serviced, the program may be resumed.
- The exception-handling routine can analyze the cause of the error via the context saved on the system stack and can pick up information suitable for inclusion in an error message (for example, the address of the instruction which caused the error). In the case of fatal errors, the saved context is not restored.

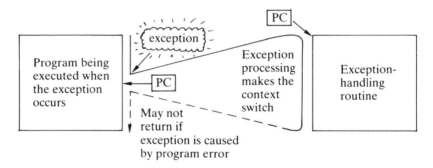

Fig. 14.2

14.3.1 Exception groups

Exceptions are classified into three groups according to their priority and the time at which exception processing commences. Priorities are discussed further when multiple exceptions are considered in Section 14.4.

Group 0 exceptions (the highest priority group) are:

  RESET.
  Bus Error.
  Address Error.

The current instruction is not completed if a group 0 exception occurs and exception processing commences at the next minor cycle of the processor. Within the group, RESET has the highest priority followed by bus error then address error.

Group 1 exceptions (next highest priority) are:

Tracing.
Interrupts.
Illegal and Unimplemented Instructions.
Privilege Violation.

Exception processing commences on completion of the current instruction. Illegal, unimplemented and privileged instructions are detected when they are the next instruction to be executed. The relative priorities are tracing then interrupts and the rest have equal priority.

Group 2 exceptions (lowest priority) are:

Instruction Traps.

Exception processing commences during the course of normal execution of these instructions.

14.3.2 Internal and external exceptions

Exceptions may also be classified as internal, caused by an action of the currently executing program or external, occurring at an unpredictable time from a source external to the program currently being executed by the processor, for example, from a device.

Internal exceptions are:

- Instructions TRAP, TRAPV, CHK, DIVS, DIVU.
- Trace – after each instruction.
- Illegal address – odd address for a .W or .L operation.
- Illegal instruction – invalid bit pattern.
- Unimplemented instruction – operation codes 1010 or 1111 are intended for emulation.
- Privilege violation – a program executing in user state executes a privileged instruction, for example, an attempt to write to the system byte of the status register.

External exceptions are:

- RESET.
- Bus Error.
- Device Interrupt – an interrupt signal arrives from a device and the interrupt level of that device is higher than the current interrupt level.
- Spurious Interrupt.

In the case of internal exceptions, the interrupt mask in the status register is unchanged when exception processing commences. In the case of external exceptions, exception processing takes place at an interrupt level appropriate to the exception.

14.3.3 Transfer to the exception-handling routine

The steps involved in saving the current context and setting up a new context for exception handling vary slightly depending on the particular exception. These differences are summarized in Fig. 14.3. The basic steps are as follows:

- save SR in an internal register (see Fig. 14.3),
- set S = 1 and T = 0 in SR (always),
- set $I_2I_1I_0$ if appropriate (see Fig. 14.3),
- generate the address of the interrupt vector corresponding to the exception (see Fig. 14.3),
- stack the copy taken of SR using SSP (see Section 14.3),
- stack the PC
  (the precise address stacked will vary – see Fig. 14.3),
- set up the PC from the interrupt vector (always).

Fetch–Execute then continues from the exception-handling routine. If the saved context is to be restored, for example after a device interrupt has been serviced, the RTE instruction (return from exception) causes both PC and SR to be set up from the system stack as discussed in Section 13.6.

14.3.4 Bus error and address error

Bus error and address error are group 0 exceptions and their processing commences during instruction execution instead of being left pending until the current instruction terminates. In the case of RESET, the other group 0 exception, the current context is aborted, no attempt is made to save the current state for error analysis or later restoration. In the case of bus error and address error, SR and PC are stacked as usual so that some error analysis may be attempted but the value of PC depends on the particular stage of the fetch–execute cycle that is interrupted by the exception. The value saved for PC may be from two to ten bytes from the address of the first word of the instruction, even if the current instruction is a jump or branch and the bus error occurs during fetch of the next instruction. To assist in error analysis, further information is stacked for bus and address error including a copy of the first word of the instruction being processed, the address which was being accessed by the aborted bus cycle, whether the instruction was a read or write, etc. It is the responsibility of the exception-handling routine to perform software diagnosis and to clean up the stack.

Further details specifically related to hardware are available in the processor reference manual, ref. 4.

	Group 0			Group 1				Group 2
Exception processing begins:	At next minor cycle of processor – current instruction is aborted			These pre-empt the next instruction – current instruction is completed				Part of normal execution
Exception processing sequence	RESET	Bus Error	Address Error	Tracing	Interrupts	Illegal and unimplemented	Privilege Violation	Instructions Traps
Set up new context in SR copy SR $S=1$ $T=0$ $I_2I_1I_0$	no yes 7	yes yes unchanged	yes yes unchanged	yes yes unchanged	yes yes from device	yes yes unchanged	yes yes unchanged	yes yes unchanged
Address generation of interrupt vector	internal	internal	internal	internal	from device (or internal requested)	internal	internal	
Save the interrupted context (via SSP) Stack SR (copy) Stack PC (which address?)	no no	yes complex	yes complex	yes next instruction	yes next instruction	yes in illegal instruction (as decode)	yes first word of privileged instruction	yes next instruction
Set up PC for fetch/execute PC ← vector	SSP ← (0) PC ← (4)	yes	yes	yes	yes	yes	yes	yes

Fig. 14.3 Exception processing

14.4   MULTIPLE EXCEPTIONS

In all the discussion so far, the occurrence of a single exception has been assumed. In practice, multiple exceptions may occur, for example:

- A device interrupt arrives during an instruction which is illegal, unimplemented, privileged or a trap.
- A device interrupt is pending and abort or reset is pressed during the same instruction cycle.

It should be noted that multiple *internal* exceptions are not possible. Any combination of an internal with an external or multiple external exceptions may occur.

The priority ordering of exceptions was noted in Section 14.3.1, and, starting from the highest priority is:

group 0:   RESET
Bus Error
Address Error

group 1:   Trace
Interrupt
Illegal, Unimplemented or Privileged Instructions

group 2:   Instruction Traps

The priority relation between exceptions determines which ones are taken, or which one is taken first if exception conditions arrive simultaneously. Examples are:

- If a RESET or ABORT occurs during a TRAP instruction, the RESET or ABORT takes precedence and the TRAP instruction processing is aborted.
- If an interrupt request occurs during the execution of an instruction and tracing is enabled (T = 1 in SR), the trace exception has priority and is processed first. The interrupt is then processed, in an interrupt service routine and, on completion of this, control returns to the next instruction of the program being traced.
- If a bus error or address error occurs during exception processing for a bus error, address error or RESET, the processor is halted and all processing ceases. Only RESET can restart a halted processor.

14.5   PROCESSING STATES

The 68000 processor is always in one of three processing states:

- normal (special case 'stopped'),
- exception,
- halted.

Normal state is associated with fetching and executing instructions. A special case of the normal state is the stopped state which the processor enters when a STOP instruction is executed. In this state, no further memory references are made. This allows a fast response to subsequent arrival of an exception. Exception state is associated with exception processing, i.e. effecting the transition from one context to another on occurrence of an exception as described in Section 14.3. It should be noted that exception-handling routines are executed in normal state once they have been entered. The halted state is an indication of catastrophic hardware failure. Examples were given in Section 14.4. Only an external reset can restart a halted processor. It should be noted that a processor in the stopped state is not in the halted state.

15

Programming the peripheral interface adaptor (PIA)

15.1 INTRODUCTION

In Chapter 9, an introduction was given to the general principles of device interfacing together with some details of the connection of the devices to the MC68000. This chapter examines some ways in which a device may be attached to the PIA and controlled and signalled by both the PIA and the MC68000.

The PIA has two almost identical halves, or sides, each of which deals with eight bits in parallel. A common configuration is for the A side to be set up and physically connected for INPUT and the B side to be set up for OUTPUT. Fig. 15.1 shows the general arrangement.

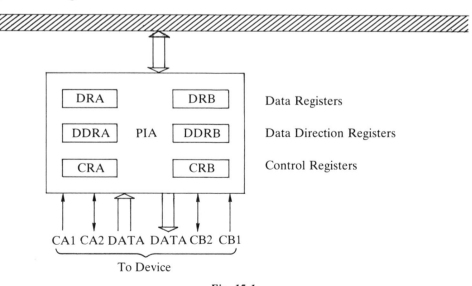

Fig. 15.1

The interface registers are used as follows:

Data Registers: PIADRA and PIADRB
                                          These are used for data input and output.
Data Direction Registers: PIADDRA and PIADDRB
                                          These are configured to identify the direction of
                                          data transfer through the Data Registers. Values 0
                                          (INPUT) and 1 (OUTPUT) in the Data Direction
                                          Registers indicate which corresponding bits in the
                                          associated data registers are for input and output
                                          values.
Control Registers: PIACRA and PIACRB
                                          These are used for control and status signals related
                                          to the flow of data.

In any physical configuration, addresses must be assigned to the device registers (see
Section 9.6.3) and, for the examples given here, addresses $30051 to $30057 will be
assumed. The following symbolic address assignments are assumed in all subsequent
examples:

```
PIA        EQU $30051    * The physical address
PIADRA     EQU PIA       * A side: Data Register
PIADDRA    EQU PIA       * Data Direction Register (same address) .
PIACRA     EQU PIA+2     * Control Register
PIADRB     EQU PIA+4     * B side: Data Register
PIADDRB    EQU PIA+4     * Data Direction Register (same address)
PIACRB     EQU PIA+6     * Control Register
```

The two instructions

```
CLR.B            PIADDRA   * configure A side for input (0's)
MOVE.B   #$FF, PIADDRB     * configure B side for output (1's)
```

are examples of directly writing to the Data Direction Registers to set them for input
and output. Full details of the initialization are given in Section 15.4.

The two instructions:

```
MOVE.B   PIADRA, D0       * transfer a byte from the A side data
                            register (input)
MOVE.B   DATA, PIADRB     * transfer a byte to the B side data register
                            (output)
```

are examples of reading to and writing from the Data Register. Individual bits of the
data registers could be set by:

```
BSET   #4, PIADRB         * set bit 4 of DRB to 1
```

But the implementation of the execution of this instruction is quite complex. It
involves the 68000 processor reading PIADRB into an internal register, setting bit 4
and writing back the updated value into PIADRB. It should be noted therefore that
this type of instruction could not be used with a read-only or write-only register since

its execution involves both reading and writing. Use of the move instruction is always preferred to avoid these side effects.

In order to use a device, its connections to the PIA must be defined explicitly. Also, in order to understand the flow of information and signals, the connections of the PIA to the MC68000 must be explained, although a detailed knowledge of every aspect is not necessary. Connection to the MC68000 is typically as shown in Fig. 15.2. This is a 40-pin package and connections are shown in the figure.

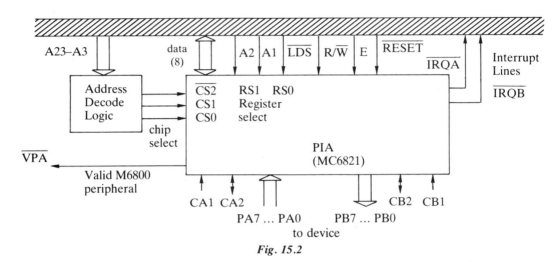

Fig. 15.2

On the device side, there are two bidirectional lines (CA2, CB2) and two unidirectional lines (CA1, CB1) which can be used to generate an interrupt or for additional control lines. There are also two parallel 8-bit channels (PA7 . . . PA0 and PB7 . . . PB0) for data. Within the interface, there are six 8-bit registers (see Fig. 15.1), which share four memory mapped addresses. Each data register shares the address of the corresponding data direction register (PIADRA with PIADDRA and PIADRB with PIADDRB). Examples are given above and full details in Section 15.4. The specific addresses used for the PIA registers are defined arbitrarily for a particular physical configuration. Any system available to the reader is likely to have different address assignments. Similarly, the devices used for examples in this chapter are connected in a specific way which is likely to be different in another system.

15.2   THE CABLE

The connections on the device side of the PIA are now defined. This is shown in Fig. 15.3 with the A side set up for input and the B side for output.

It should be noted that other systems may use different labels for the PIA terminator connections to devices.

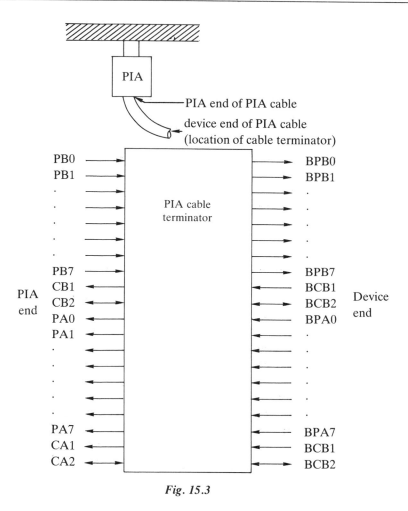

Fig. 15.3

15.3   A STEPPING MOTOR AS AN EXAMPLE OF OUTPUT

An example of the connection and use of an output device, a stepping motor, is now given. Fig. 15.4 shows how it might be connected. This is a simple device which is controlled as follows:

- A pulse on the line identified by BPB5 causes the pointer to step.
- A 1 or 0 on the line identified by BPB4 indicates whether the step should be in the clockwise (1) or anticlockwise (0) direction.

Stepping motors vary in their characteristics but typically there are 48 step positions for one complete revolution of the pointer. An associated dial or card might be

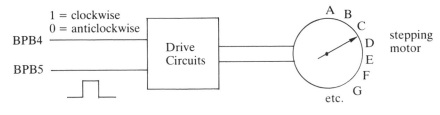

Fig. 15.4

marked with character information such as letters (A to X with two steps between successive letters) or numbers (1 to 48).

The speed at which the pointer rotates is determined by the rate of occurrence of the pulses on BPB5. Assuming that the PIA has been initialized, the code to step the motor could be as follows:

```
            MOVE.B  #S10,PIADRB  * write the bit pattern 0010000 into
                                   data register B
                                   bit 5 = 0 (destined for BPB5)
                                   bit 4 = 1 (destined for BPB4 to
                                   indicate clockwise)
STEP        EQU     *            * code to effect one step
            BSET    #5,PIADRB    * make data bit 5 = 1
            BCLR    #5,PIADRB    * then 0 again, i.e. put a pulse on
                                   BPB5 via bit 5 of PIADRB
WAIT        EQU     $FFFF        * give WAIT a large positive value
DELAY       EQU     *
            MOVE    #WAIT,D0
DELLOOP     EQU     *
            SUBQ    #1,D0        * force a delay by counting down a
            BNE     DELLOOP      * large positive value in a loop
            BRA     STEP         * do another step
```

This program fragment steps the motor indefinitely in the same direction at the same speed. The direction of rotation is changed by making bit 4 = 0. The speed of rotation is changed by changing the value of WAIT used in the DELAY loop. Decreasing the value of WAIT increases the rate at which pulses are provided and therefore the speed of rotation.

It should be noted that if the pulses are given too rapidly, i.e. the value of WAIT is made too small, the pointer may not move at all.

15.4 INITIALIZING THE PIA FOR THE STEPPING MOTOR

The PIA is a general-purpose interface which can be set up (initialized or configured) in a variety of ways. Before the stepping motor code given in Section 15.3 could be executed, the B side of the interface would need to be set up for output. In order to do this, the Data Direction and Control Registers of the PIA must be set up and this is now explained.

15.4.1 The data direction registers PIADDRA and PIADDRB

Data directed to and from the PIA always passes through the Data Registers. The PIA requires that the direction in which data is transferred is defined. This is done by setting bits to 0 for INPUT (from the device to the 68000) and 1 for OUTPUT in the Data Direction Registers.

Fig. 15.5 shows the arrangement for using the PIA configured with its A side for input and its B side for output. DDRA is all 0's defining input and DDRB is all 1's defining output.

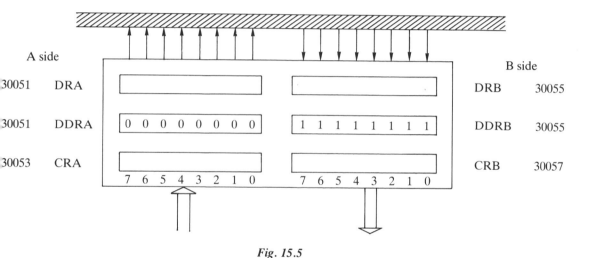

Fig. 15.5

In general, the Data Direction Registers can be set up in any way. Fig. 15.6 shows a different arrangement which might be required for the connection and use of some specific device.

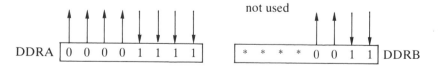

Fig. 15.6

Since the Data Direction Registers may be changed at any time, the PIA can be used to transfer 16 bits of data in parallel, one byte on the A side, the other byte on the B side. Before transfer, the Data Direction Registers must be set up for the required direction. An example of a requirement for 16-bit output is for output to a printer. A common configuration, however, is to set up the data direction once only in an initialization phase, according to the requirements of the application, and subsequently to use the data registers as prescribed by the initialization. In the example programs given in this chapter, the configuration shown in Fig. 15.5 (A side for input, B side for output) is used.

15.4.2 The control registers PIACRA and PIACRB

Each bit in the control register serves a specific purpose and Appendix C gives a complete specification. It has been shown that the Data and Data Direction Registers for each side of the PIA share an address. One of the bits in the Control register for that side indicates which register the shared address specifies.

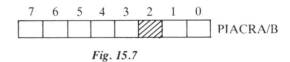

Fig. 15.7

Bit 2 = 0 indicates that the Data Direction Register is accessed. Bit 2 = 1 indicates that the Data Register is accessed. The use of the appropriate mnemonic in the program (PIADDRA or PIADRA) should make the intention of the programmer clear. Clearly the object code contains the same address whichever mnemonic is used.

15.4.3 The initialization routine

A complete initialization routine for configuring the PIA with A side for input and B side for output is as follows:

```
* set mnemonic addresses
PIA         EQU     $30051        * specify physical address
PIADRA      EQU     PIA           * A side: Data Register
PIADDRA     EQU     PIA           * Data Direction Register (same address)
PIACRA      EQU     PIA+2         * Control Register
PIADRB      EQU     PIA+4         * B side: Data Register
PIADDRB     EQU     PIA+4         * Data Direction Register (same address)
PIACRB      EQU     PIA+6         * Control Register

* Initialize the PIA
INITPIA     EQU     *
            CLR.B   PIACRA        * bit 2=0 selects DDRA
            CLR.B   PIADDRA       * DDRA all 0's for input via DRA
            BSET    #2,PIACRA     * bit 2=1 selects DRA for subse-
                                    quent use
```

```
            CLR.B    PIACRB              * bit 2=0 selects DDRB
            MOVE.B   #$FF,PIADDRB        * DDRB all 1's for output via DRB
            BSET     #2,PIACRB           * bit 2=1 selects DRB for subse-
                                           quent use
```

* End of initialization

This code leaves all 0's in DDRA, all 1's in DDRB and bit 2=1 in both CRA and CRB.

Fig. 15.8 shows the list file of a complete program to step a stepping motor continuously at a speed defined by the numerical value in WAIT, and in a direction specified by bit 4 of DRB.

```
 1                         *
 2                         *
 3                         *
 4                         *
 5                         * Program to operate the stepping motor continuously
 6                         * in one direction at a fixed speed
 7                         *
 8                         *************************************************************
 9                         * PIA MC6821
10      00030051    PIA      EQU     $30051   * PIA base address
11      00030051    PIADRA   EQU     PIA
12      00030051    PIADDRA  EQU     PIA
13      00030053    PIACRA   EQU     PIA+2
14      00030055    PIADRB   EQU     PIA+4
15      00030055    PIADDRB  EQU     PIA+4
16      00030057    PIACRB   EQU     PIA+6
17                         *************************************************************
18      00001000    STACK    EQU     $1000
19
20      00001000             ORG     $1000
21
22      00001000    START    EQU     *
23 001000 4FF81000           LEA     STACK,SP        * load stack pointer
24 001004 4EB81012           JSR     INITPIA         * set up PIA
25      00001008    LOOP     EQU     *
26 001008 4EB81058           JSR     DELAY           * wait
27 00100C 4EB81046           JSR     STEP            * step motor once
28 001010 60F6               BRA     LOOP
29                         *
30                         *************************************************************
31                         * INITPIA
32                         * subroutine to configure the PIA
33                         *
34      00001012    INITPIA EQU      *
35 001012 423900030057       CLR.B   PIACRB          * select DDRB
36 001018 13FC00FF
        00030055             MOVE.B  #$FF,PIADDRB     * B side for output
37 001020 08F90002
        00030057             BSET    #2,PIACRB        * select DRB
38                         * set direction clockwise (bit 4=1), pulse=0 (bit 5):
39 001028 13FC0010
        00030055             MOVE.B  #$10,PIADRB      * DRB=00010000
```

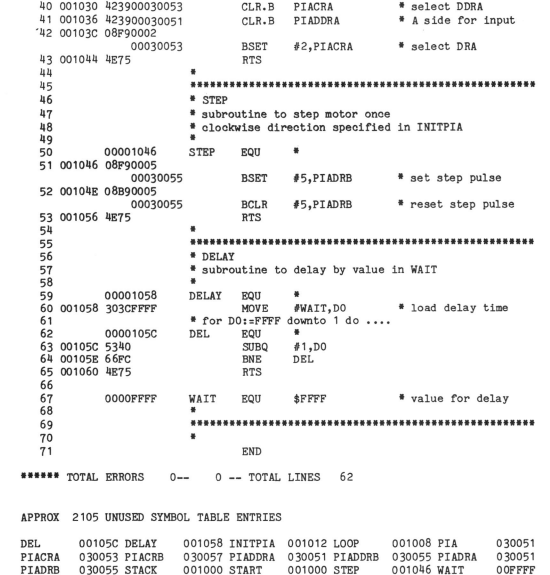

```
40 001030 423900030053              CLR.B   PIACRA      * select DDRA
41 001036 423900030051              CLR.B   PIADDRA     * A side for input
'42 00103C 08F90002
          00030053                  BSET    #2,PIACRA   * select DRA
43 001044 4E75                      RTS
44                            *
45                            ****************************************************
46                            * STEP
47                            * subroutine to step motor once
48                            * clockwise direction specified in INITPIA
49                            *
50         00001046    STEP   EQU     *
51 001046 08F90005
          00030055                  BSET    #5,PIADRB   * set step pulse
52 00104E 08B90005
          00030055                  BCLR    #5,PIADRB   * reset step pulse
53 001056 4E75                      RTS
54                            *
55                            ****************************************************
56                            * DELAY
57                            * subroutine to delay by value in WAIT
58                            *
59         00001058    DELAY  EQU     *
60 001058 303CFFFF                   MOVE    #WAIT,D0    * load delay time
61                            * for D0:=FFFF downto 1 do ....
62         0000105C    DEL    EQU     *
63 00105C 5340                       SUBQ    #1,D0
64 00105E 66FC                       BNE     DEL
65 001060 4E75                       RTS
66
67         0000FFFF    WAIT   EQU     $FFFF       * value for delay
68                            *
69                            ****************************************************
70                            *
71                                    END
```

****** TOTAL ERRORS   0--   0 -- TOTAL LINES   62

APPROX 2105 UNUSED SYMBOL TABLE ENTRIES

DEL   00105C DELAY   001058 INITPIA 001012 LOOP   001008 PIA   030051
PIACRA   030053 PIACRB   030057 PIADDRA 030051 PIADDRB 030055 PIADRA   030051
PIADRB   030055 STACK   001000 START   001000 STEP   001046 WAIT   00FFFF

Fig. 15.8 Stepping motor

15.5 GENERAL PIA CONFIGURATION

The rest of this chapter deals with some examples to illustrate how the PIA may be configured. Output, as described in Section 15.2, is fairly straightforward since it involves writing binary patterns to the relevant data register which feed through to the connected device. The stepping motor of Section 15.3 was connected to bits 4 and

5 of PIADRB. Initialization for this involved setting direction bits in PIADDRB and bit 2 of Control Register B (PIACRB). Other examples tend to be more complex largely because of the requirements of the devices.

15.5.1   Input and the control lines

The Control Line CA1 (see Fig. 15.2) is connected through Control Register A bit 7, which is usually labelled IRQ1, to the interrupt line $\overline{\text{IRQA}}$ as shown in Fig. 15.9.

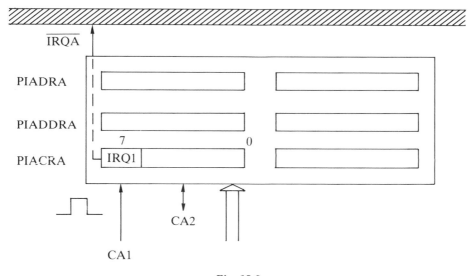

Fig. 15.9

A pulse on CA1 will cause bit 7 (IRQ1) of PIACRA to set (=1). The effect of IRQ1 becoming one is an attempt to interrupt the processor by sending an interrupt signal (asserting $\overline{\text{IRQA}}$).

The PIA must therefore be configured to specify what type of signal (pulse) on CA1 will cause IRQ1 to set, i.e.:

• whether a positive or negative edged signal on CA1 will set IRQ1, or
• whether a logic 1 in IRQ1 will cause $\overline{\text{IRQA}}$ to be asserted, i.e. whether interrupts are enabled.

This is now explained in general.

15.5.2 Control registers: CA1 control

The layout of the bits in PIACRA is shown in Fig. 15.10.

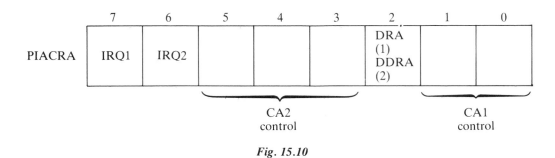

Fig. 15.10

Bits 0 and 1 of PIACRA are used to specify the control line CA1. The possible values in these bits are:

bit no *1 0*
                0 0   IRQ1 is set on the negative edge of the signal (pulse) on CA1. Interrupts are disabled.
                0 1   IRQ1 is set on the negative edge of the signal on CA1. Interrupts are enabled.
                1 0   IRQ1 is set on the positive edge of the signal on CA1. Interrupts are disabled.
                1 1   IRQ1 is set on the positive edge of the signal on CA1. Interrupts are enabled.

Thus bit 0 is used to enable the interrupt output from bit 7 (IRQ1) and assert $\overline{IRQA}$. Bit 1 is used to specify whether the negative or positive edge of the pulse on CA1 causes this to happen.

An *important point* is that IRQ1 (bit 7) is reset by reading from the associated data register and is READ ONLY. This means that in some circumstances it is necessary to read from the data register solely to clear IRQ1 and leave it in a state in which it may be triggered by a subsequent signal on CA1.

15.5.3 An example of input

An example to illustrate how the above may be used is shown in Fig. 15.11.

It is assumed that the Device (the Plant Data and its Interface) puts a pulse on CA1 when new data is available on PA7 . . . PA0 and that the positive edge of the pulse is the indicator. The code to set up the PIA to deal with this is as follows:

```
INITPIA     EQU       *
            CLR.B     PIACRA          * bit 2=0, DDRA selected
            CLR.B     PIADDRA         * all lines in DRA are for input
            MOVE.B    #$06,PIACRA     * set pattern 00000110
* end of INITPIA.
```

The above code leaves PIACRA with bit 2=1 which selects PIADRA. The

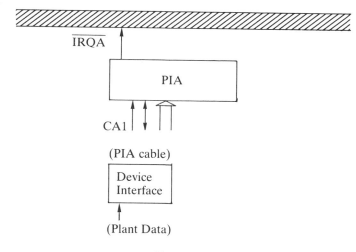

Fig. 15.11

pattern in bits 1 and 0 (CA1 control) is 10 which selects positive edge trigger without interrupts.

The routine to read the data to the processor would require some form of *POLLING* to detect when IRQ1 (bit 7 of PIACRA) becomes set (=1). One method of doing this is as follows:

```
BTST      #7,PIACRA     * Test bit 7 for 0 or 1
BEQ       EXIT          * branch to EXIT if bit 7=0
MOVE.B    PIADRA,D0     * input new data and clear IRQ1
```

or even:

```
TESTFORDATA   EQU *
              BTST      #7,PIACRA     * test bit 7
              BEQ       TESTFORDATA   * go back and test
                                        again if 0
              MOVE.B    PIADRA,D0     * read data
```

In many practical situations it is not desirable to endlessly poll a device waiting for something to occur such as the arrival of data. Although polling is simple to program it may be necessary for reasons associated with the application to use the interrupt mechanism. In the above example, use of the interrupt mechanism requires that the PIA must be set up to enable interrupts. This is achieved by the following code:

```
INITPIA   EQU       *
          CLR.B     PIACRA        * as before
          CLR.B     PIADDRA       *
          MOVE.B    #$07,PIACRA   * set pattern 00000111
* end of INITPIA.
```

In this case, bits 1 and 0 (CA1 control) are 11 which indicates that IRQ1 sets on a positive edge (as before) and that interrupts are enabled. The interrupt service routine will contain the code to fetch the data and clear IRQ1. At this stage it is left to the reader to consider the detailed coding of the interrupt service routine although a complete program is given as Fig. 15.19.

A typical situation in interrupt programming is that a number of devices may be connected at the same interrupt level. The interrupt service routine must therefore carry out some form of status testing to determine which device has raised the interrupt. The program of Fig. 15.19 illustrates this, albeit in a contrived situation.

15.5.4 Control registers: CA2 control

As shown in Fig. 15.10, bits 3, 4, and 5 of PIACRA operate in conjunction with the CA2 line. As shown in Figs. 15.1, 15.2, etc., CA2 is bi-directional and is therefore capable of dealing with both the input and output of signals. Bit 5 determines this. If bit 5=0 then CA2 can be used for input control in much the same ways as CA1, the difference being that in this case IRQ2 (bit 6) is set or not and the interrupt line $\overline{IRQB}$ asserted or not.

The full coding for input is as follows:

bit number 5 4 3	which edge sets IRQ2	Interrupts
0 0 0	negative	disabled
0 0 1	negative	enabled
0 1 0	positive	disabled
0 1 1	positive	enabled

The diagram for PIACRA is shown in Fig. 15.12.

15.5.5 Control lines, registers and output

The Control Register for the B side, PIACRB, is set up in much the same way as PIACRA. As in the examples given in this chapter, output will be described in conjuction with the B side. It should be noted, however, that, in general, the PIA can be configured in any required way, as described in Section 15.4.1.

For output, bit 5 of the control register must be 1.

If bit 5=1, then if bit 4=1, the value loaded into bit 3 will be output to CB2 (or CA2). The formal coding is:

bit number   5   4   3
                    1   1   0   0 passed to CB2 (or CA2)
                    1   1   1   1 passed to CB2 (or CA2)

This provides a mechanism for the output of a control signal (see Fig. 15.13).

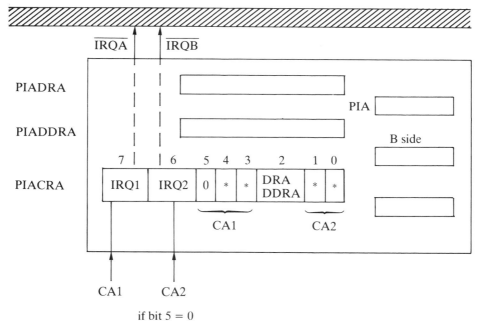

Fig. 15.12

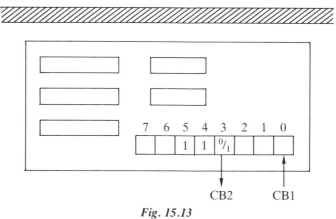

Fig. 15.13

Setting bit 4=0 provides the mechanism for the output of data to the device. The control register shown in Fig. 15.14 can be set up as follows (B side data output, A side data input):

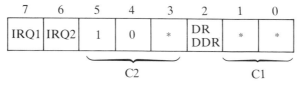

Fig. 15.14

for PIACRB:

bit number	5	4	3	
	1	0	1	A negative pulse appears on CB2 *after* a *write* into PIADRB has occurred. It lasts one clock period.
	1	0	0	A negative pulse appears on CB2. It starts *when a write* to PIADRB starts and ends when IRQ1 is set.

for PIACRA:

bit number	5	4	3	
	1	0	1	A negative pulse appears on CA2 *after* a *read* has occurred from PIADRA. It lasts one clock period.
	1	0	0	A negative pulse appears on CA2. It starts *when* PIADRA is *read* and ends when IRQ1 is set.

15.6   A SEVEN-SEGMENT DISPLAY AS AN EXAMPLE

In this example the PIA is set up so that whenever data, which is to be passed to the display device, is output to PIADRB a pulse is automatically generated which can be used to trigger the movement of data into the display.

A seven-segment display is commonly used to display decimal characters. If a signal is passed to any one of the seven segments, that segment is illuminated. Thus the shape of the required number (or letter) can be built by illuminating the appropriate segments, for example:

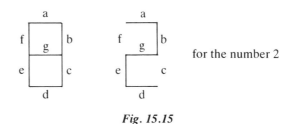

Fig. 15.15

The code used to control which collection of segments is illuminated is commonly Natural Binary Coded Decimal (BCD) (see Section 8.8 and Appendix A), in fact a BCD 7-segment decoder chip is used within the device. The BCD number 0010 for example would cause the segments shown in Fig. 15.15 to be illuminated giving number 2. The connections to the PIA could be as shown in Fig. 15.16 (refer also to Section 15.2 on the PIA cable).

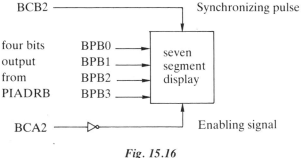

Fig. 15.16

This is an example where both CA2 and CB2 are used for output. The PIA is set up as follows:

```
INITPIA    EQU        *
           CLR.B      PIACRB        * select DDRB
           MOVE.B     #$FF,PIADDRB  * B side output
           MOVE.B     #$2C,PIACRB   * binary pattern 00101100 to
                                      CRB. This causes a negative
                                      pulse on CB2 after a write
                                      into DRB
           MOVE.B     #$34,PIACRA   * binary pattern 00110100 to
                                      CRA. This puts 0 on CA2 to
                                      enable the display.
      * end of INITPIA.
```

It should be noted that PIADRA and PIADDRA are not used. On the A side, the CA2 line is used as an output signal to enable the device. Whenever PIADRB is loaded with data, the display will automatically be triggered.

15.7   HANDSHAKING DATA AS AN EXAMPLE

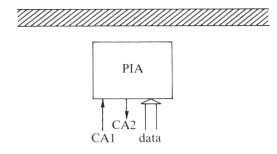

Fig. 15.17

A positive edge on CA1 is to be used to indicate that (more) data is available on PA0 . . . PA7. IRQ1 should be set and an interrupt generated. A negative pulse should be produced on CA2 to indicate that the data has been read by the processor. CA2 should remain low until new data is signalled.

```
INITPIA     EQU      *
            CLR.B    PIACRA        * select PIADDRA
            CLR.B    PIADDRA       * A side for input
            MOVE.B   #$27,PIACRA   * binary pattern 00100111 in
                                     CRA. This causes a negative
                                     pulse on CA2 which starts
                                     when DRA is read and ends
                                     when IRQ1 is set. IRQ1 is
                                     set on a positive edge. Inter-
                                     rupts are enabled.
```

* end of INITPIA.

The interrupt routine will then contain:

```
     MOVE.B  PIADRA, NEWDATA        * input data and reset IRQ1
```

which causes all of the required events to occur. This is shown on a timing diagram in Fig. 15.18:

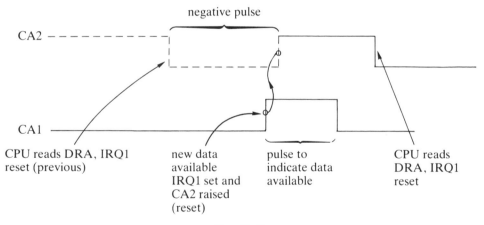

Fig. 15.18

15.8   EXAMPLE OF A PIA INTERRUPT PROGRAM

The complete code is given as Fig. 15.19 for a (contrived) example to illustrate interrupt signals coming from two sources at the same level. It has been kept as simple as possible for illustrative purposes. It assumes that a keyboard is connected to *both* an ACIA addressed through 30061 *and* a PIA addressed through 30051. Such an arrangement is unusual and is for educational rather than practical purposes. When the program is run (start address 1000) the WORK routine simply counts forever in a

```
 1                         *              Figure 15.19
 2                         *
 3                         *
 4                         *
 5                         * program to service two sources of interrupt
 6                         * at the same level
 7                         *
 8          00001000       STACK           EQU  $1000
 9
10                         ***ACIA MC6850
11          00030061       ACIA            EQU  $30061      * ACIA base address
12          00030061       ACIASTATUS      EQU  ACIA
13          00030061       ACIACONTROL     EQU  ACIA
14          00030063       ACIARXDATA      EQU  ACIA+2
15          00030063       ACIATXDATA      EQU  ACIA+2
16
17                         ***PIA MC6821
18          00030051       PIA             EQU  $30051      * PIA base address
19          00030051       PIADRA          EQU  PIA
20          00030051       PIADDRA         EQU  PIA
21          00030053       PIACRA          EQU  PIA+2
22          00030055       PIADRB          EQU  PIA+4
23          00030055       PIADDRB         EQU  PIA+4
24          00030057       PIACRB          EQU  PIA+6
25
26          00001000           ORG   $1000
27
28          00001000       START  EQU      *
29                         **************************
30                         * INITIALIZATION MODULE *
31                         **************************
32 001000 4FF81000                LEA      STACK,SP
33 001004 4EB8106A                JSR      VECTINIT
34 001008 4EB8109C                JSR      INITACIA
35 00100C 4EB810BA                JSR      INITPIA
36                         * set processor status register to level 0
37 001010 027CF8FF                ANDI     #$F8FF,SR
38 001014 4EB8101A                JSR      WORK
39 001018 4E40                    TRAP     #0
40
41
42                         ***************
43                         * WORK MODULE *
44                         ***************
45                         *
46          0000101A       WORK    EQU      *
47 00101A 4286                     CLR.L D6
48 00101C 5286             WLOOP   ADDQ.L   #1,D6
49 00101E 60FC                     BRA      WLOOP   * loop forever incrementing D
50 001020 4E75                     RTS
53                         *****************************
54                         * INTERRUPT SERVICE MODULE *
55                         *****************************
58          00001022       INT4    EQU      *
59 001022 08390000
           00030061                BTST     #0,ACIASTATUS   * looks for rx bit
```

```
60 00102A 66000010                  BNE      SERIAL       * branch if rx set
61                       * next look for IRQ1 signal (ie CA1)
62 00102E 08390007
        00030053                    BTST     #7,PIACRA
63 001036 66000014                  BNE      PARALL       * branch if set
64 00103A 4E40          ERROR       TRAP     #0           * error exit
65
66 00103C 06380001105E SERIAL      ADDI.B   #1,SCOUNT
67                       * read char from ACIA & store in buffer
68 001042 11F900030063
         105C                       MOVE.B   ACIARXDATA,SBUFF
69 00104A 4E73                      RTE
70
71 00104C 06380001105F PARALL      ADDI.B   #1,PCOUNT
72                       * read char from PIA & store in buffer
73 001052 11F900030051
         105D                       MOVE.B   PIADRA,PBUFF
74 00105A 4E73                      RTE
75
76 00105C 00           SBUFF       DC.B     0
77 00105D 00           PBUFF       DC.B     0
78 00105E 00           SCOUNT      DC.B     0        * initialized in INITACIA
79 00105F 00           PCOUNT      DC.B     0        * initialized in INITPIA
80                       *
81                       * end of level 4 interrupt service routine
83                       ******************************************************
84                       * interrupts should not occur at levels 1,2,3,5,6
85                       * the service routines cause a clean exit into TUTOR
86 001060 4E40          INT1        TRAP #0
87 001062 4E40          INT2        TRAP #0
88 001064 4E40          INT3        TRAP #0
89 001066 4E40          INT5        TRAP #0
90 001068 4E40          INT6        TRAP #0
92                       ******************************************************
93                       * set up interrupt vectors:
94         0000106A     VECTINIT         EQU    *
95 00106A 21FC00001060
         0064                       MOVE.L   #INT1,$64    * level 1
96 001072 21FC00001062
         0068                       MOVE.L   #INT2,$68    * level 2
97 00107A 21FC00001064
         006C                       MOVE.L   #INT3,$6C    * level 3
99                       * level 4 interrupt service routine for ACIA and PIA:
100 001082 21FC00001022
         0070                       MOVE.L   #INT4,$70
101 00108A 21FC00001066
         0074                       MOVE.L   #INT5,$74    * level 5
102 001092 21FC00001068
         0078                       MOVE.L   #INT6,$78    * level 6
103 00109A 4E75                     RTS
106                      * INITACIA
107                      * subroutine to RESET & configure ACIA
108                      * & to initialize serial buffer count
109                      *
110         0000109C     INITACIA        EQU    *
111                      * RESET at power-on for the ACIA
```

```
112 00109C 13FC0003
            00030061            MOVE.B   #3,ACIACONTROL
114                        * wait for RESET to take effect:
115 0010A4 303C0400            MOVE    #$400,D0
116 0010A8 5340       RLOOP    SUBQ    #1,D0
117 0010AA 66FC                BNE     RLOOP
119                        * configure the ACIA and enable receive interrupts:
120 0010AC 13FC0095
            00030061            MOVE.B   #$95,ACIACONTROL
121 0010B4 4238105E            CLR.B    SCOUNT      * serial count
122 0010B8 4E75                RTS
123                        *
124                        * end of ACIA initialization
126                        ********************************************************
127                        * INITPIA
128                        * subroutine to configure PIA
129                        * & initialize parallel buffer count
130                        *
131         000010BA       INITPIA EQU      *
132                        * configure PIA Data Direction and Control registers
133 0010BA 423900030057            CLR.B    PIACRB      * select DDRB
134 0010C0 13FC00FF
            00030055            MOVE.B   #$FF,PIADDRB * B side for output
135 0010C8 08F90002
            00030057            BSET    #2,PIACRB    * select DRB
136 0010D0 423900030053            CLR.B    PIACRA      * select DDRA
137 0010D6 423900030051            CLR.B    PIADDRA     * A side for input
138 0010DC 13FC0007
            00030053            MOVE.B   #$07,PIACRA  * IRQ1 set on + edge
139                        *                         * interrupt enabled
140 0010E4 4238105F            CLR.B    PCOUNT      * parallel count
141 0010E8 4E75                RTS
142                        *
143                        * end of PIA initialization
145                        ********************************************************
146                                END
```

****** TOTAL ERRORS   0--   0 -- TOTAL LINES 139

APPROX 2090 UNUSED SYMBOL TABLE ENTRIES

```
ACIACONT 030061 ACIARXDA 030063 ACIASTAT 030061 ACIATXDA 030063 ACIA     030061
ERROR    00103A INITACIA 00109C INITPIA  0010BA INT1     001060 INT2     001062
INT3     001064 INT4     001022 INT5     001066 INT6     001068 PARALL   00104C
PBUFF    00105D PCOUNT   00105F PIA      030051 PIACRA   030053 PIACRB   030057
PIADDRA  030051 PIADDRB  030055 PIADRA   030051 PIADRB   030055 RLOOP    0010A8
SBUFF    00105C SCOUNT   00105E SERIAL   00103C STACK    001000 START    001000
VECTINIT 00106A WLOOP    00101C WORK     00101A
```

Fig. 15.19 PIA and ACIA with interrupts

loop in D6 (as in the programs in Chapter 13). Depressing a key causes two
interrupts, the first one from the faster (parallel) PIA followed by the second from
the slower (serial) ACIA. The code stores the character read in from the keyboard in
PBUFF from the PIA and SBUFF from the ACIA.

The reader should examine the initialization sections for the PIA and ACIA. If an MC68000 system with this arrangement is available, the program could be run and it could be verified that:

- the same character does indeed appear from two sources,
- it comes from the PIA first

Variations on the example may be produced. It is left as an exercise for the reader to extend the code as follows:

- Input a character in the range 0(1)9.
- Input a character A (anticlockwise) or C (clockwise).
- Add a section which drives the stepping motor.
- Use the characters input to control the speed and direction of rotation.
- Input a character and arrange that the stepping motor stops at the point referenced by the character. Another input should cause the pointer to move to the new position.

This introduces a requirement for an interactive initialization section in which the user specifies the initial position of the pointer.

Number systems for computers

ONTENTS

NUMBER SYSTEMS FOR COMPUTERS

1. Representation of information

In any machine, system, or communication device, the information to be used or transmitted must be formalized in such a way that the machine or device can use it. This formalization is called *coding*, a particular code is the formal representation of the information the system uses. Examples are:

- Morse code, a variable length code used in telegraphy.
- Postcodes, a code used by letter sorting machines.
- Subscriber Trunk Dialling; the telephone number uses digits that are uniquely important, e.g. 01 as the first pair of digits means *London*.
- The Roman system I, II, III, IV, V, VI, VII, VIII, IX, X is the use of a code in a particular form of counting.
- ASCII; a fixed length 7-bit code used in the transfer of data by characters. (An 8-bit ASCII exists in draft form and includes the 7-bit code as a subset.)

2. Information in computers

The use of *two-state* (or *binary*) is very common in digital devices for many reasons, for example *two stable states* can be reliably and easily implemented. Some data transmission systems, however, do use *three* and others *multiple* states.

In digital computers, the use of *two stable states* or *binary* is almost universal. The symbols that are used in the real world (for communication, calculation, counting, etc.) represent information, and in order to be stored and used in a digital computer, they must be coded. The fundamental unit from which the coded system is built up in a digital computer is the *two stable state unit* (or *bistable*) called a *binary digit* – or *bit* for short.

Symbolically the *bit* is often represented as a 0 or a 1, but other forms are to be found, e.g. + or –, and in the computer hardware the 0 or 1 appears in a large variety of forms, e.g. a positive or negative current, a hole or not in paper tape or two different voltage levels.

In digital computers, a sequence of *binary digits* or *bits* collected together in an ordered way is used to represent a wide range and many different forms of information. This ordered collection of bits is called a *computer word*, e.g. 16 bits. Computer *words* which are used to store information are not to be confused with natural language *words*; the latter are normally totally variable in length from one symbol (letter) to many, and are used to convey information. In many digital computers the word is a fixed size, which often gives rise to problems. A number of computers use groups of integer multiples of a basic unit, which is typically 8 bits, e.g. the MC68000 byte, word and longword.

Thus, in the 68000, a typical unit for storing numbers is a word of size 16 bits:

15 14 13 12 11 10 9 8 7 6 5 4 3 2 1 0   digit number

A large number of words make up the computer main store. These are used to hold *information* be it numbers, characters, computer instructions, system software, etc.

3. Number systems – decimal

In the *decimal* system there are *ten* symbols:

$$0 \quad 1 \quad 2 \quad 3 \quad 4 \quad 5 \quad 6 \quad 7 \quad 8 \quad 9$$

The number *ten* is called the *base* of the system. When used in counting, 1 more than (or added to) 0 is 1, 1 more than 1 is 2, etc., and 1 more than 9 is a problem because no single symbol exists for it. This is solved in the decimal system by incrementing by 1 in a 'tens position' and resetting the 'units position' to zero. This gives the number 10 called *ten*. The counting process continues to give . . . . $1 + 19 = 20 \ldots 1 + 29 = 30 \ldots 1 + 99 = 100$, and now we have a 'hundreds position' or third digit position.

Formally, the number 34962 therefore means 2 units, plus 6 tens, plus 9 hundreds, plus 4 thousands, plus 3 ten thousands, or:

$$(3*10000) + (4*1000) + (9*100) + (6*10) + (2*1) \text{ or}$$
$$(3*10^4) + (4*10^3) + (9*10^2) + (6*10^1) + (2*10^0).$$

Since decimal is the familiar system used from earliest school days, all other systems are usually related to it.

4. Number systems – binary

In the *binary* system there are *two* symbols:

$$0 \quad 1$$

The number *two* is called the *base* of the system. When used in counting, 1 more than (or added to) 0 is 1, but 1 more than 1 is not a single symbol (since 2 is not allowed) and is therefore a problem, solved in the binary system by incrementing by 1 in a 'twos position' and resetting the 'units position' to zero. This gives the number 10 or *two*. Often such numbers are written $(10)_2$ to clearly indicate the base, as opposed to $(10)_{10}$. The counting process continues, *in binary*, to give $1 + 10 = 11$ (i.e. three), $1 + 11 = 100$ (i.e. four), so that we now have a 'fours position'; $1 + 100 = 101$ (i.e. five), $1 + 101 = 110$ (i.e.six), etc.

Formally, the binary number 101101 therefore means 1 unit plus zero twos, plus 1 fours, plus 1 eights, plus zero sixteens, plus 1 thirty twos, or:

$$(1*32) + (0*16) + (1*8) \ + (1*4) \ + (0*2) \ + (*1) \text{ or}$$
$$(1*2^5) + (0*2^4) + (1*2^2) + (1*2^2) + (0*2^1) + (1*2^0) \text{ or}$$
$$32 \ + \qquad\quad 8 \ + \ 4 \qquad\quad + \ 1$$
$$= (45)_{10}$$

So the decimal number 45 is 101101 in binary

or $(45)_{10} = (101101)_2$

Counting in binary and decimal we have:

0	1	10	11	100	101	110	111	1000	1001	1010	1011	
0	1	2	3	4	5	6	7	8	9	10	11	etc

5. Number systems – octal

In the *octal* system there are *eight* symbols:

0   1   2   3   4   5   6   7

The number *eight* is called the base of the system. As in the decimal and binary systems, for example:

$(10)_8$ means 1*8 plus 0
$(11)_8$ means 1*8 plus 1

Formally the octal number $(7053)_8$ means:

$(7*8^3) + (0*8^2) + (5*8^1) + (3*8^0)$

or   7*512   + 5*8 + 3   =   3627

So the decimal $(3627)_{10} = (7053)_8$ in octal.

Counting in binary, octal and decimal we have:

0	1	10	11	100	101	110	111	1000	1001	1010	1011
0	1	2	3	4	5	6	7	10	11	12	13
0	1	2	3	4	5	6	7	8	9	10	11

6. Number systems – hexadecimal

In the *hexadecimal* system there are *sixteen* symbols

0 1 2 3 4 5 6 7 8 9 A B C D E F

The number *sixteen* is called the base of the system. As in the decimal and binary systems, for example:

$(A)_{16}$ means   ten $= (10)_{10}$
$(10)_{16}$ means   1*16 plus 0 $= (16)_{10}$
$(1A)_{16}$ means   1*16 plus $(10)_{10} = (26)_{10}$

Counting in decimal, binary, octal and hexadecimal we have

Decimal	Binary	Octal	Hexadecimal
0	0	0	0
1	1	1	1
2	10	2	2
3	11	3	3
4	100	4	4
5	101	5	5
6	110	6	6
7	111	7	7
8	1000	10	8
9	1001	11	9
10	1010	12	A
11	1011	13	B
12	1100	14	C
13	1101	15	D
14	1110	16	E
15	1111	17	F
16	10000	20	10
17	10001	21	11
18	10010	22	12
19	10011	23	13
20	10100	24	14
21	10101	25	15
22	10110	26	16
23	10111	27	17
24	11000	30	18
25	11001	31	19
26	11010	32	1A
27	11011	33	1B
28	11100	34	1C
29	11101	35	1D
30	11110	36	1E
31	11111	37	1F
32	100000	40	20

7. Summary of common bases and number systems

Base	System
2	Binary
3	Ternary
8	Octal
10	Decimal
12	Duodecimal
16	Hexadecimal

Noting that $2^3 = 8^1$, every octal digit corresponds exactly to 3 binary digits. Noting that $2^4 = 16^1$, every hexadecimal digit corresponds exactly to 4 binary digits. The correspondence between a binary digit and a decimal digit can be determined approximately by noting that:

$$10^3 = 1000, \quad 1024 = 2^{10}, \text{ which gives that:}$$

every 3 decimal digits correspond approximately to ten binary digits *or* 1 decimal digit requires about 10/3 or 3 1/3 binary digits. Using logarithms gives the precise relationship that 1 decimal digit corresponds exactly to $1/\log_{10}2$ binary digits (this number is 3.3219 to four decimal places).

8. Conversion of positive decimal integers to binary

(i) *Binary*

To convert a decimal integer to binary, the integer is successively divided by 2, the remainder (which must be 0 or 1) being noted each time. For example, $(289)_{10}$:

$$
\begin{array}{lll}
289 \div 2 & = 144 & \text{Remainder} = 1 \text{ [least significant bit; } *2^0] \\
144 \div 2 & = 72 & \text{Remainder} = 0 \text{ [second bit; } *2^1] \\
72 \div 2 & = 36 & \text{Remainder} = 0 \text{ [third bit; } *2^2] \\
36 \div 2 & = 18 & \text{Remainder} = 0 \text{ [fourth bit; } *2^3] \\
18 \div 2 & = 9   & \text{Remainder} = 0 \text{ [fifth bit; } *2^4] \\
9 \div 2   & = 4   & \text{Remainder} = 1 \text{ [sixth bit; } *2^5] \\
4 \div 2   & = 2   & \text{Remainder} = 0 \text{ [seventh bit; } *2^6] \\
2 \div 2   & = 1   & \text{Remainder} = 0 \text{ [eighth bit; } *2^7] \\
1 \div 2   & = 0   & \text{Remainder} = 1 \text{ [ninth bit; } *2^8] \\
\end{array}
$$

the process continues until the quotient part becomes 0. Then we have:

$$(289)_{10} = (100100001)$$
$$\text{i.e. } 1*2^8 + 1*2^5 + 1$$

(ii) *Alternatively via hexadecimal or octal*

Since 1 hexadecimal digit corresponds to exactly 4 binary digits, the above process can be achieved via the conversion of decimal integers to hexadecimal (see below), then converting hexadecimal to binary (also see below) directly.

Since 1 octal digit corresponds to exactly 3 binary digits, octal may alternatively be used as an intermediate step.

9. Conversion of positive decimal integers to hexadecimal and octal

(i) *Hexadecimal*

To convert a decimal integer to hexadecimal the integer is successively divided by 16, the remainder (which must lie between 0 and 15) is noted each time. For example $(289)_{10}$:

$$289 \div 16 = 18 \quad \text{Remainder 1 [least significant digit; } *16^0]$$
$$18 \div 16 = 1 \quad \text{Remainder 2 [second digit; } *16^1]$$
$$1 \div 16 = 0 \quad \text{Remainder 1 [third digit; } *16^2]$$

The quotient part is now 0 so the process finishes. We then have:

$$(289)_{10} = (121)_{16}$$

This can be written in binary immediately:

$$\begin{array}{ccc} 1 & 2 & 1 \\ (121)_{16} = 0001 & 0010 & 0001 \end{array}$$

The conversion of a positive decimal integer to binary can thus be carried out by converting to an intermediate representation in hexadecimal (or indeed via any intermediate stage which has as base an exact number of bits, e.g. octal) then converting hexadecimal to binary.

Note that it is only familiarity with decimal that makes us think there is something absolute about a number such as $(289)_{10}$. The same number is given by:

$$(289)_{10} \text{ or } (441)_8 \text{ or } (100100001)_2 \text{ or } (121)_{16}$$

The system or base used is simply the mechanism for a formal representation of the number.

(ii) *Octal*
A very similar algorithm can be used with 8 replacing 16 in the base position.

10. Positive integers in a computer

As has been said earlier, it is now almost universal that digital computers store information (and a number is only one example of information) in binary form in *computer words*. Computers often display or output the contents of words in octal, or hexadecimal, note that this is achieved by storing and working in binary and converting to the octal or hexadecimal form. Taking as an example the 68000 computer word of 16 bits, the decimal number 289 would appear in the computer in binary as:

> 0000000100100001

This is likely to be displayed as $(0121)_{16}$.
The decimal number 2 would appear as:

> 0000000000000010

which would be displayed as $(0002)_{16}$.

The operations that the computer carries out – storing, transferring, adding, subtracting – are done by the hardware in binary on the full specified number of bits (see below) which make up the *word* (or half word or longword or whatever unit is defined).

11. Arithmetic with positive integers

Remember that in binary, $0 + 1 = 1$, $1 + 0 = 1$, $1 + 1 = 10$, and $1 + 1 + 1 = 11$.

A 16-bit word is used as an example:

Addition

0000000100100001	$(289)_{10}$
0000000010100111	$(167)_{10}$
0000000111001000	$(456)_{10}$

Subtraction

0000000100100001	$(289)_{10}$
0000000010100111	$(167)_{10}$
0000000001111010	$(122)_{10}$

Multiplication

0000000010100111	$(167)_{10}$
0000000100100001	$(289)_{10}$
0000000010100111	
0001010011100000	
1010011100000000	
1011110010000111	$(48263)_{10}$

12. Conversion of positive binary (or octal or hexadecimal) integers to decimal

(i) *Binary*

The usual way of carrying this out efficiently is to use *nested multiplication*. For example $(100100001)_2$ in *nested* form is:

$$((((((((1*2+0)*2+0)*2+1)*2+0)*2+0)*2+0)*2+0)*2+1$$

Which is, of course, $1*2^8 + 1*2^5 + 1$.

In the nested form the calculation *starts* with the innermost bracket and works outwards.

(ii) *Octal or hexadecimal*

The same form can be used for octal numbers with base 8, and hexadecimal numbers with base 16.

e.g. $(121)_{16} =$
          $((1*16)+2)*16+1$

13. Positive real numbers in binary and octal

So far only integers have been considered. Extending the types of numbers to include *real*, for example 57.296 (which is the number of degrees in one radian, accurate to 3 decimal places) gives:

$$5*10^1 + 7*10^0 + 2*10^{-1} + 9*10^{-2} + 6*10^{-3}$$

Similarly in binary:

$(1.1101)_2$ means
$1*2^0 + 1*2^{-1} + 1*2^{-2} + 0*2^{-3} + 1*2^{-4}$
$1\quad + 0.5\quad + 0.25\qquad\qquad + 0.0625$
$\qquad\quad = (1.8125)_{10}$

and in hexadecimal:

$(0.41E)_{16}$ means $4*16^{-1} + 1*16^{-2} + 14*16^{-3} = (0.2573242187)_{10}$
                                                           to ten decimal places

14. Conversion of positive real numbers

Real numbers have non-zero values for both the integer part and fractional part, and are converted by treating the two parts separately.

(i) *Integer part of the number:* This is converted as in Section 8 above.
(ii) *Fractional part:* To convert a number which lies between 0 and 1 to binary it is successively multiplied by 2, the integer part which this produces (which must be 0 or 1) is noted and removed each time.

For example, to convert $(0.9)_{10}$ to binary:

$0.9*2 = 1.8$ integer part $= 1$ [most significant bit; $*2^{-1}$]
$0.8*2 = 1.6$ integer part $= 1$ [second significant bit; 2^{-2}]
$0.6*2 = 1.2$ integer part $= 1$ [third significant bit; 2^{-3}]
$0.2*2 = 0.4$ integer part $= 0$ [fourth significant bit; 2^{-4}]
$0.4*2 = 0.8$ integer part $= 0$ [fifth significant bit; 2^{-5}]
$0.8*2 = 1.6$ integer part $= 1$ [sixth significant bit; 2^{-6}]
$0.6*2 = 1.2$ integer part $= 1$ [seventh significant bit; 2^{-6}]
etc.

This process is clearly non terminating, and repeats.
Thus $(0.9)_{10} = 0.11100110011 \ldots$

In its nested form for conversion from binary to decimal the number must first be truncated, e.g. seven binary places 0.1110011 is

$$((((((1*2^{-1})+1)*2^{-1}+0)*2^{-1}+0)*2^{-1}+1)*2^{-1}+1)*2^{-1}+1)*2^{-1}$$

which gives

$$1*2^{-1}+1*2^{-2}+1*2^{-3}+0*2^{-4}+0*2^{-5}+1*2^{-6}+1*2^{-7} = (0.89844)_{10}$$

to five decimal places

A number such as $(0.9)_{10}$ which is exact in its decimal form is thus not exact in its binary form and this leads to an error when it appears in a digital computer.

To convert positive real numbers to and from octal or hexadecimal a very similar algorithm is used with 8 and 16 replacing 2 above in the base positions. For example, convert $(27.1)_{10}$ to hexadecimal. The integer part is $(27)_{10} = (1B)_{16}$, and the fractional part is

$0.1*16 = 1.6$	integer part $= 1$	[most significant digit; $*16^{-1}$]
$0.6*16 = 9.6$	integer part $= 9$	[second significant digit; 16^{-2}]
$0.6*16 = 9.6$	integer part $= 9$	[third significant digit; 16^{-3}]
$0.6*16 = 9.6$	integer part $= 9$	[fourth significant digit; 16^{-4}]
$0.6*16 = 9.6$	integer part $= 9$	[fifth significant digit; 16^{-5}]
$0.8*16$ repeats		

Thus $(27.1)_{10} = (1B.19999\ldots\ldots\ldots)_{16}$ which is, of course, easily written in binary

11011.0001100110011001100110011001100 etc.

15. Negative binary integers

Negative integers can be stored in digital computers (and operated on by the hardware) in different ways, one of the most common is the *complement* form. One way of understanding this is to consider a negative number as its positive form subtracted from 0. Thus formally, for example, the negative form of 72 is $0 - (+72)$. This is usually written in *signed magnitude* as −72.

Carrying out this subtraction gives:

$$\begin{array}{r} 0 \\ -72 \\ \hline \ldots\ldots 99999928 \end{array}$$

Note the non-terminating sequence of 9s extending to the left, and that the implied leading zeros were used. The number .....99999928 is, in fact, another way of writing (−72); it is called the *ten's-complement* form, and can be used in all arithmetic operations in place of (−72). Similarly, in binary the common form of negative integers is *two's-complement*, produced by subtracting the positive version of the number from 0, for example $(−45)_{10}$

$$\begin{array}{r} 0 \\ 101101 \\ \hline \ldots 111111111010011 \end{array}$$

Note the non-terminating sequence of 1s extending to the left. Note also that if leading zeros are added to the 45, then the negative number is the digital opposite (change 0 for 1 and 1 for 0) with the exception of the least significant 1. This gives a simple rule for working out the *two's-complement* (or *true negative*):

- Rule: Fix the total number of bits required (see below) to represent the number, for example sixteen; write out the number with all the leading zeros inserted, e.g.:

  0000000000101101

  then change 0 for 1 and 1 for 0

  1111111111010010 which gives the *one's-complement* form. Then add 1

  $$\frac{1}{1111111111010011}$$

16. Negative binary integers in a computer

As was said in Section 10, the numbers are stored in and operated on from computer words which are of fixed size. Consider the 68000 size of 16 bits. Suppose that the operation $(19)_{10} - (45)_{10}$ is carried out

$$\frac{\begin{array}{ll}000000000010011 & (19)_{10}\\ 000000000101101 & (45)_{10}\end{array}}{111111111100110}$$

The result is the *two's-complement* form of $(-26)_{10}$. In the computer word, the extension of 1s to the left must end when the word is full. Thus, in 16 bits:

$$(+26)_{10} = (000000000011010)_2 = (000032)_8 = (001A)_{16}$$

$$(-26)_{10} = (111111111100110)_2 = (177746)_8 = (FFE6)_{16}$$

In a digital computer therefore there could be confusion between a very large positive number and a negative number; to avoid this, the sixteenth (labelled 15) or leftmost bit is reserved as a *sign bit* when signed integers are in use). If it is 0 then the number is deemed to be positive; if it is 1 then the number is deemed to be negative. This means that the largest positive integer that can be stored in a 16-bit word when using *two's-complement* for negative numbers is:

$$(0111111111111111)_2 = (077777)_8$$

$$= (7FFF)_{16} = (32767)_{10}$$

Note there are, in fact, a number of different ways of storing numbers – both positive and negative. The use of *two's-complement* for negative numbers is one (common) form; there are others, all make use of a *sign bit* to indicate negative (or indeed positive) numbers. In the 68000 there is an option of working with signed or unsigned (positive only) integers.

17. General form of a real binary number

A binary number can be written as:

$$a_m * 2^m + a_{m-1} * 2^{m-1} + \ldots a_1 * 2^1 + a_0 * 2^0 + a_{-1} * 2^{-1} + a_{-2} * 2^{-2} \ldots a_{-n} * 2^{-n}$$

where $a_m a_{m-1} \ldots a_1 a_0 a_{-1} a_{-2} \ldots a_n$ are the binary digits, each one either 0 or 1. There are (m + 1) bits for the integer part, i.e. before the binary point, and n bits for the fractional part.

For example $(11011.101)_2 = (27.625)_{10}$.

18. Fixed-point arithmetic in a computer

As has been seen in Sections 10, 11, and 16, digital computers carry out arithmetic operations with a fixed number of bits. The 68000 has 16 bits for each word. Many computers allow multi-word working (double length is common). Arithmetic with these numbers is often more complicated and takes longer.

To use a computer word to store a real fixed point number involves a decision by the user of where the binary point is going to be. For example, $(27.5)_{10} = (11011.1)_2 = (33.4)_8 = (1B.8)_{16}$. How can this be stored in a 16-bit word?

One solution is $\boxed{00011011.10000000}$ i.e. to 8 b. p.

Another is $\boxed{00000011011.10000}$ i.e. to 5 b. p.

Suppose that is to be added to $(41.75)_{10} = (101001.11)_2$. How must this number be stored?

- Rule: ADDITION
  All fixed-point numbers must be operated upon with the binary point in the same position.

Thus to 8 b. p.	+	00011011.10000000	27.5
		00101001.11000000	41.75
	ans	01000101.01000000	69.25

or to 5 b. p.	+	00000011011.10000	27.5
		00000101001.11000	41.75
	ans	00001000101.01000	69.25

If many fixed-point numbers are added (or accumulated) into a single word, overflow may occur.

Integers are the special case of numbers stored fixed-point with zero binary places.

- Rule: <u>SUBTRACTION</u>
  The same as <u>ADDITION</u>.

    It should be noted that the subtraction of a number that is positive is the same as the addition of that number in its negative form.

- Rule: <u>MULTIPLICATION</u>
  If one single length number with b_1 binary places is multiplied by another with b_2 binary places, the result has $(b_1 + b_2)$ binary places and is nearly always left as a double word (or double length) product. What the user does with the product must then be related to the requirements of the program; for example it may be possible to contract the product to be stored in a single word.

For example

	00011011.10000000
	00000101001.11000
0000000010001111	100.0010000000000

27.5 to 8 b. p.
41.75 to 5 b. p.
product 1148.125 to 13 b. p.

This can be stored in a single word

0010001111100.001

to 3 b. p.

- Rule: <u>DIVISION</u>
  Fixed point division is the converse of multiplication.

19. Floating-point numbers

The major problem associated with numbers in a fixed-point form is the severe restriction on the *range* of the numbers. Associated with this is that arithmetic operations may cause the numbers to go out of range.

   Floating-point form is a method that extends the *range* of numbers; frequently it does it at the expense of the *accuracy* (i.e. the number of *significant digits*) of the number.

   A number in floating form is $A*B^N$

   where   A is called the *mantissa*
              N is called the *exponent*, a positive or negative integer
              B is the *base* of the number.

A, B and N can, in general, be any number (see Knuth, ref. 5). In practice, there are two main forms:

- Decimal: $A * 10^N$, A is a real fixed-point decimal number and N is a decimal integer. For example:

    $31.4159*10^{-1}$

- Binary: $A * 2^N$, A is a real fixed-point binary number, and N is a binary integer. For example:

    $11.01100011*2^3$

The floating-point number is called *standard* (or sometimes *normal*) *floating-point* if the range of the mantissa is restricted.

- Decimal: $0.1 \leqslant A < 1.0$ or $-1.0 \leqslant A < -0.1$

- Binary: $0.5 \leqslant A < 1.0$ or $-1.0 \leqslant A < -0.5$

The Exponent, N, is a +ve or –ve integer.

Examples	*Decimal*	*Binary*
	$0.625*10^{-1}$	$0.1*2^{-11}$
	$0.25*10^{1}$	$0.101*2^{10}$
	$0.275*10^{2}$	$0.110111*2^{101}$
	$0.4175*10^{4}$	$0.1000001001111*2^{1101}$

The reason for the name floating-point can be understood from the fact that the integer exponent simply shifts (or scales) the decimal point or binary point from the standard position.

20. Floating-point numbers in a computer

A standard floating-point binary number is in the form $a*2^{n}$. Frequently, and sometimes confusingly, the words standard and binary are omitted.

One problem about (standard) floating-point (binary) numbers is that there are always two parts required to define a number – the mantissa and the exponent. These two parts are stored in a variety of ways which depend on the type of floating-point hardware available with any particular computer. A 16-bit minicomputer typically uses one computer word for the mantissa, so this is stored fixed-point with fifteen binary places, and one computer word for the integer exponent. Thus a single number with this system requires *two* store locations. Some floating-point hardware units use two-, three-, and five-word formats. The five-word format could be:

word 1	word 2	word 3	word 4	word 5

79   64 62   48 47   32 31   16 15   0

mantissa   exponent

A common arrangement to be found in mainframe computers such as the DEC System 10 (word length 36 bits) is the *packing* of the mantissa and the exponent into a single computer word. The format of the DEC-10 floating-point number is:

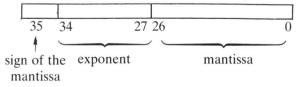

35   34   27 26   0

sign of the   exponent   mantissa
mantissa

Clearly this is a totally different arrangement. The packed single word of the DEC-10 has 27 bits for the mantissa and thus each number is *accurate* to 27 significant binary digits (just greater than 8 decimal digits) compared with 36 bits (nearly 11 decimal digits) of the full word used for fixed-point numbers. The power of the floating-point form is shown by the *range*. Considering the DEC-10 form:

the exponent has 8 bits available:

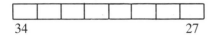

34   27

This can be used for numbers in the range 0 to 255, but, since +ve and −ve values for the exponent are required, the permitted values for n are −128 to +127 and it is stored as a positive integer with 128 added. This gives:

Positive numbers

- Largest value of mantissa = very nearly 1.0, largest value of exponent +127
  therefore the largest number is almost $1.0*2^{127}$ which is just greater than 10^{+38}.

- Smallest value of mantissa = $\frac{1}{2}$, smallest value of exponent is −128
  therefore the smallest number is $\frac{1}{2}*2^{-128} = 2^{-129}$ which is very nearly 10^{-39}.

The usual operating range for numbers on the DEC-10 is taken as from 10^{+38} down to 10^{-38} and any numbers that are outside this range cause a hardware error condition, *overflow* if the number is too large (typically caused by a divide by zero), and *underflow* if the number is too small.

21. Computer languages and numbers

It is almost universal that variables declared as *type real* appear as numbers in floating point format in the computer. Variables declared as *type integer* always appear as integers – that is numbers in fixed-point format with zero binary places. But note that some languages differentiate between constants such as 1.0 and 1; 1.0 is a real number and would appear in floating-point form, e.g. on the DEC-10:

1.0 is $\boxed{0 \mid 10000001 \mid 100 \dots\dots\dots 0}$
     35   34   27 26   0

Whereas 1 is an integer and would appear in the DEC-10 as

$\boxed{000000000000\dots\dots\dots\dots 1}$

In some languages (e.g. BASIC) it is not always clear which form an *integer* actually takes in the computer. This largely depends on the whims of the compiler or interpreter.

22. Arithmetic operations on floating-point numbers

- ADDITION and SUBTRACTION – Binary numbers

$$(a_1*2^{n_1}) \pm (a_2*2^{n_2})$$

The principle of floating-point addition and subtraction is to make the two exponents equal by shifting one mantissa to the right – dividing by 2^2, note $a*2^n = (a/2)*2^{n+1}$. When the two exponents are equal, the mantissa may be added (or subtracted) as fixed-point real numbers.

For example $(27.5)_{10}$ + $(41.75)_{10}$

$$(0.110111*2^{101})_2 + (0.10100111*2^{110})_2$$

The exponents are different so the smaller number is shifted right until they are equal, one place in this case

$$(0.0110111*2^{110})   +   (0.10100111*2^{110})_2$$

Adding gives $(1.00010101*2^{110})_2$

but this is not in the standard form. One shift right gives the result in standard form

$$(0.100010101*2^{111})_2$$

- MULTIPLICATION

$$(a_1*2^{n_1}) * (a_2*2^{n_2})$$

The process is much simpler since there is no need to make the exponents equal. The result is

$$a_1*a_2*2^{n_1+n_2}$$

Since the range of each mantissa is $\frac{1}{2}$ to 1 the range of the product a_1*a_2 is $\frac{1}{4}$ to 1, so that the final operation may involve a shift left to get the product into standard form.

- DIVISION

is very similar to multiplication.

23. Block floating-point form

This is sometimes used when a compromise between the *accuracy* of the fixed-point form and the *range* of the floating-point form is needed. It is commonly used with *arrays* where all the numbers in the array (or *block*) (for example a vector of one hundred numbers) have a single exponent which applies to all numbers in that array. Each number is stored in fixed-point format with full word accuracy. Note that these numbers will not, in general, be in standard form.

24. Binary-coded decimal

The numbers used in this Appendix have all appeared in their *natural* (Decimal, Binary, Octal, Hexadecimal) form. Some digital computers give the option of working with the numeric information in *decimal*, rather than binary. Where this happens, it is common that the decimal form in the computer is stored and dealt with by the hardware in Binary Coded Decimal.

In Binary Coded Decimal, each of the Decimal Digits of the number is coded into binary using four bits. *Natural binary-coded decimal* (NBCD) is perhaps most common in computers but there are other codes.

		Other examples		
Decimal character or digit	NBCD or 8421 code	2421 Code	Excess 3 Code	Gray Code
0	0000	0000	0011	0000
1	0001	0001	0100	0001
2	0010	0010	0101	0011
3	0011	0011	0110	0010
4	0100	0100	0111	0110
5	0101	0101	1000	0111
6	0110	0110	1001	0101
7	0111	0111	1010	0100
8	1000	1110	1011	1100
9	1001	1111	1100	1101

The different codes each have useful properties for control and data-logging applications. Thus, for example, the decimal number:

314159

in NBCD is:

0011   0001   0100   0001   0101   1001

i.e. 24 bits are required

or in Gray Code is

0010   0001   0110   0001   0111   1101

Whereas, as a natural binary integer, it is:

1001100101100101111

i.e. 19 bits are required.

In order to represent *real numbers* a further character code is needed for the decimal point.

The Asynchronous Communications Interface Adapter (ACIA) MC6850

ASYNCHRONOUS COMMUNICATIONS INTERFACE ADAPTER (ACIA)

The MC6850 Asynchronous Communications Interface Adapter provides the data formatting and control to interface serial asynchronous data communications information to bus organized systems such as the MC6800 Microprocessing Unit.

The bus interface of the MC6850 includes select, enable, read/write, interrupt and bus interface logic to allow data transfer over an 8-bit bi-directional data bus. The parallel data of the bus system is serially transmitted and received by the asynchronous data interface, with proper formatting and error checking. The functional configuration of the ACIA is programmed via the data bus during system initialization. A programmable Control Register provides variable word lengths, clock division ratios, transmit control, receive control, and interrupt control. For peripheral or modem operation three control lines are provided. These lines allow the ACIA to interface directly with the MC6860L 0-600 bps digital modem.

- Eight and Nine-Bit Transmission
- Optional Even and Odd Parity
- Parity, Overrun and Framing Error Checking
- Programmable Control Register
- Optional ÷1, ÷16, and ÷64 Clock Modes
- Up to 500 kbps Transmission
- False Start Bit Deletion
- Peripheral/Modem Control Functions
- Double Buffered
- One or Two Stop Bit Operation

MOS

(N-CHANNEL, SILICON-GATE)

ASYNCHRONOUS COMMUNICATIONS INTERFACE ADAPTER

L SUFFIX
CERAMIC PACKAGE
CASE 716

NOT SHOWN: **P SUFFIX**
PLASTIC PACKAGE
CASE 709

M6800 MICROCOMPUTER FAMILY
BLOCK DIAGRAM

MC6850 ASYNCHRONOUS COMMUNICATIONS INTERFACE ADAPTER
BLOCK DIAGRAM

MAXIMUM RATINGS

Rating	Symbol	Value	Unit
Supply Voltage	V_{CC}	–0.3 to +7.0	Vdc
Input Voltage	V_{in}	–0.3 to +7.0	Vdc
Operating Temperature Range	T_A	0 to +70	°C
Storage Temperature Range	T_{stg}	–55 to +150	°C
Thermal Resistance	θ_{JA}	82.5	°C/W

This device contains circuitry to protect the inputs against damage due to high static voltages or electric fields; however, it is advised that normal precautions be taken to avoid application of any voltage higher than maximum rated voltages to this high-impedance circuit.

ELECTRICAL CHARACTERISTICS (V_{CC} = 5.0 V ±5%, V_{SS} = 0, T_A = 0 to 70°C unless otherwise noted.)

Characteristic		Symbol	Min	Typ	Max	Unit
Input High Voltage		V_{IH}	V_{SS} + 2.0	–	V_{CC}	Vdc
Input Low Voltage		V_{IL}	V_{SS} –0.3	–	V_{SS} + 0.8	Vdc
Input Leakage Current (V_{in} = 0 to 5.25 Vdc)	R/W,CS0,CS1,$\overline{CS2}$,Enable	I_{in}	–	1.0	2.5	μAdc
Three-State (Off State) Input Current (V_{in} = 0.4 to 2.4 Vdc)	D0-D7	I_{TSI}	–	2.0	10	μAdc
Output High Voltage (I_{Load} = –205 μAdc, Enable Pulse Width <25 μs)		V_{OH}	V_{SS} + 2.4	–	–	Vdc
(I_{Load} = –100 μAdc, Enable Pulse Width <25 μs)	Tx Data, $\overline{RTS}$		V_{SS} + 2.4	–	–	
Output Low Voltage (I_{Load} = 1.6 mAdc, Enable Pulse Width <25 μs)		V_{OL}	–	–	V_{SS} + 0.4	Vdc
Output Leakage Current (Off State) (V_{OH} = 2.4 Vdc)	$\overline{IRQ}$	I_{LOH}	–	1.0	10	μAdc
Power Dissipation		P_D	–	300	525	mW
Input Capacitance		C_{in}				pF
(V_{in} = 0, T_A = 25°C, f = 1.0 MHz)	D0-D7		–	10	12.5	
	E, Tx Clk, Rx Clk, R/W, RS, Rx Data, CS0, CS1, $\overline{CS2}$, $\overline{CTS}$, $\overline{DCD}$		–	7.0	7.5	
Output Capacitance	$\overline{RTS}$, Tx Data	C_{out}	–	–	10	pF
(V_{in} = 0, T_A = 25°C, f = 1.0 MHz)	$\overline{IRQ}$		–	–	5.0	
Minimum Clock Pulse Width, Low (Figure 1)	÷16, ÷64 Modes	PW_{CL}	600	–	–	ns
Minimum Clock Pulse Width, High (Figure 2)	÷16, ÷64 Modes	PW_{CH}	600	–	–	ns
Clock Frequency	÷1 Mode	f_C	–	–	500	kHz
	÷16, ÷64 Modes		–	–	800	
Clock-to-Data Delay for Transmitter (Figure 3)		t_{TDD}	–	–	1.0	μs
Receive Data Setup Time (Figure 4)	÷1 Mode	t_{RDSU}	500	–	–	ns
Receive Data Hold Time (Figure 5)	÷1 Mode	t_{RDH}	500	–	–	ns
Interrupt Request Release Time (Figure 6)		t_{IR}	–	–	1.2	μs
Request-to-Send Delay Time (Figure 6)		t_{RTS}	–	–	1.0	μs
Input Transition Times (Except Enable)		t_r, t_f	–	–	1.0*	μs

*1.0 μs or 10% of the pulse width, whichever is smaller.

BUS TIMING CHARACTERISTICS

READ (Figures 7 and 9)

Characteristic	Symbol	Min	Typ	Max	Unit
Enable Cycle Time	t_{cycE}	1.0	–	–	μs
Enable Pulse Width, High	PW_{EH}	0.45	–	25	μs
Enable Pulse Width, Low	PW_{EL}	0.43	–	–	μs
Setup Time, Address and R/W valid to Enable positive transition	t_{AS}	160	–	–	ns
Data Delay Time	t_{DDR}	–	–	320	ns
Data Hold Time	t_H	10	–	–	ns
Address Hold Time	t_{AH}	10	–	–	ns
Rise and Fall Time for Enable input	t_{Er}, t_{Ef}	–	–	25	ns

WRITE (Figure 8 and 9)

Characteristic	Symbol	Min	Typ	Max	Unit
Enable Cycle Time	t_{cycE}	1.0	–	–	μs
Enable Pulse Width, High	PW_{EH}	0.45	–	25	μs
Enable Pulse Width, Low	PW_{EL}	0.43	–	–	μs
Setup Time, Address and R/W valid to Enable positive transition	t_{AS}	160	–	–	ns
Data Setup Time	t_{DSW}	195	–	–	ns
Data Hold Time	t_H	10	–	–	ns
Address Hold Time	t_{AH}	10	–	–	ns
Rise and Fall Time for Enable input	t_{Er}, t_{Ef}	–	–	25	ns

FIGURE 1 – CLOCK PULSE WIDTH, LOW-STATE

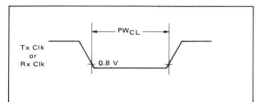

FIGURE 2 – CLOCK PULSE WIDTH, HIGH-STATE

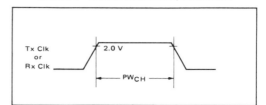

FIGURE 3 – TRANSMIT DATA OUTPUT DELAY

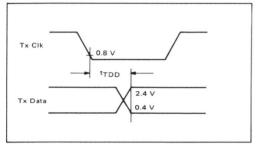

FIGURE 4 – RECEIVE DATA SETUP TIME
($\div$1 Mode)

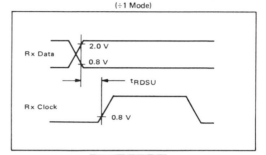

FIGURE 5 – RECEIVE DATA HOLD TIME
($\div$1 Mode)

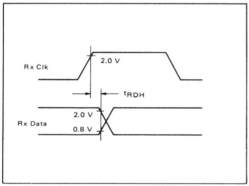

FIGURE 6 – $\overline{\text{REQUEST-TO-SEND}}$ DELAY AND
$\overline{\text{INTERRUPT-REQUEST}}$ RELEASE TIMES

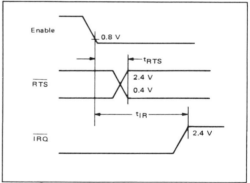

FIGURE 7 – BUS READ TIMING CHARACTERISTICS
(Read information from ACIA)

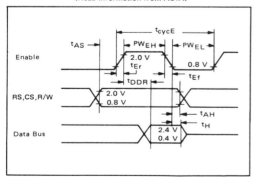

FIGURE 8 – BUS WRITE TIMING CHARACTERISTICS
(Write information into ACIA)

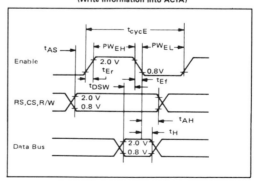

FIGURE 9 – BUS TIMING TEST LOADS

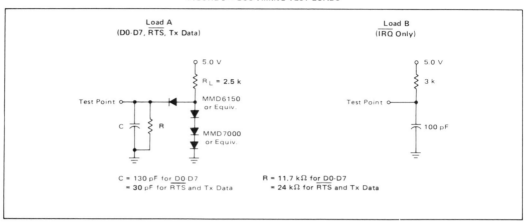

Load A
(D0-D7, RTS, Tx Data)

Load B
(IRQ Only)

5.0 V
R_L = 2.5 k
MMD6150
or Equiv.
Test Point
C   R
MMD7000
or Equiv.

5.0 V
3 k
Test Point
100 pF

C = 130 pF for D0-D7   R = 11.7 kΩ for D0-D7
  = 30 pF for RTS and Tx Data   = 24 kΩ for RTS and Tx Data

EXPANDED BLOCK DIAGRAM

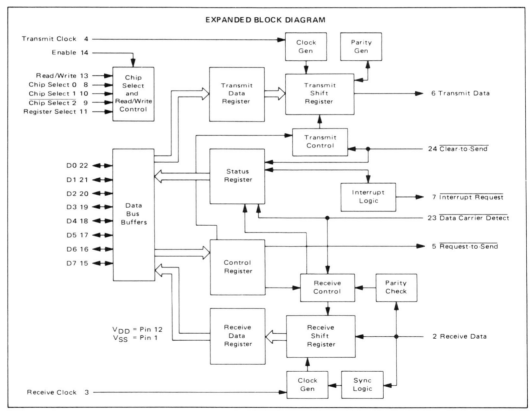

DEVICE OPERATION

At the bus interface, the ACIA appears as two address-able memory locations. Internally, there are four registers: two read-only and two write-only registers. The read-only registers are Status and Receive Data; the write-only registers are Control and Transmit Data. The serial interface consists of serial input and output lines with independent clocks, and three peripheral/modem control lines.

POWER ON/MASTER RESET

The master reset (CR0, CR1) should be set during system initialization to insure the reset condition and prepare for programming the ACIA functional configuration when the communications channel is required. Control bits CR5 and CR6 should also be programmed to define the state of $\overline{RTS}$ whenever master reset is utilized. The ACIA also contains internal power-on reset logic to detect the power line turn-on transition and hold the chip in a reset state to prevent erroneous output transitions prior to initialization. This circuitry depends on clean power turn-on transitions. The power-on reset is released by means of the bus-programmed master reset which must be applied prior to operating the ACIA. After master resetting the ACIA, the programmable Control Register can be set for a number of options such as variable clock divider ratios, variable word length, one or two stop bits, parity (even, odd, or none), etc

TRANSMIT

A typical transmitting sequence consists of reading the ACIA Status Register either as a result of an interrupt or in the ACIA's turn in a polling sequence. A character may be written into the Transmit Data Register if the status read operation has indicated that the Transmit Data Register is empty. This character is transferred to a Shift Register where it is serialized and transmitted from the Transmit Data output preceded by a start bit and followed by one or two stop bits. Internal parity (odd or even) can be optionally added to the character and will occur between the last data bit and the first stop bit. After the first character is written in the Data Register, the Status Register can be read again to check for a Transmit Data Register Empty condition and current peripheral status. If the register is empty, another character can be loaded for transmission even though the first character is in the process of being transmitted (because of double buffering). The second character will be automatically transferred into the Shift Register when the first character transmission is completed. This sequence continues until all the characters have been transmitted.

RECEIVE

Data is received from a peripheral by means of the Receive Data input. A divide-by-one clock ratio is provided for an externally synchronized clock (to its data) while the divide-by-16 and 64 ratios are provided for internal synchronization. Bit synchronization in the divide-by-16 and 64 modes is initiated by the detection of the leading mark-to-space transition of the start bit. False start bit deletion capability insures that a full half bit of a start bit has been received before the internal clock is synchronized to the bit time. As a character is being received, parity (odd or even) will be checked and the error indication will be available in the Status Register along with framing error, overrun error, and Receive Data Register full. In a typical receiving sequence, the Status Register is read to determine if a character has been re-

ceived from a peripheral. If the Receiver Data Register is full, the character is placed on the 8-bit ACIA bus when a Read Data command is received from the MPU. When parity has been selected for an 8-bit word (7 bits plus parity), the receiver strips the parity bit (D7 = 0) so that data alone is transferred to the MPU. This feature reduces MPU programming. The Status Register can continue to be read again to determine when another character is available in the Receive Data Register. The receiver is also double buffered so that a character can be read from the data register as another character is being received in the shift register. The above sequence continues until all characters have been received.

INPUT/OUTPUT FUNCTIONS

ACIA INTERFACE SIGNALS FOR MPU

The ACIA interfaces to the MC6800 MPU with an 8-bit bi-directional data bus, three chip select lines, a register select line, an interrupt request line, read/write line, and enable line. These signals, in conjunction with the MC6800 VMA output, permit the MPU to have complete control over the ACIA.

ACIA Bi-Directional Data (D0-D7) — The bi-directional data lines (D0-D7) allow for data transfer between the ACIA and the MPU. The data bus output drivers are three-state devices that remain in the high-impedance (off) state except when the MPU performs an ACIA read operation.

ACIA Enable (E) — The Enable signal, E, is a high impedance TTL compatible input that enables the bus input/output data buffers and clocks data to and from the ACIA. This signal will normally be a derivative of the MC6800 $\phi 2$ Clock.

Read/Write (R/W) — The Read/Write line is a high impedance input that is TTL compatible and is used to control the direction of data flow through the ACIA's input/output data bus interface. When Read/Write is high (MPU Read cycle), ACIA output drivers are turned on and a selected register is read. When it is low, the ACIA output drivers are turned off and the MPU writes into a selected register. Therefore, the Read/Write signal is used to select read-only or write-only registers within the ACIA.

Chip Select (CS0, CS1, $\overline{CS2}$) — These three high impedance TTL compatible input lines are used to address the ACIA. The ACIA is selected when CS0 and CS1 are high and $\overline{CS2}$ is low. Transfers of data to and from the ACIA are then performed under the control of the Enable signal, Read/Write, and Register Select.

Register Select (RS) — The Register Select line is a high impedance input that is TTL compatible. A high level is used to select the Transmit/Receive Data Registers and a low level the Control/Status Registers. The Read/Write signal line is used in conjunction with Register Select to select the read-only or write-only register in each register pair.

Interrupt Request ($\overline{IRQ}$) — $\overline{Interrupt\ Request}$ is a TTL compatible, open-drain (no internal pullup), active low output that is used to interrupt the MPU. The $\overline{IRQ}$ output remains low as long as the cause of the interrupt is present and the appropriate interrupt enable within the ACIA is set. The IRQ status bit, when high, indicates the $\overline{IRQ}$ output is in the active state.

Interrupts result from conditions in both the transmitter and receiver sections of the ACIA. The transmitter section causes an interrupt when the Transmitter Interrupt Enabled condition is selected (CR5 · $\overline{CR6}$), and the Transmit Data Register Empty (TDRE) status bit is high. The TDRE status bit indicates the current status of the Transmitter Data Register except when inhibited by Clear-to-Send ($\overline{CTS}$) being high or the ACIA being maintained in the Reset condition. The interrupt is cleared by writing data into the Transmit Data Register. The interrupt is masked by disabling the Transmitter Interrupt via CR5 or CR6 or by the loss of $\overline{CTS}$ which inhibits the TDRE status bit. The Receiver section causes an interrupt when the Receiver Interrupt Enable is set and the Receive Data Register Full (RDRF) status bit is high, an Overrun has occurred, or Data Carrier Detect ($\overline{DCD}$) has gone high. An interrupt resulting from the RDRF status bit can be cleared by reading data or resetting the ACIA. Interrupts caused by Overrun or loss of $\overline{DCD}$ are cleared by reading the status register after the error condition has occurred and then reading the Receive Data Register or resetting the ACIA. The receiver interrupt is masked by resetting the Receiver Interrupt Enable.

CLOCK INPUTS

Separate high impedance TTL compatible inputs are provided for clocking of transmitted and received data. Clock frequencies of 1, 16 or 64 times the data rate may be selected.

Transmit Clock (Tx Clk) — The Transmit Clock input is used for the clocking of transmitted data. The transmitter initiates data on the negative transition of the clock.

Receive Clock (Rx Clk) — The Receive Clock input is used for synchronization of received data. (In the ÷ 1 mode, the clock and data must be synchronized externally.) The receiver samples the data on the positive transiton of the clock.

SERIAL INPUT/OUTPUT LINES

Receive Data (Rx Data) — The Receive Data line is a high impedance TTL compatible input through which data is received in a serial format. Synchronization with a clock for detection of data is accomplished internally when clock rates of 16 or 64 times the bit rate are used. Data rates are in the range of 0 to 500 kbps when external synchronization is utilized.

Transmit Data (Tx Data) — The Transmit Data output line transfers serial data to a modem or other peripheral. Data rates are in the range of 0 to 500 kbps when external synchronization is utilized.

PERIPHERAL/MODEM CONTROL

The ACIA includes several functions that permit limited control of a peripheral or modem. The functions included are Clear-to-Send, Request-to-Send and Data Carrier Detect.

Clear-to-Send ($\overline{CTS}$) — This high impedance TTL compatible input provides automatic control of the transmitting end of a communications link via the modem Clear-to-Send active low output by inhibiting the Transmit Data Register Empty (TDRE) status bit.

Request-to-Send ($\overline{RTS}$) — The Request-to-Send output enables the MPU to control a peripheral or modem via the data bus. The $\overline{RTS}$ output corresponds to the state of the Control Register bits CR5 and CR6. When CR6 = 0 or both CR5 and CR6 = 1, the $\overline{RTS}$ output is low (the active state). This output can also be used for Data Terminal Ready ($\overline{DTR}$).

Data Carrier Detect ($\overline{DCD}$) — This high impedance TTL compatible input provides automatic control, such as in the receiving end of a communications link by means of a modem Data Carrier Detect output. The $\overline{DCD}$ input inhibits and initializes the receiver section of the ACIA when high. A low to high transition of the Data Carrier Detect initiates an interrupt to the MPU to indicate the occurrence of a loss of carrier when the Receive Interrupt Enable bit is set.

ACIA REGISTERS

The expanded block diagram for the ACIA indicates the internal registers on the chip that are used for the status, control, receiving, and transmitting of data. The content of each of the registers is summarized in Table 1.

TRANSMIT DATA REGISTER (TDR)

Data is written in the Transmit Data Register during the negative transition of the enable (E) when the ACIA has been addressed and RS · $\overline{R/W}$ is selected. Writing data into the register causes the Transmit Data Register Empty bit in the Status Register to go low. Data can then be transmitted. If the transmitter is idling and no character is being transmitted, then the transfer will take place within one bit time of the trailing edge of the Write command. If a character is being transmitted, the new data character will commence as soon as the previous character is complete. The transfer of data causes the Transmit Data Register Empty (TDRE) bit to indicate empty.

RECEIVE DATA REGISTER (RDR)

Data is automatically transferred to the empty Receive Data Register (RDR) from the receiver deserializer (a shift register) upon receiving a complete character. This event causes the Receive Data Register Full bit (RDRF) in the status buffer to go high (full). Data may then be read through the bus by addressing the ACIA and selecting the Receive Data Register with RS and R/W high when the ACIA is enabled. The non-destructive read cycle causes the RDRF bit to be cleared to empty although

TABLE 1 — DEFINITION OF ACIA REGISTER CONTENTS

Data Bus Line Number	Buffer Address			
	RS • R̄/W̄ Transmit Data Register (Write Only)	RS • R/W Receive Data Register (Read Only)	R̄S̄ • R̄/W̄ Control Register (Write Only)	R̄S̄ • R/W Status Register (Read Only)
0	Data Bit 0*	Data Bit 0	Counter Divide Select 1 (CR0)	Receive Data Register Full (RDRF)
1	Data Bit 1	Data Bit 1	Counter Divide Select 2 (CR1)	Transmit Data Register Empty (TDRE)
2	Data Bit 2	Data Bit 2	Word Select 1 (CR2)	Data Carrier Detect (D̄C̄D̄)
3	Data Bit 3	Data Bit 3	Word Select 2 (CR3)	Clear to Send (C̄T̄S̄)
4	Data Bit 4	Data Bit 4	Word Select 3 (CR4)	Framing Error (FE)
5	Data Bit 5	Data Bit 5	Transmit Control 1 (CR5)	Receiver Overrun (OVRN)
6	Data Bit 6	Data Bit 6	Transmit Control 2 (CR6)	Parity Error (PE)
7	Data Bit 7***	Data Bit 7**	Receive Interrupt Enable (CR7)	Interrupt Request (IRQ)

* Leading bit = LSB = Bit 0
** Data bit will be zero in 7 bit plus parity modes.
*** Data bit is "don't care" in 7 bit plus parity modes.

the data is retained in the RDR. The status is maintained by RDRF as to whether or not the data is current. When the Receive Data Register is full, the automatic transfer of data from the Receiver Shift Register to the Data Register is inhibited and the RDR contents remain valid with its current status stored in the Status Register.

CONTROL REGISTER

The ACIA Control Register consists of eight bits of write-only buffer that are selected when RS and R/W are low. This register controls the function of the receiver, transmitter, interrupt enables, and the Request-to-Send peripheral/modem control output.

Counter Divide Select Bits (CR0 and CR1) — The Counter Divide Select Bits (CR0 and CR1) determine the divide ratios utilized in both the transmitter and receiver sections of the ACIA. Additionally, these bits are used to provide a master reset for the ACIA which clears the Status Register (except for external conditions on C̄T̄S̄ and D̄C̄D̄) and initializes both the receiver and transmitter. Master reset does not affect other Control Register bits. Note that after power-on or a power fail/restart, these bits must be set high to reset the ACIA. After reseting, the clock divide ratio may be selected. These counter select bits provide for the following clock divide ratios:

CR1	CR0	Function
0	0	÷ 1
0	1	÷ 16
1	0	÷ 64
1	1	Master Reset

Word Select Bits (CR2, CR3, and CR4) — The Word

Select bits are used to select word length, parity, and the number of stop bits. The encoding format is as follows:

CR4	CR3	CR2	Function
0	0	0	7 Bits + Even Parity + 2 Stop Bits
0	0	1	7 Bits + Odd Parity + 2 Stop Bits
0	1	0	7 Bits + Even Parity + 1 Stop Bit
0	1	1	7 Bits + Odd Parity + 1 Stop Bit
1	0	0	8 Bits + 2 Stop Bits
1	0	1	8 Bits + 1 Stop Bit
1	1	0	8 Bits + Even Parity + 1 Stop Bit
1	1	1	8 Bits + Odd Parity + 1 Stop Bit

Word length, Parity Select, and Stop Bit changes are not buffered and therefore become effective immediately.

Transmitter Control Bits (CR5 and CR6) — Two Transmitter Control bits provide for the control of the interrupt from the Transmit Data Register Empty condition, the Request-to-Send (R̄T̄S̄) output, and the transmission of a Break level (space). The following encoding format is used:

CR6	CR5	Function
0	0	R̄T̄S̄ = low, Transmitting Interrupt Disabled.
0	1	R̄T̄S̄ = low, Transmitting Interrupt Enabled.
1	0	R̄T̄S̄ = high, Transmitting Interrupt Disabled.
1	1	R̄T̄S̄ = low, Transmits a Break level on the Transmit Data Output. Transmitting Interrupt Disabled.

Receive Interrupt Enable Bit (CR7) — The following interrupts will be enabled by a high level in bit position 7 of the Control Register (CR7): Receive Data Register Full, Overrun, or a low to high transistion on the Data Carrier Detect (D̄C̄D̄) signal line.

STATUS REGISTER

Information on the status of the ACIA is available to the MPU by reading the ACIA Status Register. This read-only register is selected when RS is low and R/W is high. Information stored in this register indicates the status of the Transmit Data Register, the Receive Data Register and error logic, and the peripheral/modem status inputs of the ACIA.

Receive Data Register Full (RDRF), Bit 0 — Receive Data Register Full indicates that received data has been transferred to the Receive Data Register. RDRF is cleared after an MPU read of the Receive Data Register or by a master reset. The cleared or empty state indicates that the contents of the Receive Data Register are not current. Data Carrier Detect being high also causes RDRF to indicate empty.

Transmit Data Register Empty (TDRE), Bit 1 — The Transmit Data Register Empty bit being set high indicates that the Transmit Data Register contents have been transferred and that new data may be entered. The low state indicates that the register is full and that transmission of a new character has not begun since the last write data command.

Data Carrier Detect (DCD), Bit 2 — The Data Carrier Detect bit will be high when the DCD input from a modem has gone high to indicate that a carrier is not present. This bit going high causes an Interrupt Request to be generated when the Receive Interrupt Enable is set. It remains high after the DCD input is returned low until cleared by first reading the Status Register and then the Data Register or until a master reset occurs. If the DCD input remains high after read status and read data or master reset has occurred, the interrupt is cleared, the DCD status bit remains high and will follow the DCD input.

Clear-to-Send (CTS), Bit 3 — The Clear-to-Send bit indicates the state of the Clear-to-Send input from a modem. A low CTS indicates that there is a Clear-to-Send from the modem. In the high state, the Transmit Data Register Empty bit is inhibited and the Clear-to-Send status bit will be high. Master reset does not affect the Clear-to-Send Status bit.

Framing Error (FE), Bit 4 — Framing error indicates that the received character is improperly framed by a start and a stop bit and is detected by the absence of the 1st stop bit. This error indicates a synchronization error, faulty transmission, or a break condition. The framing error flag is set or reset during the receive data transfer time. Therefore, this error indicator is present throughout the time that the associated character is available.

Receiver Overrun (OVRN), Bit 5 — Overrun is an error flag that indicates that one or more characters in the data stream were lost. That is, a character or a number of characters were received but not read from the Receive Data Register (RDR) prior to subsequent characters being received. The overrun condition begins at the midpoint of the last bit of the second character received in succession without a read of the RDR having occurred. The Overrun does not occur in the Status Register until the valid character prior to Overrun has been read. The RDRF bit remains set until the Overrun is reset. Character synchronization is maintained during the Overrun condition. The Overrun indication is reset after the reading of data from the Receive Data Register or by a Master Reset.

Parity Error (PE), Bit 6 — The parity error flag indicates that the number of highs (ones) in the character does not agree with the preselected odd or even parity. Odd parity is defined to be when the total number of ones is odd. The parity error indication will be present as long as the data character is in the RDR. If no parity is selected, then both the transmitter parity generator output and the receiver parity check results are inhibited.

Interrupt Request (IRQ), Bit 7 — The IRQ bit indicates the state of the IRQ output. Any interrupt condition with its applicable enable will be indicated in this status bit. Anytime the IRQ output is low the IRQ bit will be high to indicate the interrupt or service request status. IRQ is cleared by a read operation to the Receive Data Register or a write operation to the Transmit Data Register.

PIN ASSIGNMENT

1	V$_{SS}$	CTS	24
2	Rx Data	DCD	23
3	Rx Clk	D0	22
4	Tx Clk	D1	21
5	RTS	D2	20
6	Tx Data	D3	19
7	IRQ	D4	18
8	CS0	D5	17
9	CS2	D6	16
10	CS1	D7	15
11	RS	E	14
12	V$_{DD}$	R/W	13

PACKAGE DIMENSIONS

CASE 716-02
(CERAMIC)

SEE PAGE 165 FOR PLASTIC PACKAGE DIMENSIONS

DIM	MILLIMETERS		INCHES	
	MIN	MAX	MIN	MAX
A	29.97	30.99	1.180	1.220
B	14.88	15.62	0.585	0.615
C	3.05	4.19	0.120	0.165
D	0.38	0.53	0.015	0.021
F	0.76	1.40	0.030	0.055
G	2.54 BSC		0.100 BSC	
H	0.76	1.78	0.030	0.070
J	0.20	0.30	0.008	0.012
K	2.54	4.19	0.100	0.165
L	14.88	15.37	0.585	0.605
M	–	10⁰	–	10⁰
N	0.51	1.52	0.020	0.060

NOTE:
1. LEADS TRUE POSITIONED WITHIN 0.25mm (0.010) DIA (AT SEATING PLANE) AT MAXIMUM MATERIAL CONDITION.

The Peripheral Interface Adapter (PIA) MC6821

MOTOROLA
Semiconductors
3501 ED BLUESTEIN BLVD., AUSTIN, TEXAS 78721

MC6821

PERIPHERAL INTERFACE ADAPTER (PIA)

The MC6821 Peripheral Interface Adapter provides the universal means of interfacing peripheral equipment to the MC6800 Microprocessing Unit (MPU). This device is capable of interfacing the MPU to peripherals through two 8-bit bidirectional peripheral data buses and four control lines. No external logic is required for interfacing to most peripheral devices.

The functional configuration of the PIA is programmed by the MPU during system initialization. Each of the peripheral data lines can be programmed to act as an input or output, and each of the four control/interrupt lines may be programmed for one of several control modes. This allows a high degree of flexibility in the over-all operation of the interface.

- 8-Bit Bidirectional Data Bus for Communication with the MPU
- Two Bidirectional 8-Bit Buses for Interface to Peripherals
- Two Programmable Control Registers
- Two Programmable Data Direction Registers
- Four Individually-Controlled Interrupt Input Lines; Two Usable as Peripheral Control Outputs
- Handshake Control Logic for Input and Output Peripheral Operation
- High-Impedance 3-State and Direct Transistor Drive Peripheral Lines
- Program Controlled Interrupt and Interrupt Disable Capability
- CMOS Drive Capability on Side A Peripheral Lines
- Two TTL Drive Capability on All A and B Side Buffers
- TTL-Compatible
- Static Operation

MOS

(N-CHANNEL, SILICON-GATE, DEPLETION LOAD)

PERIPHERAL INTERFACE ADAPTER

L SUFFIX
CERAMIC PACKAGE
CASE 715

NOT SHOWN: **P SUFFIX**
PLASTIC PACKAGE
CASE 711

M6800 MICROCOMPUTER FAMILY BLOCK DIAGRAM

- MC6800 Microprocessor
- Read Only Memory
- Random Access Memory
- MC6821 Interface Adapter
- Interface Adapter — Modem

Address Bus   Data Bus

MC6821 PERIPHERAL INTERFACE ADAPTER BLOCK DIAGRAM

Data Bus — Data Bus Buffers — A Buffers and Data Register — Peripheral Data

Memory Address and Control Interrupt — Selection and Control — B Buffers and Data Register — Peripheral Data

ELECTRICAL CHARACTERISTICS (V_{CC} = 5.0 V ± 5%, V_{SS} = 0, T_A = 0 to 70°C unless otherwise noted.)

Characteristic	Symbol	Min	Typ	Max	Unit
Input High Voltage	V_{IH}	V_{SS} + 2.0	–	V_{CC}	Vdc
Input Low Voltage	V_{IL}	V_{SS} – 0.3	–	V_{SS} + 0.8	Vdc
Input Leakage Current R/W, $\overline{Reset}$, RS0, RS1, CS0, CS1, $\overline{CS2}$, CA1, (V_{in} = 0 to 5.25 Vdc) CB1, Enable	I_{in}	–	1.0	2.5	µAdc
Three-State (Off State) Input Current D0–D7, PB0–PB7, CB2 (V_{in} = 0.4 to 2.4 Vdc)	I_{TSI}	–	2.0	10	µAdc
Input High Current PA0–PA7, CA2 (V_{IH} = 2.4 Vdc)	I_{IH}	–200	–400	–	µAdc
Input Low Current PA0–PA7, CA2 (V_{IL} = 0.4 Vdc)	I_{IL}	–	–1.3	–2.4	mAdc
Output High Voltage (I_{Load} = –205 µAdc) D0–D7 (I_{Load} = –200 µAdc) Other Outputs	V_{OH}	V_{SS} + 2.4 V_{SS} + 2.4	– –	– –	Vdc
Output Low Voltage (I_{Load} = 1.6 mAdc) D0–D7 (I_{Load} = 3.2 mAdc) Other Outputs	V_{OL}	– –	– –	V_{SS} + 0.4 V_{SS} + 0.4	Vdc
Output Leakage Current (Off State) $\overline{IRQA}$, $\overline{IRQB}$ (V_{OH} = 2.4 Vdc)	I_{LOH}	–	1.0	10	µAdc
Power Dissipation	P_D	–	–	550	mW
Capacitance (V_{in} = 0, T_A = 25°C, f = 1.0 MHz) D0–D7 PA0–PA7, PB0–PB7, CA2, CB2 Enable, R/W, $\overline{Reset}$, RS0, RS1, CS0, CS1, $\overline{CS2}$, CA1, CB1	C_{in}	– – –	– – –	12.5 10 7.5	pF
$\overline{IRQA}$, $\overline{IRQB}$	C_{out}	–	–	5.0	pF
Peripheral Data Setup Time (Figure 1)	t_{PDSU}	200	–	–	ns
Peripheral Data Hold Time (Figure 1)	t_{PDH}	0	–	–	ns
Delay Time, Enable negative transition to CA2 negative transition (Figure 2, 3)	t_{CA2}	–	–	1.0	µs
Delay Time, Enable negative transition to CA2 positive transition (Figure 2)	t_{RS1}	–	–	1.0	µs
Rise and Fall Times for CA1 and CA2 input signals (Figure 3)	t_r, t_f	–	–	1.0	µs
Delay Time from CA1 active transition to CA2 positive transition (Figure 3)	t_{RS2}	–	–	2.0	µs
Delay Time, Enable negative transition to Peripheral Data Valid (Figures 4, 5)	t_{PDW}	–	–	1.0	µs
Delay Time, Enable negative transition to Peripheral CMOS Data Valid (V_{CC} – 30% V_{CC}, Figure 4; Figure 12 Load C) PA0–PA7, CA2	t_{CMOS}	–	–	2.0	µs
Delay Time, Enable positive transition to CB2 negative transition (Figure 6, 7)	t_{CB2}	–	–	1.0	µs
Delay Time, Peripheral Data Valid to CB2 negative transition (Figure 5)	t_{DC}	20	–	–	ns
Delay Time, Enable positive transition to CB2 positive transition (Figure 6)	t_{RS1}	–	–	1.0	µs
Peripheral Control Output Pulse Width, CA2/CB2 (Figures 2, 6)	PW_{CT}	550	–	–	ns
Rise and Fall Time for CB1 and CB2 input signals (Figure 7)	t_r, t_f	–	–	1.0	µs
Delay Time, CB1 active transition to CB2 positive transition (Figure 7)	t_{RS2}	–	–	2.0	µs
Interrupt Release Time, $\overline{IRQA}$ and $\overline{IRQB}$ (Figure 9)	t_{IR}	–	–	1.6	µs
Interrupt Response Time (Figure 8)	t_{RS3}	–	–	1.0	µs
Interrupt Input Pulse Width (Figure 8)	PW_I	500	–	–	ns
Reset Low Time* (Figure 10)	t_{RL}	1.0	–	–	µs

*The Reset line must be high a minimum or 1.0 µs before addressing the PIA.

MAXIMUM RATINGS

Rating	Symbol	Value	Unit
Supply Voltage	V_{CC}	−0.3 to +7.0	Vdc
Input Voltage	V_{in}	−0.3 to +7.0	Vdc
Operating Temperature Range	T_A	0 to +70	°C
Storage Temperature Range	T_{stg}	−55 to +150	°C
Thermal Resistance	θ_{JA}	82.5	°C/W

This device contains circuitry to protect the inputs against damage due to high static voltages or electric fields; however, it is advised that normal precautions be taken to avoid application of any voltage higher than maximum rated voltages to this high impedance circuit.

BUS TIMING CHARACTERISTICS

READ (Figures 11 and 13)

Characteristic	Symbol	Min	Typ	Max	Unit
Enable Cycle Time	t_{cycE}	1.0	–	–	µs
Enable Pulse Width, High	PW_{EH}	0.45	–	–	µs
Enable Pulse Width, Low	PW_{EL}	0.43	–	–	µs
Setup Time, Address and R/W valid to Enable positive transition	t_{AS}	160	–	–	ns
Data Delay Time	t_{DDR}	–	–	320	ns
Data Hold Time	t_H	10	–	–	ns
Address Hold Time	t_{AH}	10	–	–	ns
Rise and Fall Time for Enable input	t_{Er}, t_{Ef}	–	–	25	ns

WRITE (Figures 12 and 13)

Characteristic	Symbol	Min	Typ	Max	Unit
Enable Cycle Time	t_{cycE}	1.0	–	–	µs
Enable Pulse Width, High	PW_{EH}	0.45	–	–	µs
Enable Pulse Width, Low	PW_{EL}	0.43	–	–	µs
Setup Time, Address and R/W valid to Enable positive transition	t_{AS}	160	–	–	ns
Data Setup Time	t_{DSW}	195	–	–	ns
Data Hold Time	t_H	10	–	–	ns
Address Hold Time	t_{AH}	10	–	–	ns
Rise and Fall Time for Enable input	t_{Er}, t_{Ef}	–	–	25	ns

FIGURE 1 – PERIPHERAL DATA SETUP AND HOLD TIMES
(Read Mode)

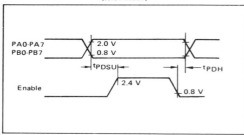

FIGURE 2 – CA2 DELAY TIME
(Read Mode; CRA-5 = CRA-3 = 1, CRA-4 = 0)

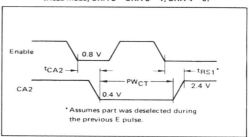

FIGURE 3 – CA2 DELAY TIME
(Read Mode; CRA-5 = 1, CRA-3 = CRA-4 = 0)

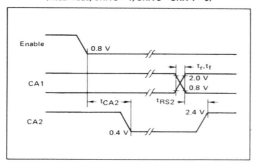

FIGURE 4 – PERIPHERAL CMOS DATA DELAY TIMES
(Write Mode; CRA-5 = CRA-3 = 1, CRA-4 = 0)

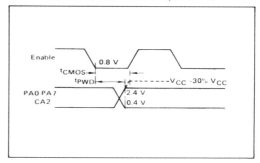

FIGURE 5 – PERIPHERAL DATA AND CB2 DELAY TIMES
(Write Mode; CRB-5 = CRB-3 = 1, CRB-4 = 0)

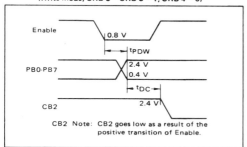

CB2 Note: CB2 goes low as a result of the positive transition of Enable.

FIGURE 6 – CB2 DELAY TIME
(Write Mode; CRB-5 = CRB-3 = 1, CRB-4 = 0)

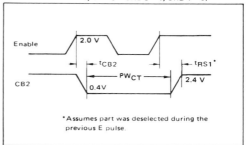

*Assumes part was deselected during the previous E pulse.

FIGURE 7 – CB2 DELAY TIME
(Write Mode; CRB-5 = 1, CRB-3 = CRB-4 = 0)

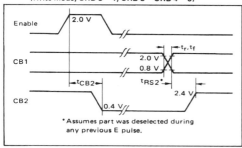

*Assumes part was deselected during any previous E pulse.

FIGURE 8 – INTERRUPT PULSE WIDTH and $\overline{IRQ}$ RESPONSE

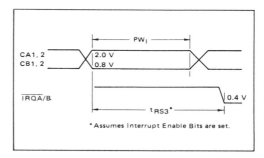

*Assumes Interrupt Enable Bits are set.

FIGURE 9 – $\overline{IRQ}$ RELEASE TIME

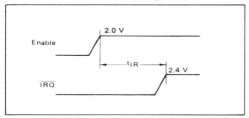

FIGURE 10 – $\overline{RESET}$ LOW TIME

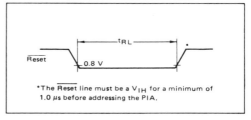

*The Reset line must be a V_{IH} for a minimum of 1.0 μs before addressing the PIA.

FIGURE 11 – BUS READ TIMING CHARACTERISTICS
(Read Information from PIA)

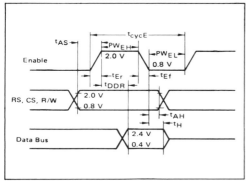

FIGURE 12 – BUS WRITE TIMING CHARACTERISTICS
(Write Information into PIA)

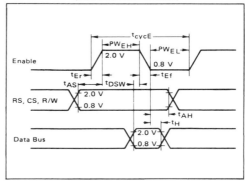

FIGURE 13 – BUS TIMING TEST LOADS

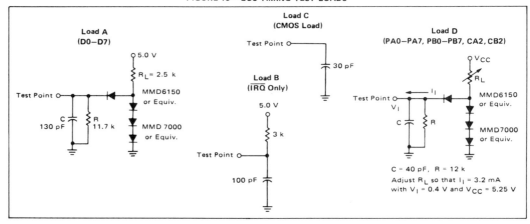

PIA INTERFACE SIGNALS FOR MPU

The PIA interfaces to the MC6800 MPU with an eight-bit bi-directional data bus, three chip select lines, two register select lines, two interrupt request lines, read/write line, enable line and reset line. These signals, in conjunction with the MC6800 VMA output, permit the MPU to have complete control over the PIA. VMA should be utilized in conjunction with an MPU address line into a chip select of the PIA.

PIA Bi-Directional Data (D0-D7) – The bi-directional data lines (D0-D7) allow the transfer of data between the MPU and the PIA. The data bus output drivers are three-state devices that remain in the high-impedance (off) state except when the MPU performs a PIA read operation. The Read/Write line is in the Read (high) state when the PIA is selected for a Read operation.

PIA Enable (E) – The enable pulse, E, is the only timing signal that is supplied to the PIA. Timing of all other signals is referenced to the leading and trailing edges of the E pulse. This signal will normally be a derivative of the MC6800 φ2 Clock.

PIA Read/Write (R/W) – This signal is generated by the MPU to control the direction of data transfers on the Data Bus. A low state on the PIA Read/Write line enables the input buffers and data is transferred from the MPU to the PIA on the E signal if the device has been selected. A high on the Read/Write line sets up the PIA for a transfer of data to the bus. The PIA output buffers are enabled when the proper address and the enable pulse E are present.

Reset – The active low Reset line is used to reset all register bits in the PIA to a logical zero (low). This line can be used as a power-on reset and as a master reset during system operation.

PIA Chip Select (CS0, CS1 and CS2) – These three input signals are used to select the PIA. CS0 and CS1 must be high and CS2 must be low for selection of the device. Data transfers are then performed under the control of the Enable and Read/Write signals. The chip select lines must be stable for the duration of the E pulse. The device is deselected when any of the chip selects are in the inactive state.

PIA Register Select (RS0 and RS1) – The two register select lines are used to select the various registers inside the PIA. These two lines are used in conjunction with internal Control Registers to select a particular register that is to be written or read.

The register and chip select lines should be stable for the duration of the E pulse while in the read or write cycle.

Interrupt Request (IRQA and IRQB) – The active low Interrupt Request lines (IRQA and IRQB) act to interrupt the MPU either directly or through interrupt priority circuitry. These lines are these "open drain" (no load device on the chip). This permits all interrupt request lines to be tied together in a wire-OR configuration.

Each Interrupt Request line has two internal interrupt flag bits that can cause the Interrupt Request line to go low. Each flag bit is associated with a particular peripheral interrupt line. Also four interrupt enable bits are provided in the PIA which may be used to inhibit a particular interrupt from a peripheral device.

Servicing an interrupt by the MPU may be accomplished by a software routine that, on a prioritized basis, sequentially reads and tests the two control registers in each PIA for interrupt flag bits that are set.

The interrupt flags are cleared (zeroed) as a result of an

EXPANDED BLOCK DIAGRAM

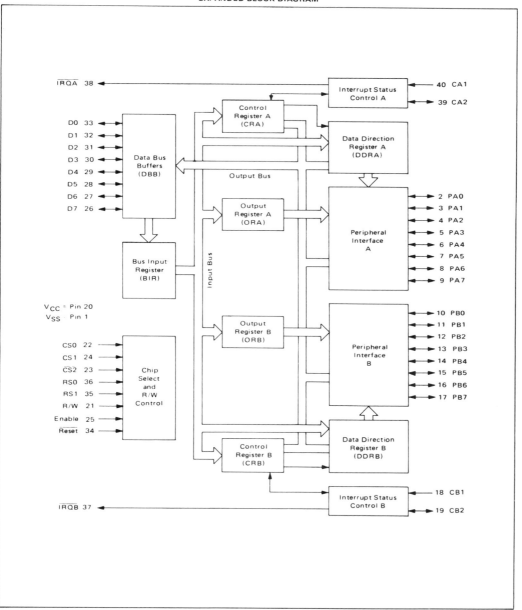

MPU Read Peripheral Data Operation of the corresponding data register. After being cleared, the interrupt flag bit cannot be enabled to be set until the PIA is deselected during an E pulse. The E pulse is used to condition the interrupt control lines (CA1, CA2, CB1, CB2). When these lines are used as interrupt inputs at least one E pulse must occur from the inactive edge to the active edge of the interrupt input signal to condition the edge sense network. If the interrupt flag has been enabled and the edge sense circuit has been properly conditioned, the interrupt flag will be set on the next active transition of the interrupt input pin.

PIA PERIPHERAL INTERFACE LINES

The PIA provides two 8-bit bi-directional data buses and four interrupt/control lines for interfacing to peripheral devices.

Section A Peripheral Data (PA0-PA7) — Each of the peripheral data lines can be programmed to act as an input or output. This is accomplished by setting a "1" in the corresponding Data Direction Register bit for those lines which are to be outputs. A "0" in a bit of the Data Direction Register causes the corresponding peripheral data line to act as an input. During an MPU Read Peripheral Data Operation, the data on peripheral lines programmed to act as inputs appears directly on the corresponding MPU Data Bus lines. In the input mode the internal pullup resistor on these lines represents a maximum of 1.5 standard TTL loads.

The data in Output Register A will appear on the data lines that are programmed to be outputs. A logical "1" written into the register will cause a "high" on the corresponding data line while a "0" results in a "low". Data in Output Register A may be read by an MPU "Read Peripheral Data A" operation when the corresponding lines are programmed as outputs. This data will be read properly if the voltage on the peripheral data lines is greater than 2.0 volts for a logic "1" output and less than 0.8 volt for a logic "0" output. Loading the output lines such that the voltage on these lines does not reach full voltage causes the data transferred into the MPU on a Read operation to differ from that contained in the respective bit of Output Register A.

Section B Peripheral Data (PB0-PB7) — The peripheral data lines in the B Section of the PIA can be programmed to act as either inputs or outputs in a similar manner to PA0-PA7. However, the output buffers driving these lines differ from those driving lines PA0-PA7. They have three-state capability, allowing them to enter a high impedance state when the peripheral data line is used as an input. In addition, data on the peripheral data lines PB0-PB7 will be read properly from those lines programmed as outputs even if the voltages are below 2.0 volts for a "high". As outputs, these lines are compatible with standard TTL and may also be used as a source of up to 1 milliampere at 1.5 volts to directly drive the base of a transistor switch.

Interrupt Input (CA1 and CB1) — Peripheral Input lines CA1 and CB1 are input only lines that set the interrupt flags of the control registers. The active transition for these signals is also programmed by the two control registers.

Peripheral Control (CA2) — The peripheral control line CA2 can be programmed to act as an interrupt input or as a peripheral control output. As an output, this line is compatible with standard TTL; as an input the internal pullup resistor on this line represents 1.5 standard TTL loads. The function of this signal line is programmed with Control Register A.

Peripheral Control (CB2) — Peripheral Control line CB2 may also be programmed to act as an interrupt input or peripheral control output. As an input, this line has high input impedance and is compatible with standard TTL. As an output it is compatible with standard TTL and may also be used as a source of up to 1 milliampere at 1.5 volts to directly drive the base of a transistor switch. This line is programmed by Control Register B.

INTERNAL CONTROLS

There are six locations within the PIA accessible to the MPU data bus: two Peripheral Registers, two Data Direction Registers, and two Control Registers. Selection of these locations is controlled by the RS0 and RS1 inputs together with bit 2 in the Control Register, as shown in Table 1.

TABLE 1 — INTERNAL ADDRESSING

RS1	RS0	Control Register Bit CRA-2	CRB-2	Location Selected
0	0	1	X	Peripheral Register A
0	0	0	X	Data Direction Register A
0	1	X	X	Control Register A
1	0	X	1	Peripheral Register B
1	0	X	0	Data Direction Register B
1	1	X	X	Control Register B

X = Don't Care

INITIALIZATION

A low reset line has the effect of zeroing all PIA registers. This will set PA0-PA7, PB0-PB7, CA2 and CB2 as inputs, and all interrupts disabled. The PIA must be configured during the restart program which follows the reset.

Details of possible configurations of the Data Direction and Control Register are as follows.

DATA DIRECTION REGISTERS (DDRA and DDRB)

The two Data Direction Registers allow the MPU to control the direction of data through each corresponding peripheral data line. A Data Direction Register bit set at "0" configures the corresponding peripheral data line as an input; a "1" results in an output.

CONTROL REGISTERS (CRA and CRB)

The two Control Registers (CRA and CRB) allow the MPU to control the operation of the four peripheral control lines CA1, CA2, CB1 and CB2. In addition they allow the MPU to enable the interrupt lines and monitor the status of the interrupt flags. Bits 0 through 5 of the two registers may be written or read by the MPU when the proper chip select and register select signals are applied. Bits 6 and 7 of the two registers are read only and are modified by external interrupts occurring on control lines CA1, CA2, CB1 or CB2. The format of the control words is shown in Table 2.

TABLE 2 — CONTROL WORD FORMAT

	7	6	5	4	3	2	1	0
CRA	IRQA1	IRQA2	CA2 Control			DDRA Access	CA1 Control	

	7	6	5	4	3	2	1	0
CRB	IRQB1	IRQB2	CB2 Control			DDRB Access	CB1 Control	

Data Direction Access Control Bit (CRA-2 and CRB-2) — Bit 2 in each Control register (CRA and CRB) allows selection of either a Peripheral Interface Register or the Data Direction Register when the proper register select signals are applied to RS0 and RS1.

Interrupt Flags (CRA-6, CRA-7, CRB-6, and CRB-7) — The four interrupt flag bits are set by active transitions of signals on the four Interrupt and Peripheral Control lines when those lines are programmed to be inputs. These bits cannot be set directly from the MPU Data Bus and are reset indirectly by a Read Peripheral Data Operation on the appropriate section.

TABLE 3 — CONTROL OF INTERRUPT INPUTS CA1 AND CB1

CRA-1 (CRB-1)	CRA-0 (CRB-0)	Interrupt Input CA1 (CB1)	Interrupt Flag CRA-7 (CRB-7)	MPU Interrupt Request IRQA (IRQB)
0	0	↓ Active	Set high on ↓ of CA1 (CB1)	Disabled — IRQ remains high
0	1	↓ Active	Set high on ↓ of CA1 (CB1)	Goes low when the interrupt flag bit CRA-7 (CRB-7) goes high
1	0	↑ Active	Set high on ↑ of CA1 (CB1)	Disabled — IRQ remains high
1	1	↑ Active	Set high on ↑ of CA1 (CB1)	Goes low when the interrupt flag bit CRA-7 (CRB-7) goes high

Notes: 1. ↑ indicates positive transition (low to high)

2. ↓ indicates negative transition (high to low)

3. The Interrupt flag bit CRA-7 is cleared by an MPU Read of the A Data Register, and CRB-7 is cleared by an MPU Read of the B Data Register.

4. **If CRA-0 (CRB-0) is low when an interrupt occurs (Interrupt disabled) and is later brought high, IRQA (IRQB) occurs after CRA-0 (CRB-0) is written to a "one".**

Control of CA1 and CB1 Interrupt Input Lines (CRA-0, CRB-0, CRA-1, and CRB-1) — The two lowest order bits of the control registers are used to control the interrupt input lines CA1 and CB1. Bits CRA-0 and CRB-0 are used to enable the MPU interrupt signals $\overline{IRQA}$ and $\overline{IRQB}$, respectively. Bits CRA-1 and CRB-1 determine the active transition of the interrupt input signals CA1 and CB1 (Table 3).

TABLE 4 — CONTROL OF CA2 AND CB2 AS INTERRUPT INPUTS
CRA5 (CRB5) is low

CRA-5 (CRB-5)	CRA-4 (CRB-4)	CRA-3 (CRB-3)	Interrupt Input CA2 (CB2)	Interrupt Flag CRA-6 (CRB-6)	MPU Interrupt Request $\overline{IRQA}$ ($\overline{IRQB}$)
0	0	0	↓ Active	Set high on ↓ of CA2 (CB2)	Disabled — $\overline{IRQ}$ remains high
0	0	1	↓ Active	Set high on ↓ of CA2 (CB2)	Goes low when the interrupt flag bit CRA-6 (CRB-6) goes high
0	1	0	↑ Active	Set high on ↑ of CA2 (CB2)	Disabled — $\overline{IRQ}$ remains high
0	1	1	↑ Active	Set high on ↑ of CA2 (CB2)	Goes low when the interrupt flag bit CRA-6 (CRB-6) goes high

Notes: 1. ↑ indicates positive transition (low to high)
2. ↓ indicates negative transition (high to low)
3. The Interrupt flag bit CRA-6 is cleared by an MPU Read of the A Data Register and CRB-6 is cleared by an MPU Read of the B Data Register.
4. If CRA-3 (CRB-3) is low when an interrupt occurs (Interrupt disabled) and is later brought high, $\overline{IRQA}$ ($\overline{IRQB}$) occurs after CRA-3 (CRB-3) is written to a "one".

TABLE 5 — CONTROL OF CB2 AS AN OUTPUT
CRB-5 is high

CRB-5	CRB-4	CRB-3	CB2	
			Cleared	Set
1	0	0	Low on the positive transition of the first E pulse following an MPU Write "B" Data Register operation.	High when the interrupt flag bit CRB-7 is set by an active transition of the CB1 signal.
1	0	1	Low on the positive transition of the first E pulse after an MPU Write "B" Data Register operation.	High on the positive edge of the first "E" pulse following an "E" pulse which occurred while the part was deselected.
1	1	0	Low when CRB-3 goes low as a result of an MPU Write in Control Register "B".	Always low as long as CRB-3 is low. Will go high on an MPU Write in Control Register "B" that changes CRB-3 to "one".
1	1	1	Always high as long as CRB-3 is high. Will be cleared when an MPU Write Control Register "B" results in clearing CRB-3 to "zero".	High when CRB-3 goes high as a result of an MPU Write into Control Register "B".

Control of CA2 and CB2 Peripheral Control Lines (CRA-3, CRA-4, CRA-5, CRB-3, CRB-4, and CRB-5) — Bits 3, 4, and 5 of the two control registers are used to control the CA2 and CB2 Peripheral Control lines. These bits determine if the control lines will be an interrupt input or an output control signal. If bit CRA-5 (CRB-5) is low, CA2 (CB2) is an interrupt input line similar to CA1 (CB1) (Table 4). When CRA-5 (CRB-5) is high, CA2 (CB2) becomes an output signal that may be used to control peripheral data transfers. When in the output mode, CA2 and CB2 have slightly different characteristics (Tables 5 and 6).

TABLE 6 — CONTROL OF CA-2 AS AN OUTPUT
CRA-5 is high

CRA-5	CRA-4	CRA-3	CA2	
			Cleared	Set
1	0	0	Low on negative transition of E after an MPU Read "A" Data operation.	High when the interrupt flag bit CRA-7 is set by an active transition of the CA1 signal.
1	0	1	Low on negative transition of E after an MPU Read "A" Data operation.	High on the negative edge of the first "E" pulse which occurs during a deselect.
1	1	0	Low when CRA-3 goes low as a result of an MPU Write to Control Register "A".	Always low as long as CRA-3 is low. Will go high on an MPU Write to Control Register "A" that changes CRA-3 to "one".
1	1	1	Always high as long as CRA-3 is high. Will be cleared on an MPU Write to Control Register "A" that clears CRA-3 to a "zero".	High when CRA-3 goes high as a result of an MPU Write to Control Register "A".

PACKAGE DIMENSIONS

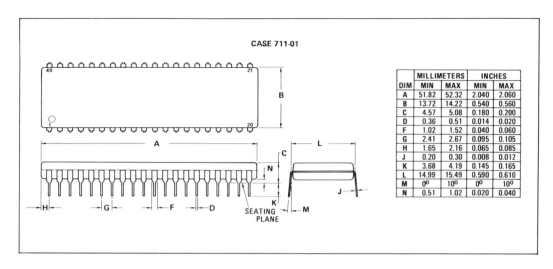

CASE 711-01

DIM	MILLIMETERS		INCHES	
	MIN	MAX	MIN	MAX
A	51.82	52.32	2.040	2.060
B	13.72	14.22	0.540	0.560
C	4.57	5.08	0.180	0.200
D	0.36	0.51	0.014	0.020
F	1.02	1.52	0.040	0.060
G	2.41	2.67	0.095	0.105
H	1.65	2.16	0.065	0.085
J	0.20	0.30	0.008	0.012
K	3.68	4.19	0.145	0.165
L	14.99	15.49	0.590	0.610
M	0^0	10^0	0^0	10^0
N	0.51	1.02	0.020	0.040

PIN ASSIGNMENT

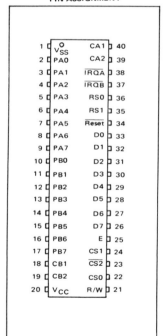

1	V_{SS}	CA1	40
2	PA0	CA2	39
3	PA1	$\overline{IRQA}$	38
4	PA2	$\overline{IRQB}$	37
5	PA3	RS0	36
6	PA4	RS1	35
7	PA5	$\overline{Reset}$	34
8	PA6	D0	33
9	PA7	D1	32
10	PB0	D2	31
11	PB1	D3	30
12	PB2	D4	29
13	PB3	D5	28
14	PB4	D6	27
15	PB5	D7	26
16	PB6	E	25
17	PB7	CS1	24
18	CB1	$\overline{CS2}$	23
19	CB2	CS0	22
20	V_{CC}	R/W	21

PACKAGE DIMENSIONS

CASE 715-02
(CERAMIC)

SEE PAGE 165 FOR
PLASTIC PACKAGE
DIMENSIONS.

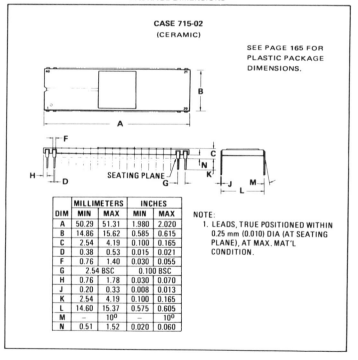

DIM	MILLIMETERS		INCHES	
	MIN	MAX	MIN	MAX
A	50.29	51.31	1.980	2.020
B	14.86	15.62	0.585	0.615
C	2.54	4.19	0.100	0.165
D	0.38	0.53	0.015	0.021
F	0.76	1.40	0.030	0.055
G	2.54 BSC		0.100 BSC	
H	0.76	1.78	0.030	0.070
J	0.20	0.33	0.008	0.013
K	2.54	4.19	0.100	0.165
L	14.60	15.37	0.575	0.605
M	–	10^0	–	10^0
N	0.51	1.52	0.020	0.060

NOTE:
1. LEADS, TRUE POSITIONED WITHIN
   0.25 mm (0.010) DIA (AT SEATING
   PLANE), AT MAX. MAT'L
   CONDITION.

THE MC68000 family and peripherals

Microprocessors

Device #	Description	Speeds (MHz)	Package Types	
MC68000	16/32-Bit Microprocessor	8, 10, 12.5	64-lead L, G 68-lead R, ZB, ZC, FN*	
MC68008	Reduced Bus 8-Bit Version	8, 10	48-lead L, P 52-lead FN**	
MC68010	16-Bit Virtual Memory MPU	8, 10, 12.5	64-lead L, G 68-lead R	
MC68012	16-Bit Extended Virtual MPU	8, 10, 12.5	84-lead R	* available 1984
MC68020	32-Bit Microprocessor	12.5, 16.67	114-lead R	** available 1985

MC68000 32-bit internal/16-bit external MPU

The MC68000 is the first member of the Motorola Family of advanced 16/32 bit microprocessors. It is a fully-implemented 16-bit microprocessor with 17 general purpose 32-bit data and address registers. The MC68000 possesses an asynchronous bus structure with non-multiplexed 24-bit address bus and 16-bit data bus. This provides for a direct addressing range of 16 megabytes. The higher level language oriented instruction set allows for mainframe-like performance.

MC68008 32-bit internal/8-bit external MPU

The MC68008 is the 8-bit data bus version of the MC68000. It is completely user object code compatible with the MC68000, allowing software developed to be run on either MPU. With a one-megabyte non-segmented linear address space, large modular programs can be developed and executed efficiently without the performance limitations forced by the segmented architecture of other, non-Motorola 8-bit MPUs. In addition, the MC68008 provides extensive exception processing. The use of an 8-bit data bus conserves PC board space and money, making the MC68008 the choice for high-performance, cost-effective, 8-bit designs.

MC68010 Virtual Memory MPU

The MC68010 is the virtual memory version of the M68000 microprocessor family. Its internal architecture, instruction set and bus structures are identical to the MC68000, making the MC68010 fully upward object code compatible. In addition to all of the resources of the MC68000, the MC68010 offers high speed loop-mode operation which allows for faster execution of tight software loops. The added features of virtual memory support and enhanced instruction execution timing make the MC68010 one of the fastest and most versatile MPUs on the market.

Package Designator	Description
L	Ceramic Dual-In-Line-Package (DIP)
G	Plastic DIP with internal heat spreader
P	Plastic DIP
R	Ceramic Pin-Grid-Array (PGA)
ZB	Ceramic Leadless Chip Carrier (LCC) - socketable
ZC	Ceramic LCC - surface mount
FN	Plastic Quad Pack - surface mount

MC68012 Extended Virtual Memory MPU

The MC68012 provides all the resources of the MC68010 and maintains the upward compatibility of the M68000 Family. Extended virtual memory capabilities are provided by additional addressing resources which allow for a linear two-gigabyte range. Additional resources provide improved multiprocessor operation.

MC68020 32-bit internal/32-bit external MPU

The MC68020 is the newest member of the M68000 Family. While it is the first complete, commercially available 32-bit microprocessor and has several features which make it unique, the MC68020 is fully upward object code compatible with all members of the M68000 family. It has non-multiplexed 32-bit address and data buses with innovative techniques to improve bus efficiency, an enhanced instruction set and instruction cache for high-speed performance advantages, and new instructions and addressing modes for improved operating system support. In addition, the MC68020 is the first MPU to have a coprocessor interface which extends the capabilities of an M68000 system beyond the limits of any single processing element. As the MC68000 set the performance standard for 16-bit microprocessor systems, so will the MC68020 be the performance standard for all 32-bit micro systems.

The M68000 Peripherals

CoProcessors

MC68881 Floating Point CoProcessor (FPCP)
The MC68881 FPCP provides full support for IEEE specified (Revision 10.0) floating point high level math functions.

In addition to the IEEE set of computations, full support for transcendental functions (trigonometrics, hyperbolics, exponentials, logarithmics, etc.) and non-transcendental functions (absolute value, square root, negate, etc.) is provided. All calculations are performed to 80 bits of precision and no software "envelope" is required. The FPCP can perform either as a tightly coupled coprocessor to the 32-bit MC68020 microprocessor (via the standard MC68020 coprocessor interface) or as a peripheral device with the MC68000, MC68010 or MC68012.

Memory Management

MC68451 Memory Management Unit (MMU)
The MC68451 MMU is the basic element of a memory management mechanism in an M68000-based system. The MMU provides address translation and protection for the entire 16-megabyte addressing range of the M68000 microprocessor family. It provides 32 segments of variable memory size and also allows for multiple MMU capabilities to expand to any number of segments. Virtual memory support is also provided for the MC68010 MPU as is full support for the UNIX™-derived SYSTEM V/68™ Operating System.

MC68851 Paged Memory Management Unit (PMMU)
The MC68851 is a 32-bit memory manager which provides full support for a demand-paged virtual environment. It supports a 4-gigabyte addressing space when used as a coprocessor with the MC68020. An on-chip address translation cache ensures single-cycle translation delays and maximum system performance.

DMA Controllers

MC68440 Dual DMA (DDMA)
The MC68440 complements the performance capabilities of M68000 microprocessors by moving blocks of data in a quick efficient manner with a minimum of intervention from the MPU. The DDMA performs memory-to-memory, peripheral-to-memory, and memory-to-peripheral transfers through each of two completely independent DMA channels. Either 8- or 16-bit transfers are supported and the DDMA also offers two interrupt vectors per channel.

MC68450 DMA Controller (DMAC)
The MC68450 maintains high-performance data movement for even more complex M68000 MPU-based systems. While pin-compatible with the MC68440 DDMA, the DMAC offers four completely independent DMA channels. In addition to all the features of the DDMA, the DMAC also provides very sophisticated manipulation of data through block-, array-, and linked array-chained addressing capabilities.

Disk Controllers

MC68454 Intelligent Multiple Disk Controller (IMDC)
The MC68454 directly interfaces to an M68000 system bus and has the capability of controlling any combination of up to four floppy or hard disks. Both single- and dual-density formats are supported. A 256-byte FIFO smooths the transfer of data to and from the disk, and a four-gigabyte on-board DMA controller guarantees proper data movement.

MC68459 Disk Phase Lock Loop (DPLL)
This device is used to interface disk drives to the MC68454 IMDC. At the present, this device is only available from a designated M68000 alternate source. For additional information on the DPLL, contact the Signetics Corporation.

MC68465 Floppy Disk Controller (FDC)
The FDC (presently available only from a designated M68000 alternate source) can interface two single- or double-density floppy disk drives to an M68000 system bus. More information is available on this device from Rockwell International, Semiconductor Products Division.

Synchronous and Asynchronous Data Communications

MC68561 Multi Protocol Communication Controller II (MPCC-II)
The MPCC-II is a single-channel multi-protocol data communication device that interfaces directly to an M68000 system bus. Asynchronous, bisync, and SDLC protocols are supported by the MPCC-II. For more information, contact Rockwell International, the only present source for this device.

MC68562 Dual Universal Serial Communication Controller (DUSCC)

The MC68562 offers two completely independent, multi-protocol, full duplex receiver/transmitter channels. All major data communication formats are recognized, including asynchronous (5 to 8 bits plus parity), byte control (BI/SYNC, DDCMP, X.21), and bit oriented (HDLC/ADCCP, SDLC, X.25). Also included in the part are a 16-bit multi-function counter/timer, fully programmable bit rate generator, and a DMA interface compatible with the MC68440 DDMA and the MC68450 DMAC.

MC68564 Serial I/O (SI/O)

The SI/O, presently available only from a designated M68000 alternate source, is a dual-channel device which supports asynchronous, bisync, and SDLC formats. Further information is available from the Mostek division of United Technologies.

MC68652 Multi Protocol Communication Controller (MPCC)

The MC68652 is a single-channel serial data communications device that recognizes byte-control and bit-oriented protocols. Also included within the device is CRC (programmable error-detection) circuitry. The MPCC handles data transfers of 8- or 16-bit widths at a maximum 2.5 Mbit/second rate.

MC68653 Polynomial Generator Checker (PGC)

The MC68653 is an error correction, code generation and comparitor circuit that complements a receiver/transmitter set in the support of character-oriented data-link controls. It is an excellent companion chip for the MC68652 MPCC or MC68661 EPCI. Since the PGC operates on parallel characters, the data transmission format may be serial (asynchronous or synchronous) or parallel.

MC68661 Enhanced Peripheral Communication Interface (EPCI)

The MC68661 is a univeral synchronous/asynchronous data communications controller that interfaces to the M68000 Family and most other 8- and 16-bit microprocessors. Its receiver and transmitter are double buffered for efficient full- and half-duplex operation. An internal baud rate clock (with various baud rate sets available) is provided, eliminating the need for a system clock. The EPCI converts parallel data characters accepted from the microprocessor data bus into transmit-serial data. Simultaneously, the EPCI can convert receive-serial data to parallel data characters for input to the MPU.

MC68681, MC2681, MC2682 Dual Universal Asynchronous Receiver/Transmitter (DUART)

The MC68681 features two completely independent full duplex asynchronous receiver/transmitter channels that interface directly to the M68000 microprocessor bus. Receiver data registers are quadruple buffered and transmitter data registers are double buffered for minimum MPU intervention. Each has its own independently selectable baud rate. Multi-function 6-bit input port and 8-bit output port, a 16-bit programmable counter/timer, interrupt handling capabilities, and a maximum one-megabyte transfer rate make the DUART an extremely powerful device for complex data-communication applications.

Full device functionality without an M68000 bus interface is provided by the MC2681.

Partial functionality (in a space-saving package) is provided by the MC2682.

Local Area Network Controllers

MC68590 Local Area Network Controller for Ethernet™ (LANCE)

The MC68590 provides complete IEEE specification (P802.3) Ethernet™ communication control for M68000-based systems. The LANCE can operate either as a bus master or as a peripheral to the processor. A 16-megabyte DMA controller on board ensures the proper movement of data to and from the processor via the Ethernet™ connection.

68802 Local Network Controller (LNET)

The LNET is a local area network controller that implements the IEEE 802 network specification. This device is available only from a designated alternate source. For more information, contact Rockwell International.

General Purpose I/O

MC68120, MC68121 Intelligent Peripheral Controller (IPC)

The MC68120 is a general-purpose peripheral controller which provides the interface between an M68000 or M6800 Family microprocessor and the final peripheral devices through a system bus and control lines. The intelligence of this device comes from its MC6801 MPU core. System bus data is transferred to and from the IPC via 128 bytes of on-board dual-port RAM. Multiple operating modes are supported ranging from single-chip control (with 21 I/O lines and two control lines) to expanded mode (with 64K address space). Also included are 2K of ROM, a serial communications interface, a 16-bit timer, and six shared semaphore registers.

The MC68121 is identical to the MC68120 except that it is without ROM.

MC68230 Parallel Interface/Timer (PI/T)

The MC68230 provides versatile double-buffered parallel interfaces and a system-oriented timer for M68000 systems. The parallel interfaces operate either in a uni-directional or bidirectional mode, either 8- or 16-bits wide. The timer is 24 bits with full programmability and a 5-bit prescaler. The PI/T has a complete M68000 bus interface and is also fully compatible with the MC68450 DMAC.

MC68901 Multi Function Peripheral (MFP)

The MC68901 provides basic microcomputer function requirements as a single companion chip to the M68000 Family of microprocessors. Features provided via a direct M68000 system bus interface include a full-function single-channel universal serial asynchronous receiver/transmitter (USART) for data communication, an 8-source interrupt controller, eight parallel I/O lines, and four 8-bit timers.

System Interface

MC68153 Bus Interrupt Module (BIM)

The MC68153 interfaces an M68000 microcomputer system bus to multiple slave devices which require interrupt capabilities. It allows up to four independent sources of interrupt requests to be routed to any of the seven M68000 interrupt levels. The BIM is VERSAbus™- and VMEbus- compatible and fully programmable.

MC68172 VMEbus Controller (E-BUSCON)
MC68173 VMSbus Controller (S-BUSCON)
MC68174 VMEbus Arbiter (E-BAM)

The MC68172, MC68173 and MC68174 are designed to facilitate development of VMEbus compatible boards and systems. The E-BUSCON performs VMEbus/local bus arbitration, VMEbus requests, and bus transceiver control, and guarantees VMEbus timing requirements. The S-BUSCON handles the interface of operations between the high-speed serial peripheral VMSbus and the central controlling VMEbus. Finally, the E-BAM performs round-robin and four-level priority arbitration for VMEbus systems or round-robin and five-level priority arbitration for VERSAbus™ systems.

MC68452 Bus Arbitration Module (BAM)

The MC68452 arbitrates the control of an M68000 system bus when multiple bus masters are involved. These bus masters can be processors, DMA controllers, and serial or parallel data communication controllers. Up to eight masters can be handled by each BAM device.

Graphics Controllers

MC68486 Raster Memory Interface (RMI)
MC68487 Raster Memory Controller (RMC)

The MC68486 and the MC68487 together make up what is known as the Motorola Raster Memory System (RMS). RMS performs most of the functions required by a bit-mapped or object-oriented color graphics or alphanumeric display system. The two devices are fully compatible with M68000 microprocessors and feature true (movable) and fixed object definition, manipulation, collision detection, light pen input, x/y capture and interrupt, x/y settable raster interrupt, choice of 32 out of 4096 colors, virtual and visual screens, smooth horizontal and vertical scrolling, and much more.

Device #	Description	Speeds	Package Types
CoProcessors			
68881*	Floating Point CoProcessor	12.5, 16.67 MHz	64 lead L, 68 lead R
Memory Management			
68451	Memory Management Unit	8, 10, 12.5 MHz	64 lead L, 68 lead R
68851**	Paged Memory Management Unit	12.5, 16.67 MHz	124 lead R
DMA Controllers			
68440	Dual DMA	6, 8, 10 MHz	64 lead L, 68 lead R
68450	DMA Controller	6, 8, 10 MHz	64 lead L, 68 lead R
Disk Controllers			
68454	Intelligent Multiple Disk Controller	2-10 Mbits/sec	48 lead L, P
68459[1]	Disk Phase Lock Loop	N/A	N/A
68465[2]	Floppy Disk Controller	N/A	N/A
Synch & Asynch Data Communications			
68561[2]	Multi Protocol Communication Controller II	4Mbits/sec	48 lead ceramic
68562*	Dual Universal Serial Communication Controller	4Mbits/sec	48 lead L
68564[3]	Serial I/O	1Mbit/sec	N/A
68652 2652	Multi Protocol Communication Controller	2Mbits/sec	40 lead L, P
68653 2653	Polynomial Generator Checker	N/A	16 lead L, P
68661 2661	Enhanced Peripheral Communication Interface	1Mbit/sec	28 lead L, P
68681 2681 2682	Dual Universal Asynchronous Receiver/Transmitter	1Mbit/sec	40 lead L, P 40 lead L, P 28 lead L, P
Local Area Network Controllers			
68590	Local Area Network Controller for Ethernet™	N/A	48 lead L
68802[2]	IEEE 802 Network Controller	N/A	40 lead plastic
General Purpose I/O			
68120/121	Intelligent Peripheral Controller	N/A	48 lead L, P
68230	Parallel Interface/Timer	8, 10 MHz	48 lead L, P
68901	Multi Function Peripheral	1Mbit/sec	48 lead L
System Interface			
68153	Bus Interrupt Module	N/A	40 lead L
68172**	VMEbus Controller	N/A	28 lead L, P
68173**	VMSbus Controller	N/A	28 lead L, P
68174**	VMEbus Arbiter	N/A	20 lead L, P
68452	Bus Arbitration Module	N/A	28 lead L, P
Graphics Controllers			
68486*	Raster Memory Interface	N/A	28 lead L, P
68487*	Raster Memory Controller	N/A	28 lead L, P

* available 1984
** available 1985
1 available only from designated alternate source - contact Signetics
2 available only from designated alternate source - contact Rockwell
3 available only from designated alternate source - contact Mostek

Index